Violence, hate crimes, theft, drug possession, se[...] sion, underage drinking, rape, along with many [...] plague all campuses. College and university staff, administrators, and policy makers are under increasing parental and legislative pressure to demonstrate that they have adopted measures to prevent crime and keep students safe.

This book serves as a sourcebook to enhance and evaluate safety programs, generate new solutions and interventions, comply with new legislation, and present practical steps and guidelines to establish best practices.

This book pays particular attention to the factors that may give rise to crime. It considers high-risk drinking and examines the intersection between hate crimes and violence. It devotes chapters to discrimination in all its forms, whether against international students, students of color, or on the basis of ethnicity or sexual orientation. It reviews the range of issues relating to harassment and violence against women and engages with hazing and the presence of guns on campus.

The authors pay attention to the different circumstances that may apply in specific institutional types, such as community colleges and minority-serving institutions. The book offers perspectives from administrators, campus security, student affairs personnel, and faculty and policy makers, as well as a review of legal considerations.

The purpose is to provide readers with the context and tools to devise a comprehensive safety plan. For administrators operating with few formal support systems, advice is given on how to co-opt individuals and resources from around the campus and the local community to assist in the common goal of maintaining a safe and welcoming campus.

WITHDRAWN UofM

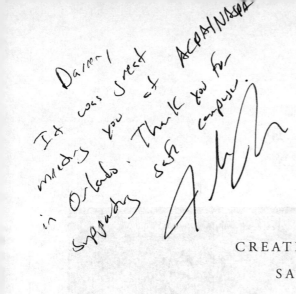

Darren!

It was great meeting you at ACPA/NASPA in Orlando. Thank you for supporting safe campuses.

CREATING AND MAINTAINING

SAFE COLLEGE CAMPUSES

CREATING AND MAINTAINING SAFE COLLEGE CAMPUSES

A Sourcebook for Evaluating and Enhancing Safety Programs

Edited by

Jerlando F. L. Jackson and
Melvin Cleveland Terrell

Foreword by Constance B. Clery
Preface by Gregory Roberts

Sty/us

STERLING, VIRGINIA

St/us

COPYRIGHT © 2007 BY STYLUS PUBLISHING, LLC.

Published by Stylus Publishing, LLC
22883 Quicksilver Drive
Sterling, Virginia 20166-2102

All rights reserved. No part of this book may be reprinted or
reproduced in any form or by any electronic, mechanical, or
other means, now known or hereafter invented, including
photocopying, recording, and information storage and
retrieval, without permission in writing from the publisher.

Library of Congress Cataloging-in-Publication-Data
Creating and maintaining safe college campuses : a
sourcebook for evaluating and enhancing safety programs /
edited by Jerlando F. L. Jackson and Melvin Cleveland
Terrell ; foreword by Constance B. Clery ; preface by
Gregory Roberts.—1st ed.
   p. cm.
   Includes bibliographical references and index.
   ISBN 1-57922-124-6 (cloth : alk. paper)—ISBN 1-57922-
196-3 (pbk. : alk. paper)
1. Universities and colleges—Security measures—United
States.   2. Universities and colleges—United
States—Safety measures.   3. Campus violence—United
States—Prevention. I. Jackson, Jerlando F. L., 1973–
II. Terrell, Melvin C.
LB2866.C74 2007
378.1′9782—dc22   2006030838

ISBN: 978-1-57922-124-9 (hardcover)
ISBN: 978-1-57922-196-6 (paper)

Printed in the United States of America

All first editions printed on acid free paper
that meets the American National Standards Institute
Z39-48 Standard.

Bulk Purchases

Quantity discounts are available for use in workshops
and for staff development.
Call 1-800-232-0223

First Edition, 2007

10 9 8 7 6 5 4 3 2 1

CONTENTS

v

INSTITUTIONAL CONTEXT AND RESPONSES

INSTITUTIONAL RESOURCES

ACKNOWLEDGMENTS

The editors are indebted to individuals who supported them in the process of writing this book. Dr. Terrell wishes to express his appreciation to Northeastern Illinois University President Salme Harju Steinberg for her support of his professional development through the years. He looks forward to continuing his scholarship and research during Dr. Sharon K. Hahs's tenure as Northeastern Illinois University president. Further, he must acknowledge his parents, the late Ethel Lee and Cleveland Terrell, for providing financial and moral support throughout his education. Many thanks are in order to his graduate assistants, Jose Fernandez and Wambui Njuguna, for their contributions toward this project. In addition, he would like to thank his editorial assistant, Kerri A. Kadow, for lending her expertise to the project. Trusted colleagues, including Mr. James Lyon Jr., Director of Public Safety at Northeastern Illinois University, have reviewed the manuscript and made helpful suggestions and comments.

Dr. Jackson would like to thank the Wisconsin Center for the Advancement of Postsecondary Education at the University of Wisconsin-Madison for research funding to complete this book project. He would also like to acknowledge research assistance provided by two graduate students: Consuelo Contreras, for her help in the initial stages of this project, and Brandon D. Daniels, for his work in the final stages. Last, Dr. Jackson would like to thank his family and friends for their support throughout the duration of this book project.

Last but not least, the editors would like to thank the authors for their valuable contributions.

This comprehensive and insightful book will be a great resource for college administrators who care about the safety and well-being of our college students.

My only daughter was once studying at college and full of dreams. Jeanne was pure *joy*, adored by her brothers, her father, and me. You can imagine the *horror* when we arrived home from a business trip her freshman year at Lehigh University to the news she'd been murdered that morning at 6 a.m. in her dorm room. The murderer was a fellow student. He was robbing her room and she awakened. He beat her, suffocated her, cut her neck with a broken bottle, raped and sodomized her, strangled her to death, and then bit her on her cheeks and breasts to make sure she was dead!

In the aftermath of Jeanne's death, Howard and I heard from many victims of campus crimes or their families. We were shocked at the prevalence of campus crime. We knew this was a national scandal, endangering student lives on college campuses, and that the parents were completely unaware, as we had been unaware. What Jeanne didn't know and we didn't know cost Jeanne her life. Howard and I were determined to make the public aware of this "best kept secret." If it happened to Jeanne in what seemed like the most idyllic and perfect circumstances, it could happen to anyone. So on the very day the murder trial ended, we announced the establishment of Security On Campus, Inc. (SOC), to help save lives on college campuses by making the public aware of the extent of campus crimes.

Thus began a heart-wrenching period in our lives that we would never have attempted or desired under normal circumstances. I started passing out petitions locally to help us begin to make people aware of campus crimes. That didn't work—too many parents were afraid to sign for fear their children would be blackballed by the colleges.

Howard and I decided the quickest and best way to raise awareness was to do a lot of TV interviews—though the prospect made both of us extremely nervous. Our lawyer also advised us not to. But we ignored his advice, thinking nothing could hurt us if we told the truth about this national scandal endangering college students' lives.

Howard wrote a College Security Questionnaire for parents, students, and high school and college advisors, which we promoted and sent out free of charge. It cost us a fortune, but we didn't care! Our daughter's life was beyond monetary value, and if it could save anyone else from becoming a victim of or from death—it would mean Jeanne's death and life had not been in vain.

We began to work for campus crime legislation passage in our home state of Pennsylvania first. Quickly, we learned the power of the vote and the tremendous public support through our TV, radio, and newspaper coverage. Within one year, the very first campus crime bill was enacted into law: the Pennsylvania College and University Security Information Act (May 26, 1988).

After Pennsylvania, we started working on similar legislation for other states from Florida to Massachusetts to California—traveling to state capitals to testify with other campus crime victims and parents of victims to pass legislation similar to Pennsylvania's. By 1989, we had at least 13 state laws passed—but they weren't uniform. Some were weak and some were strong. So, we decided to try for a federal law. In 1998, the Jeanne Clery Disclosure of Campus Security Policy and Campus Crime Statistics Act was passed into law, amending the 1990 Campus Security Act to eliminate loopholes and expand reporting requirements.

In all, 6 federal laws and more than 30 state laws have been passed in less than 20 years. It is amazing to Howard and me that Security On Campus, Inc., has accomplished so much. None of this could have happened without the tremendous caring and support of parents and students writing and calling their legislators to pass our bills into law.

SOC has done so much to advance the protection of women on college campuses. Violence against women is one of the biggest problems on college campuses and far too prevalent. The Jeanne Clery Act mandates reporting of sexual assaults, rapes, and other crimes against women. In 1992, Congress passed the "Campus Sexual Assault Victims' Bill of Rights" into law, further refining the fair treatment of victims of this all too prevalent crime.

As we know, alcohol is connected to sexual assault in up to 90% of cases. Many college students say they drink to excess simply because "There's nothing else to do." I think this represents a problem with the college culture in general. Students aren't even taking classes on Fridays anymore, so they can start partying earlier in the week. Of course, I don't think students should stop having fun while in school, but I think they should be more cautious when choosing the activities they *do* get involved in.

Many college students might say they are just having fun, but sometimes it doesn't seem like our nation's college kids are having much fun at all. Many of them are so busy with schoolwork and campus activities that they get increasingly overwhelmed; eating disorders and depression run rampant on America's campuses, but most students keep on a happy face. Suicide is the second-leading cause of death of college students, with 1,100 students per year taking their own lives.

Keeping in tune with our quest for awareness and openness, SOC established something very important in September 2006. Thanks to massive action by our supporters and dedicated employees, we were able to achieve unanimous congressional permission for SOC to designate September as National Campus Safety Awareness Month (NCSAM). This is a huge milestone in SOC's history. The idea is simple—National Campus Safety Awareness Month is meant to focus even more attention on safety for students, administrators, parents, and the general public.

SOC encourages colleges to creatively embrace NCSAM as an opportunity to enhance a comprehensive, campus-wide initiative. SOC is supporting this effort through a special website, http://www.campussafetymonth.org.

In spite of all this, we are hopeful. We see colleges nationwide trying to deal with the awesome binge drinking problem and truly showing interest in and wanting to comply with the Jeanne Clery Act. We know college administrators *can* change the environment. Why are these precious young students attending college? Let's help them *learn* and *live safely* while having some fun. Working together, it's possible, because we *care*. You care, and parents care. Good luck and God bless you in your important and difficult work.

Constance B. Clery
Co-founder, Security On Campus, Inc.

This is a timely addition to the resources available to college student educators on campuses in the United States and abroad. I would like to thank the editors and authors for taking the bold step of bringing to the profession a comprehensive and timely book exploring the nuances of campus safety.

Given the increasing number of incidents of violence, harassment, and disrespect on campuses, it is appropriate to challenge ourselves to look carefully at the reasons contributing to this change in behavior and weakened expectations. We must examine our reactions to this trend in American higher education. If we focus on the trends and responses from our colleagues in the K–12 sector, the trend toward violence should come as no surprise. For the last decade, K–12 institutions have had to reallocate instructional and other educational funds to campus safety initiatives to ensure elementary and secondary students may learn in a safe and secure learning environment. This situation has not been restricted to the classroom environment, but from the time a child leaves his or her home and steps onto the school bus, this has been necessary. Unfortunately, there were 16 reported student deaths in American elementary schools during the 2002–2003 school year (National School Safety and Security Services, 2003). This trend is unacceptable, and higher education cannot allow it a strong hold on the educational process, thus the need for this kind of research and the impetus for writing this book.

This book is not just for the college student educators on urban campuses that are located on the fringes of "undesirable" neighborhoods, but on all American campuses. The unfortunate death of Jeanne Ann Clery on the campus of Lehigh University in 1986 was not an incident that happened on a campus in the middle of a major urban community; it happened in rural Pennsylvania. In 2003, there were 10 reported murders on American college campuses (U.S. Department of Education, 2003). We are all at risk. This is a national dilemma based on changing moral values, and economic and social conditions have minimized the value placed on life and property.

The current national issues that support the timely release of this publication are rooted in a concern for national safety, following the tragic events of September 11, 2001, and the concern that college campuses are too lax on students and their access to the American higher education system. This speaks to a greater problem of cultural and religious understanding or lack thereof, particularly in the United States.

We continue to be plagued with increasing numbers of hate crimes, primarily targeted at African Americans and members of the gay and lesbian community. Since September 11, 2001, we have seen Muslim citizens and persons of Middle Eastern descent the target of increased harassment and crimes, an alarming trend that is grounded in privilege, power, and lack of concern for "the common good." The recent economic cycles that create particular pressures on the socially deprived and economically disadvantaged tend to result in more property crimes and crimes of opportunity (on most residential campuses).

The 21st century, with all of its electronic advantages over previous centuries, has challenged us to address more "white collar" crimes in addition to the challenges of resolving intellectual property issues, computer-generated data thefts, and the verbal/written threats and harassment that have become a by-product of the Internet. Identity theft is a major criminal act that may be rooted on college campuses. The Internet is a quality tool that has become an accessory to crime.

The new century will challenge us to understand a much smaller and better-connected world. Those familiar with technology have the opportunity to use it as another mechanism to abuse knowledge and access to information that was created to enhance education and quality of life.

I hope you will agree, after reading this book, that we are able to craft the future agenda and form our response to a major threat to American higher education. We must not wait for the situation to deteriorate further. We must take bold steps to increase cultural understanding among all members of the university community. We must teach at home and at school the value of life and the respect and dignity of each person. We must address issues of access and affordability in education and work collaboratively with parents and local and campus law enforcement authorities. In addition, we must create a campus environment that has zero tolerance for behaviors that marginalize any member of the community. We must find ways to address the increasing need to create an environment that is both physically and psychologically safe for our campus community members. With increasing advances of computers and other technology, we must acknowledge not only threats to our physical safety, but also threats to our psychological safety and our well-being.

The 21st century brings with it many global thoughts and challenges, and American higher education must broaden our responsibilities to include a safe and secure environment, both physical and virtual. This is just the first step in a collaborative partnership between college student educators and others to create and maintain safe college campuses. Many thanks to the editors and authors for sharing these perspectives with us. It is our responsibility to move this agenda to the next level.

Are you ready?

Gregory Roberts
Executive Director
ACPA–College Student Educators International

References

National School Safety and Security Services. (2003). *School shootings and high-profile incidents of school violence.* Retrieved June 30, 2006, from http://www.schoolsecurity.org/trends/school_violence.html

U.S. Department of Education. (2003). *Murder/non-negligent manslaughter.* Retrieved June, 30, 2006, from http://www.ed.gov/admins/lead/safety/crime/criminaloffenses/edlite-murder.html

IDENTIFYING THE PROBLEM

THE COMPLEXITY OF MAINTAINING A SAFE CAMPUS IN HIGHER EDUCATION

An Administrative Dilemma

Jerlando F. L. Jackson, Melvin Cleveland Terrell, and Richie L. Heard

V iolence and crime on college and university campuses are major concerns for many campus-based officials. The issues surrounding these topics range from theft to bioterrorism and from substance abuse to hate crimes (Barr, Desler, & Associates, 2000; Hoffman, Schuh, & Fenske, 1998; Whitaker & Pollard, 2002). These are key issues plaguing the entire higher education community—particularly college students. Consequently, these occurrences beg the question, "What are campus leaders doing to protect and ensure community safety, not just from the threat of terrorism, but from the violence and crime on their campus?" College and university administrators, as central campus leaders, need to examine measures taken on their campuses to protect the students and the greater campus community. Through campus safety departments, universities offer many needed services to the general student body (e.g., protection, transportation, personal safety classes, and publication of crime statistics on campus). Accordingly, the most effective and productive administrative practices need to be documented and published more broadly for the higher education community.

Disseminating this information is of critical importance because the complicated law requiring campus crime reports makes it difficult to increase awareness of campus crime (Janosik & Gehring, 2003). Thus, there is a consistent need for current research and statistics on campus safety and violence as a resource for administrators and law enforcement officials. Although there are some published statistics and reports from the U.S. Congress and the departments of Justice and Education (Pezza, 1995), these resources are quickly dated due to the protean environment of higher education (Pezza, 1995). Unfortunately, minimal research, outside of law enforcement bulletins and websites, is available for individuals involved with campus security.

Violence, hate crimes, theft, drug possession, sexual harassment, concealed weapons, underage drinking, rape, and many other major and minor offenses are infractions that college and university administrators must be able to handle (Hoffman et al., 1998; Nichols, 1997). Accordingly, this book addresses the aforementioned set of problems college and university administrators encounter in creating and maintaining safe campuses. *Creating and Maintaining Safe College Campuses* serves as an informative sourcebook to enhance and evaluate safety programs, generate new studies in this area, and facilitate the creation of safe campuses. The contributing authors bring a diverse set of voices, representing researchers and practitioners investigating critical aspects of campus safety. The remainder of this chapter describes the historical development of campus safety legislation, a national status report of crime on campuses, and an outline of the remaining chapters.

Historical Review of the Law apropos Campus Safety Legislation

On August 21, 1974, President Gerald Ford signed the Family Educational Rights and Privacy Act (FERPA) into law. Referred to commonly as the "Buckley Amendment," this legislation addressed campus safety issues encountered by U.S. education institutions (Baker, 2005). Specifically, in postsecondary education, it required institutions to retain all information pertaining to their students, until those students elected to release the information, and any deviation meant the risk of losing access to federal funds. Under FERPA, parents or legal guardians are given certain access rights to their child's educational records. These rights transfer to their child when he or she reaches the age of 18 or attends school beyond secondary education. The student is then considered "eligible." Furthermore, particularly in postsecondary education, eligible students have the right under FERPA to view all educational records pertinent to them. Eligible students also can contest information on their records that they believe to be inaccurate.

However, not all information pertaining to college and university constituents is subject to gag order under FERPA, and the law requires institutions to provide a directory of their constituents' contact information. When an emergency occurs, postsecondary institutions are at liberty to release students' personal information and academic records, without court order, if the incident relates to the safety of others. On one hand, some (e.g., Essex, 2004; Gose, 2002) argue that the law is drawn too ambiguously and could lead to problematic abuse. On the other hand, others (e.g., Baker, 2005; Clark, 2001; Foster, 2003) contend that the needs of the institutions' constituents outweigh the consequences. Still, many argue that the Buckley Amendment helps higher education institutions conceal campus safety information.

Congress answered many of the concerns by continually streamlining the Buckley Amendment in an effort to remove ambiguity, which led to FERPA's being amended a total of nine times, including passage of the original act:

1. P.L. 93-568, Buckley/Pell Amendment
2. P.L. 96-46, Amendments to Education Amendments
3. P.L. 96-88, Establishment of Department of Education
4. P.L. 101-542, Campus Security Act
5. P.L. 102-325, Higher Education Amendments of 1992
6. P.L. 103-382, Improving America's Schools Act of 1994
7. P.L. 105-244, Higher Education Amendments of 1998
8. P.L. 106-386, Campus Sex Crimes Prevention Act
9. P.L. 107-56, USA Patriot Act of 2001

The following section highlights major legislative changes in the act.

The first change took place August 6, 1979, when Congress set a bright-line rule to delineate clearly the freedom of state and local education officials to access student records for reason of necessity. This clarification applied to auditing or evaluation issues of any state or federal aided educational program that may be governed by accountability procedures at the local or federal level. Subsequently, the Crime Awareness and Campus Security Act of 1990 sought to erase further ambiguity, which its predecessor failed to resolve. That amendment declared that all postsecondary institutions were now bound by law to relinquish to the alleged victim all information regarding an alleged perpetrator's institutional hearing.

In reference to organizational freedom, the Improving America's Schools Act of 1994 permitted organizations, if they were education agencies or institutions whose main purpose was research, to access postsecondary student records. Access was rendered under the stipulation that student confidentiality was upheld; however, if a violation occurred, the organization lost access rights to student data for five or more years. Later the legislation evolved even further. The Jeanne Clery Disclosure of Campus Security Policy and Campus Crime Statistics Act of 1998 addressed other inequities with which the earlier acts did not deal, such as intensifying reporting requirements to postsecondary institutions (Security On Campus, Inc., 2003). Statistical data for certain off-campus locations now had to be documented, and institutions with a security department had to retain daily criminal records.

The Foley Amendment of 1998 stipulated additional constraints on postsecondary institutions by indicating that students who commit a violent act, including nonforcible sex, are exempt from federal student privacy protection. In 2000, the Campus Sex Crimes Prevention Act delved further into incidents of sexual wrongdoing; thus, institutions were now required to release all information relating to sexual offenders—employees or student affiliates. Yielding, yet again, a more stringent blueprint of the previous legislation, the aftermath of September 11, 2001, gave birth to the USA Patriot Act (H.R. 3162). Under this mandate, law enforcement officials gained easier access to student information, even in the absence of probable cause.

The National Context for Crimes on College and University Campuses

Institutions of higher education are increasingly under pressure to make certain that their campuses are rendered safe for all of the constituents they serve (Keels, 2004). Increasing concerns in postsecondary education regarding the rise in criminal occurrences has policymakers overwhelmed. Colleges and universities have had mixed results with improving the overall safety on campus during the past ten years (see Table 1.1). There has been a significant decrease in murder offenses occurring on campus between 1997 and 2003; during this period, murder offenses declined 44%. However, during the

TABLE 1.1
On-Campus Criminal Offenses in Higher Education

Offense	1997	2003	% Change
Murder	18	10	− 44
Forcible Sex	1,668	2,581	55
Nonforcible Sex	472	55	− 88
Robbery	1,810	2,086	15
Aggravated Assault	3,754	3,050	− 19
Burglary	26,757	29,125	9
Motor Vehicle Theft	6,732	6,594	− 2

Note: Calculations based on data from the U.S. Department of Education, Office of Post-secondary Education.

same period, the number of forcible sex offenses[1] increased from 1,668 to 2,581, a 55% increase between 1997 and 2003. In contrast, there was an 88% decrease in nonforcible sex offenses[2] on campus between 1997 and 2003. During the same seven-year period, there was a modest increase in robbery on campuses, from 1,810 in 1997 to 2,086, or 15%, in 2003. Between 1997 and 2003, aggravated assault on campus decreased 19%. Burglary is the most common offense on campus: there were 26,757 burglaries in 1997 and 29,125 in 2003. During this period, the rate of burglaries on campuses increased 9%; however, motor vehicle thefts on campus decreased 2% between 1997 and 2003.

Equally interesting are the institutions that rank among the top five in campus criminal offenses involving alcohol, drugs, and weapons (see Table 1.2). For example, the institutions that rank in the top five for on-campus offenses related to alcohol share some similar characteristics. For the most part, these institutions are located in the Midwest, are large research institutions, and have developed reputations as "party schools." As for the top five institutions related to drug arrests, while for the most part they are large research institutions, they are located all across the United States. In addition, smaller institutions, like the University of North Carolina-Greensboro,

---

[1] Sex Offenses—Forcible refers to any sexual act directed against another person, forcibly and/or against that person's will, or not forcibly or against the person's will, where the victim is incapable of giving consent. For example, forcible rape, forcible sodomy, sexual assault with an object, and forcible fondling.

[2] Sex Offenses—Nonforcible refers to unlawful, nonforcible sexual intercourse, for example, incest and statutory rape.

TABLE 1.2
Campuses Reporting the Most Alcohol, Drug, and Weapons Arrests

Offense/Institution	Number of arrests	Enrollment
Alcohol		
University of Wisconsin	792	39,699
Michigan State University	655	42,603
University of Minnesota	606	45,410
Western Michigan University	405	26,132
University of California-Berkeley	382	30,290
Drug		
University of California-Berkeley	280	30,290
Rutgers University	138	34,420
U. of North Carolina-Greensboro	132	12,535
University of Arizona	123	33,737
Virginia Commonwealth	122	22,702
Weapons		
Michigan State University	49	42,603
University of California-Berkeley	34	30,290
U. of North Carolina-Charlotte	26	16,511
U. of North Carolina-Greensboro	23	12,535
San Jose State University	20	26,897

Note: Arrests are for calendar year 1998, and enrollments are for academic year 1997–98.
Source: The Chronicle of Higher Education, A49. Available at http://chronicle.com.

are among those with the most arrests for drugs on-campus. Likewise, the top five institutions for weapons-related arrests on campus are located across the United States. It is interesting to note that two small institutions—the University of North Carolina-Charlotte and the University of North Carolina-Greensboro—ranked in the top five for weapons offenses.

Conclusion

Interventions in the form of administrative policies and practices are crucial in preventing such crimes. Having such protocols in place before violent occurrences can prevent or resolve negative situations before they become chronic on college and university campuses. Institution type, location, and campus composition individually and collectively affect and cultivate the unique campus environment. These factors, in turn, influence the types of administrative practices and policies that are appropriate for a specific institution. Understanding how to develop appropriate institutional responses in light of these institutional characteristics will likely be the primary challenge for college and university administrators for the next decade.

The remaining chapters discuss these factors and strategies for addressing them at various types of institutions. In chapter 2, Sudakshina L. Ceglarek and Aaron M. Brower explore the role student of affairs administrators, in partnership with their academic affairs colleagues, in addressing high-risk drinking using an environmental approach. The authors argue that only through a student affairs/academic affairs partnership can effective solutions be found that engage "whole students" and "whole environments." Darnell G. Cole, Meechai Orsuwan, and Anna Ah Sam address in chapter 3 the intersection between violence and hate crimes on college campuses by identifying rates of victimization, the role of race/ethnicity, and international status. The gaps in reporting acts of violence further clarify this intersection.

Despite heightened awareness, education, and even state laws prohibiting the practice of hazing, students continue to engage in increasingly more dangerous forms of the activity. In chapter 4, Walter M. Kimbrough traces the history of hazing in higher education, discusses recent cases, and attempts to explain from a student development perspective why some students are willing victims of hazing or are even insistent on being hazed to obtain membership in a student organization. Susan R. Rankin, Elizabeth A. Roosa Millar, and Christian Matheis address in chapter 5 specific challenges facing sexual minority (non-heterosexual) students and how institutions of higher education can respond appropriately to their needs.

Women comprise the majority of students on college campuses and account for a growing number of academic personnel and faculty on college campuses today. Unfortunately, violence against them continues to be a critical issue for college and university administrators. Chapter 6, by Elizabeth M. O'Callaghan, analyzes the impact of sexual harassment, sexual assault, rape, stalking, and dating/domestic violence on women's collegiate and workplace experiences. Community college students often find themselves in challenging situations and circumstances that extend far beyond the physical boundaries of the campus. Chapter 7, by Charlene Dukes and Tracy Harris, examines issues of safety on an open campus, including situations that may blur physical and intellectual borders of community college campuses wherein the potential for violence exists. Community college students often find themselves in challenging situations and circumstances that extend far beyond the physical boundaries of the campus.

Marybeth Gasman and Noah D. Drezner explore issues that manifest at the nation's minority-serving institutions (e.g., historically Black colleges and universities, Hispanic-serving institutions, and tribal colleges and universities) in chapter 8. More specifically, they examine how administrators at minority-serving institutions are responding to campus safety issues. The role of campus police or security departments in cultivating an environment where the community is successfully engaged and a partnership exists both within and external to the institution is described by James A. Perrotti in chapter 9.

In chapter 10, Charles Cychosz challenges campus administrators to understand the reasons why weapons are coming to campus and to develop meaningful policies and practices that address this problem. John Wesley Lowery examines legal implications of campus crime for student affairs professionals in chapter 11, and in chapter 12, Jerry D. Stewart and John H. Schuh discuss public safety best practices. They examine contemporary issues of emphasis for campus police agencies and explore how various units on college campuses can collaborate with police agencies to address mutual problems and concerns.

Robert D. Reason and Brenda R. Lutovsky recommend credible, up-to-date resources, including individuals who may currently be on campuses, to assist administrators with the charge of maintaining a safe and welcoming campus in chapter 13. The chapter reviews and highlights national organizations, print resources, and credible websites to provide a comprehensive assessment of administrative resources. Last, in chapter 14, Delight E. Champagne describes elements of a comprehensive safety plan.

References

Baker, T. R. (2005). Notifying parents following a college student suicide attempt: A review of case law and F.E.R.P.A., and recommendations for practice. *NASPA Journal, 42*(4), 513–533.

Barr, M. J., Desler, M., & Associates. (2000). *The handbook of student affairs administration* (2nd ed.). San Francisco: Jossey-Bass.

Clark, S. G. (2001). Confidentiality and disclosure: A lesson in sharing. *Principal Leadership (Middle School Ed.), 1*(8), 40–43.

Essex, N. L. (2004). Confidentiality and student records: Ten ways to invite legal challenges. *The Clearing House, 77*(3), 111–113.

Foster, A. L. (2003). Rule change would let students approve release of data online. *The Chronicle of Higher Education, 50*(2), A40.

Gose, Ben (2002). Supreme Court weighs whether students can sue under privacy law. *The Chronicle of Higher Education, 48*(34), A23.

Hoffman, A., Schuh, J. H., & Fenske, R. (1998). *Violence on campus: Defining the problems, strategies for action.* Gaithersburg, MD: Aspen Publishers.

Janosik, S. M., & Gehring, D. D. (2003). The impact of the Clery Campus Crime Disclosure Act on student behavior. *Journal of College Student Development, 44*(1), 81–91.

Keels, C. (2004). The best-kept secret: Crime on campus. *Black Issues in Higher Education, 21*(6), 30.

Nichols, D. (1997). *Creating a safe campus: A guide for college and university administrators.* Springfield, IL: Charles C. Thomas Publishers.

Pezza, P. E. (1995). College campus violence: The nature of the problem and its frequency. *Educational Psychology Review, 7*(1), 93–103.

Security On Campus, Inc. (2003). *Complying with the Jeanne Clery Act.* Security On Campus, Inc. Retrieved February 5, 2004, from http://www.securityoncampus.org/schools/cleryact/index.html

Whitaker, L. C., & Pollard, J. W. (2002). *Campus violence: Kinds, causes, and cures.* New York: Haworth Press.

INSTITUTIONAL AND INDIVIDUAL-BASED CHALLENGES

2

CHANGING THE CULTURE OF HIGH-RISK DRINKING

Sudakshina L. Ceglarek and Aaron Brower

Across the nation, binge drinking, also called high-risk drinking, is a major public health challenge on college campuses that leads to a number of harmful consequences, including violence, noise complaints, vandalism, transports to detox caused by overconsumption, and sexual assaults, among others (see DeJong et al., 1998; Hingson, Heeren, Zakocs, Kopstein, & Wechsler, 2002; Hingson & Howland, 2002; Institute of Medicine, 1989; National Institutes of Health [NIH], 2002; Wechsler, Lee, Hall, Wagenaar, & Lee, 2002a; Wechsler et al., 2002b). The negative effects of high-risk drinking are substantial, with 25% of college students reporting that problems involving missing classes, falling behind in course work, and receiving poor grades have been due to their problematic drinking (Presley, Meilman, & Cashin, 1996; Wechsler et al., 2002b). Furthermore, high-risk drinking significantly affects others—common "secondhand effects," as they are called, result in unwanted sexual advances, getting into serious arguments and physical violence, disruptions in sleeping and study habits, having to take care of drunken peers, and damage to property (Hingson et al., 2002; Wechsler et al., 2002a). Additionally, college presidents view campus high-risk drinking as a very serious health and safety problem on today's college campuses (Higher Education Center for Alcohol and Other Drug Prevention, 2003).

Given the complexity of the problem and the extent of its effects on college campuses and surrounding communities, it has not been a simple task to find solutions that can address the issue itself, along with its myriad consequences. This problem necessitates adopting a broad-based environmental approach—one that will facilitate engaging both the campus and community in developing collaborative solutions involving clear expectations for appropriate behaviors; an examination of campus-community traditions that inadvertently reinforce high-risk drinking; and consistent enforcement of policies when campus and community expectations are violated. In fact, a recent study evaluating strategies to address student high-risk drinking revealed that those universities most effective in combating this problem were ones that applied key campus and community partners from diverse constituencies, including local businesses, law enforcement, campus security, student affairs, health agencies, and neighborhood associations, to name a few (Weitzman, Nelson, Lee, & Wechsler, 2004).

Traditionally, addressing students' high-risk drinking has been the responsibility of those frontline offices that operate under the auspices of student affairs with little involvement of academic affairs, though partnerships between these two units are essential (Ryan & DeJong, 1998). These include university-based student health and counseling services, orientation programs, offices of the dean of students, and related units. However, these offices cannot effectively shoulder the responsibility of dealing with problematic student drinking without also partnering with academic affairs in an effort to develop solutions that can help address the dangers and consequences related to the behavior comprehensively (Ryan & DeJong, 1998).

It is with this concept of a broad environmental and collaborative framework that we explore the problem of and solutions to what is considered to be one of the most difficult public health problems facing college campuses today (NIH, 2002). No doubt, every institution differs concerning strategies that apply on its own campuses, and no doubt, each campus is unique in its challenges and resources when addressing high-risk drinking. Nevertheless, we argue that campuses must adopt campus-community collaborative strategies, within an environmental framework, to address high-risk drinking effectively on their campuses and in their communities.

First we address some of the traditional ways in which campuses have dealt with high-risk drinking. Next, we elaborate further on the need for broad-based environmental strategies followed by specific approaches that have been shown to be effective in addressing the problem. Wherever possible, we contextualize the discussion based on our experiences, particularly as they relate to our work within the PACE (Policy, Alternatives, Community & Education) Project, which seeks to decrease high-risk drinking and its negative consequences at the University of Wisconsin (UW)-Madison campus using an environmental management approach.

Environmental Approach and High-Risk Drinking on College Campuses

In 1998, the U.S. Department of Education's Higher Education Center, which deals with high-risk drinking on college campuses, articulated environmental management as strategies moving beyond general awareness and other education programs to identify and change those factors in the physical, social, legal, and economic environment that promote or abet alcohol and other drug problems (see DiFulvio, 2005). Within this broader premise, research has identified numerous factors that contribute to high-risk drinking on college campuses.

Some of these factors can involve developmental processes that lead to student lifestyles that are centered on partying and risk taking. In addition, structural elements such as year in school and social class can also influence consumption. Economic issues regarding easy access to cheap alcohol and specific college-bar marketing tactics have also been shown to influence student drinking. Moreover, living arrangements and the lack of peer accountability, social expectations about drinking in college, and even the overall drinking rates of a state and its culture of alcohol consumption based on its immigration history have all been shown to affect student drinking habits and patterns (Chaloupka & Wechsler, 1996; Erenberg & Hacker, 1997; NIH, 2002; Nelson, Naimi, Brewer, & Wechsler, 2005; O'Hare, 1990; Schulenberg et al., 2001; Wechsler, Kuo, Lee, & Dowdall, 2000).

An examination of the underlying reasons for high-risk drinking suggests numerous factors at multiple levels within the college environment that tend to influence consumption patterns. It is certain that engaging in particular risk behaviors is an individual decision; however, it is equally important to recognize that individuals make their behavioral choices and decisions within a larger social and cultural context that involves community norms and interactions. Therefore, focusing on building solutions at one of these levels without also addressing the other has generally not been effective (NIH, 2002).

Institutions generally have addressed high-risk drinking at campuses with strategies offered at an individual level. Larimer and Cronce (2002), in a review presented to the National Institutes of Health, classify these individual-focused interventions into educational awareness, cognitive-behavioral approaches, and motivational enhancement techniques. Numerous campus-based student health centers, usually operating as a unit of student affairs administration, provide these much-needed services to help reduce problematic drinking among college students.

However, a review on the efficacy for these initiatives suggests mixed results (Larimer & Cronce, 2002). For example, Larimer and Cronce's evaluation indicates weak support for education-based awareness initiatives and somewhat stronger support for cognitive-behavioral and motivational enhancement models, although studies evaluating cognitive-behavioral approaches have usually depended on smaller samples and are prone to higher rates of attrition.

On the whole, the evaluation sees individually oriented treatment and prevention services as one piece of the puzzle and reiterates the need for a broad-based approach toward addressing student drinking problems, a recommendation also emphasized elsewhere (see Chaloupka & Wechsler, 1995; Wechsler et al., 2000; Weitzman et al., 2004). Such an approach is also in step with the National Institutes of Health's landmark report that articulates a unique three-in-one framework wherein campuses are urged to focus simultaneously on individuals, then the student body as a whole, and, finally, the surrounding community, to facilitate comprehensive models of intervention to address high-risk drinking on college campuses (NIH, 2002).

At the same time, we also note here that focusing only on macro-level interventions can yield limited results. For example, although research does indicate that a macro-level approach such as social norms might moderate drinking on college campuses (Perkins, 2002), this technique has been found to have limited impact, particularly with students from a variety of high-risk drinking environments (American Medical Association [AMA], 2002; Steffain, 1999; Thombs, 2000) who also need other initiatives to manage their drinking behaviors.

Common Strategies Within the Environmental Approach

Space considerations do not allow us to review all of the strategies currently being implemented at various campuses that fall within the purview of the environmental model, though excellent overviews may be found in Hingson, Heeren, Winter, and Wechsler (2005) and Wechsler et al. (2000). What follows is a discussion of some of the more common strategies that have been implemented or are currently being considered at various universities, including here at UW-Madison. A common theme linking these strategies is that the environmental approaches described endeavor to engage both the academic and student affairs units on campus in addition to including the broader community in highly collaborative programs and activities. Addressing issues related to high-risk drinking involves not only an examination of policies and procedures that govern student behaviors, but also reviewing academic infrastructures such as class schedules, academic advisor training and availability, and larger issues surrounding academic calendars.

Importance of Partnerships Between Academic and Student Affairs

Environmental approaches emphasize broad-based coalitions—environmental change requires changes to be made at many levels and involve many stakeholders. Often these approaches highlight the role of campus-based collaborations working with external nonuniversity entities, including local businesses, neighborhood associations, and agencies; law enforcement; local government; and so forth. Proponents of environmental approaches also describe the importance of working across various student affairs units on campus such as health services, dean of students, visitors' center, admissions, chancellor's office, and others (NIH, 2002).

Campus-community partnerships and coordinated student affairs efforts are both extremely important. However, our work in addressing high-risk drinking suggests that frequently missing from these on-campus discussions is academic affairs. While the problem of high-risk drinking on college campuses has received much deserved attention, little research exists on the nature of partnerships between academic and student affairs that can help to address the consequences of the problem in a concerted manner. At the same time, our experience suggests that these are much needed and indispensable collaborations that must occur at multiple levels.

The first level is perhaps so obvious that it is often overlooked: the impact of high-risk drinking affects all aspects of student life, including academic performance and academic environment. Like no other issue in the college environment, high-risk drinking brings together student health and decision making, academic engagement and performance, social behaviors and town/gown relations.

Second, traditional divisions between student affairs and academic affairs create artificial boundaries in the manner in which a campus addresses its students' alcohol misuse. For example, student problems with alcohol use are generally relegated to campus counseling centers, health services, and units under the dean of students' office. On the other hand, poor classroom performance, regardless of the cause, is generally dealt with by faculty within individual courses. Moreover, if a consequence due to risky consumption entails violation of a policy, then, depending on the nature of the infraction, such issues might be handled by the city police (or if violations occur on campus, by the campus police, who may or may not collaborate with the dean of students office).

Third, the setting in which students receive information on university expectations about student behavior can be equally as fragmented—with "view books" coordinated through an admissions office or by campus tours and orientation programs organized through visitors' centers. In addition, on most campuses, university housing provides its own student orientations. On the other hand, student classroom experiences remain completely separate and are fragmented further through the individual and largely uncoordinated orientations that each instructor gives to students in his or her own first class of the semester.

Particularly within the context of student drinking issues, it has been our experience that all of these stakeholders must work together to clarify and coordinate expectations for student behavior, to communicate these expectations clearly, and to assist in enforcing expectations. Provosts' offices have as much stake in this process as do dean of students units, advisors are as vital to this as are housing staff, and individual faculty must coordinate their own classroom expectations with broader university expectations so that students hear a uniform message that continuously articulates what it means to be a college student.

Finally, student affairs personnel are in a unique position to discuss topics related to broader student development, including judicial processes that oversee violation of policies affecting student life issues and, at times, academic guidelines. Academic affairs personnel and faculty are in an excellent position to discuss topics related to a student's overall academic development. Of course, both groups have much to learn from each other's domains.

Here at the UW-Madison campus, we have had very good success creating strategies and programs when we have brought together subgroups from both academic and student affairs. Wherever possible, we have sought out opportunities for partnership between student affairs and academic affairs to develop comprehensive solutions that take into consideration academic performance *and* student health and development issues. For example, it is common for project investigator and staff to address alcohol issues affecting student academic performance during orientations and special sessions created specifically for academic advisors. In addition to serving as platforms to provide information regarding high-risk drinking and its influence on academic outcomes, these sessions are helpful in generating broader discussions on matters that cut across both student life and academic issues. At the other end of the spectrum (from orientation to infractions), UW-Madison has enacted a joint judicial hearing board whose responsibilities are to hear cases that cut across both academic and nonacademic areas. This board consists of both faculty and student affairs staff and is coordinated through the dean of students' office.

Faculty members remain concerned about the welfare of their students. However, with their primary role as educators, faculty have faced unique challenges while engaging in issues pertaining to student high-risk drinking, most often trying to identify an appropriate role as they endeavor to address the problem. Likewise, senior staff from our project worked with key student affairs and student health offices, and it was essential that campus and community efforts were brought forward by the faculty and staff leadership team. In doing so, we intentionally modeled the type of collaboration we sought across campus and in the community.

Some faculty members were motivated by the recognition that students' alcohol abuse negatively affected their classes, and where possible, we involved these faculty members as often as we could. Other faculty members were engaged by emphasizing that the best strategies to address high-risk drinking were those that were developed carefully through empirically driven research, which could be then be evaluated.

With faculty discussions, it was important that we tailored the message about student engagement and academic performance when we discussed the influence of high-risk drinking on our campus community. When we made presentations, we backed up our decisions with data about drinking behaviors and consequences gathered from our own campus and nationally. We found opportunities to present results at various faculty and senate meetings and within specific academic departments. In the end, by sharing information on ways in which a student development issue such as drinking affects academic performance, we were able to create common grounds for collaboration between faculty and staff dealing with academic and student life issues.

A step of paramount importance and one that we want to emphasize to any institution that is planning to address alcohol issues *and* wishes to engage its faculty in the process, is gathering data on student health and related issues. We have continued to collect information on student drinking rates, patterns, and attitudes for several years. Collecting and sharing these data has also helped to create avenues for faculty involvement, as it provided them with opportunities to study student health and their effects on academic performance. Overall, every opportunity for faculty partnerships was nurtured.

Based on our experience, we continue to encourage student affairs personnel to explore developing work groups or collaborations with faculty to facilitate partnerships with academic affairs in an effort to keep faculty informed about general issues of student health as these affect academic outcomes. In addition to encouraging communications between the two units, we believe that such collaboration might further create potential research opportunities on joint topics related to academic and student development processes.

Clarifying Broader Institutional Expectations

Ultimately, creating a campus environment that is conducive to student learning is the goal of every academic institution. It may go without saying that the overarching mission of a university—teaching and learning—must be communicated clearly to students and to the broader university community by faculty, administration at every level, and staff as they interact with students. Here it is important that institutions communicate and reiterate to students the university's expectations for their behavior as college students, that not only outline "rules" for acceptable behavior, but also expectations about engaging in learning involving all aspects of their college life. Disseminating messages to students on the central mission of the university can help to promote education, individual growth, and a sense of community, and at the same time help to influence student drinking patterns and behaviors positively (NIH, 2002).

Of course, an ongoing challenge that large universities continue to face is devising optimal ways to focus high-risk drinking at a level that addresses all students, regardless of their attitudes toward alcohol. Vehicles that help to disseminate university expectations invariably differ depending on each institution as well as the tools and resources that are available to students. Preliminary research in this area indicates that students generally receive information about the university from a variety of sources, including their parents, friends, university literature, campus visits, and orientation programs (Singer, 2003).

In this regard, frontline offices that oversee new student orientation and student visitors' programs provide excellent opportunities for an academic and student affairs partnership that can help to communicate messages regarding the institution's overall mission and expectations. Universities can encourage forming collaborative work groups comprising members representing both divisions that could then review, discuss, and develop overall university expectations related to policies that can be disseminated to incoming students through various frontline offices. For example, in the case of the UW-Madison, a partnership with various units, including admissions, dean of students, and the chancellor's office, resulted in a letter sent to all new students from the chancellor's office that outlines expectations and how they fit within the university's mission.

In this letter, expectations about high-risk drinking and the university's perception of it as a public health issue are discussed specifically, though also in the context of broader expectations about how students should treat each other and other members of the university community as individuals who are engaged in learning at this exciting time in their lives. UW-Madison uses this letter-writing campaign as an opportunity to communicate with incoming students and their parents about ways in which the institution encourages academic and social development of all its students and the role alcohol overconsumption can play in hindering the process.

Availability of Alcohol on Campus

Research suggests a direct association between the density of licensed liquor establishments in an area and the levels of drinking (Scribner, Mackinnon, &

Dwyer, 1995). Drinking, and especially binge drinking, is higher when there are more alcohol outlets situated near a campus (see Chaloupka & Wechsler, 1996).

Moreover, studies show that the availability of alcohol at different places where individuals drink affects drinking patterns and the nature of the incidence, prevalence, and geographic distribution of alcohol-related problems in the community (Gruenewald, Millar, & Treno, 1993; Maxwell & Immergluck, 1997; Scribner et al., 1995). Therefore, it is important that campuses work with community members to examine density issues.

Numerous strategies may be adopted to address this concern. For example, campus-community coalitions can work initially with local health and law enforcement agencies to acquire last-drink data that can ultimately help to inform health officials and policymakers of commonly frequented venues where individuals consume alcohol in an effort to examine policies to maximize the health and safety of a community.

In addition, local communities can review the geographic distribution of drinking-related problems by mapping crime and other data using geographic information systems. Creating these types of maps has helped to raise awareness within the city of Madison's city council and Alcohol License Review Committee (ALRC) on matters of consumption and crime. Furthermore, we expanded the definition of density to include capacity within specified areas of the city by showing the vast number of "seats" that are available in a given time within a small section of downtown Madison. For example, by looking at capacity, we discovered that a six-block area of downtown currently allows about 16,000 patrons to drink at one time. This information is motivating the ALRC to address bar density in the downtown area and related law enforcement issues that might stem from such a high concentration of consumers.

With such initial procedures completed, campus communities may choose to deal with density-related matters in several ways, including commercial density—communities might want to determine the percentage of alcohol outlets in relation to the total number of commercial outlets in a given planning area and population density, in which density of alcohol outlets is calculated per population unit, overall number of licenses being issued, and location of outlets (see Stevenson, Bronwyn & Weatherburn, 1999; U.S. Department of Health and Human Services [USDHHS], 1999). In addition, mapping activities related to density issues can also aid in allocating resources more effectively to address alcohol consumption and safety concerns further.

Dangers of Overconsumption in Nonlicensed Settings

As discussed earlier, while numerous factors contribute to overconsumption on college campuses, research has identified the supply of cheap alcohol in large volume as a critical component of this phenomenon (Chaloupka & Wechsler, 1995; Erenberg & Hacker, 1997). In addition to price-reduction strategies used by licensed establishments, are the equally important unsupervised venues such as dorms, fraternities/sororities, and house parties. Here at UW-Madison, most of the problems in these unsupervised venues occur at large house parties in the high-density student neighborhoods, as evidenced by the fact that the majority of noise complaints citations are issued at these parties. As a strategic position to head off a "displacement effect"— the possibility that students would drink more at house parties as police increase monitoring of local bars—it was critical that our campus and community coalition addressed high-risk drinking at these unsupervised venues, along with consumption at licensed establishments.

To address the house party problem, the Madison Police Department decided to view these parties as unsupervised, unlicensed taverns, since the majority of the problem parties involved students purchasing a cup at the door for "all you can drink." Thus, hosts were dispensing alcohol at cost, and students not only drank as much as they wanted to but also as much as they could before the alcohol ran out. Furthermore, there is no control over the number of people attending, which raises concerns about capacity. Only in the rarest circumstances were IDs checked at these parties, and that was generally to screen out high school students. These problem house parties were rarely concerned with screening for individuals under age 21, an issue also reflected in the literature on high-risk drinking involving unsupervised parties (College Alcohol Study [CAS], 2005). When trouble occurs because of alcohol overconsumption, a frequent occurrence at house parties, the police arrive and most students simply disperse. Police often come only after problems have reached serious levels, since attendees might be hesitant to call for help, either because they are unable to detect a problem early on or due to the problematic nature of the party (e.g., underage consumption and dispensing alcohol without a license).

Given these and other negative consequences associated with house parties, universities might consider examining this problem in more depth in an effort to create workable solutions that will help to address the safety and legal consequences that arise from drinking in such unsupervised settings. Within our broad principles of engaging the campus and community together under the environmental management model, we undertook a multi-part strategy that included the development of educational and enforcement strategies that would address house parties broadly across the communities immediately surrounding the UW-Madison's central campus.

The first step toward a more concerted effort to address house parties took the form of a campus-community work group with representation from diverse agencies, including neighborhood associations, students, city and university police, local government, chancellor's office, mayor's office, health services, apartment associations, and project staff. Work group discussions led to identifying three overarching purposes: (a) to facilitate developing a set of policies and procedures to make house parties safe; (b) to develop procedures to deal with unsafe situations; and (c) to create a set of campus-community expectations that will serve as a guideline for house parties.

One of the first solutions undertaken by our campus-community coalition was to develop the "safe house party guide" outlining policies and procedures that students could use to keep their parties under control, to keep them safe, and to help them know how to handle situations when they did escalate in unsafe ways. An important partner in the development of this safe party guide was the Madison Police Department, an agency that students needed to see as a source of assistance when their party escalated out of control. Through extensive focus group discussion, we learned that students were very often aware of when they lost control of their parties, but were afraid to call the police for fear of fines and other punishments. However, the police were able to use these discussions as opportunities to clarify that if hosts did contact them, the agency's priority was to address the unsafe situations that were occurring and that they would take into consideration that students took the initiative to contact the police.

In the past, when police have arrived at these parties, inebriated students have tended to scatter to escape being cited while increasing their chances of getting injured. However, our work group discussions helped the police in clarifying further that when they did arrive at a party, it was usually the host who was cited for operating an "unlicensed tavern." Depending on the specific situation, the fines levied at these parties have sometimes been enormous, since the base fine was compounded by the total number of guests present, with the presence of underage drinking further compounding fines. Publicizing the excessive high penalties that can be issued has served as a deterrent to hosting large parties that can quickly get out of hand and has served as reinforcement for students to "call in" for help at their own parties.

We have found that one of the effective interventions is the city police department contacting property owners when their tenants receive citations at house parties. Most standard leases include a clause stating that tenants may not engage in illegal behaviors, and police actions help the property owners to enforce this clause and follow up with their tenants. Initial communications with the police department seem to indicate that repeat citations are rare in the house of those property owners who do follow up with their tenants. We will continue to work with the police department to conduct a systematic evaluation on the outcome of this initiative as data become available.

Our work on addressing house party issues is ongoing. However, a welcome spin-off of this initiative is that our efforts have helped to facilitate stronger partnerships between the city police department and the dean of students office, both having taken on leadership roles in intervening and following up with student-hosts who are cited for house party-related infractions.

As the house party initiative demonstrates, we started with broadly accepted goals targeting the health and safety of all individuals and the community, and we worked within our principles of environmental approaches based on strong campus and community partnerships. In this case, our attention to the problem of house parties gave us an opportunity to integrate educational approaches with enforcement of existing laws.

Risks of Overconsumption in Licensed Settings

As is clear by now, a core principle of an environmental approach is to address the environment holistically by simultaneously addressing the dangers of overconsumption in both licensed and unlicensed settings within the community. Based on the evidence of effectiveness available in the literature, we also developed a list of "best practices" that can be applied to licensed settings that we have forwarded to the city's ALRC, along with our other key campus and community partners. The following list briefly describes these best practices, and the PACE website, http://pace.uhs.wisc.edu/, offers additional information:

1. Consider the impact of price on consumption, specifically, discounted drinks (see Chaloupka & Wechsler, 1996; Coate & Grossman, 1988; Grossman, Coate, & Arluck, 1987; Kuo, Wechsler, Greenberg, & Lee, 2003).

2. Implement rigorous ID-check programs. Evidence suggests that outlets conducting such checks, along with closer supervision of sales by employees, report lower rates of sale to minors (see Wolfson, Toomey, Forster, Murray, & Wagenaar, 1996a; Wolfson et al. 1996b).

3. Provide uniform server training initiatives. Research suggests that these initiatives can increase an individual's knowledge about services to minors and intoxicated patrons (see McKnight, 1993; McKnight & Streff, 1994; Wolfson et al., 1996b). Server trainings are interventions specifically designed to create safer drinking venues by reducing the likelihood of overserving. Examples of such interventions include educating servers about alcohol sales-related policies in a particular state, food service, crowd control, and the ability to identify intoxicated patrons early.

4. Examine advertising practices by alcohol outlets (see Engs & Hanson, 1993).

5. Provide food service and nonalcoholic beverages for patrons (see Fraser, Rosalki, Gamble, & Pounder, 1995; National Institute on Alcohol Abuse and Alcoholism [NIAAA], 1997).

6. Provide entertainment by offering nonalcohol events for all ages.

Importance of Campus-Community Coalitions

Last, it is imperative that any institution undertaking the task of addressing problems related to high-risk drinking on its campus nurture a campus-community coalition. We hope we have made it clear that addressing consequences stemming from high-risk drinking on a college campus is a complex task requiring the development of interventions at multiple levels, as they relate to on- and off-campus arenas. This issue necessitates campus-community coalitions that can examine the problem from a broader perspective, engage diverse "stakeholders" across the university and city, and help design a wide range of appropriate strategies.

Here at UW-Madison, it would have been impossible for staff to propel project initiatives without the support of a wide range of campus and community partners who have facilitated our work. Our project's comprehensive efforts to address alcohol issues are both collaborative and catalytic in nature. We collaborate heavily with other organizations to start up relevant initiatives and then facilitate "spin-offs" such that appropriate entities can take on ownership of issues with project staff staying on to fill an advisory role. Some examples of offices with which we collaborate include dean of students, chancellor's office, alumni association, housing (both university and private), ALRC, fraternities and sororities, and the athletic department. We initiate our work with these and other organizations by first identifying common areas around decreasing the consequences of high-risk drinking. Our work on house parties is a good example. In yet another instance, we helped the Wisconsin Union to provide more systematic campus-wide nonalcohol recreational opportunities by collaborating on grant proposals soliciting funding for such activities.

While our collaborations have been extremely fruitful, there have been a few instances (though understandable and perhaps expected) of "turf protection" in which there was concern about role definition. However, by demonstrating to concerned parties that project efforts were complementary to and not competitive with their efforts, such problems were resolved quickly.

Conclusion

At times, the extent of high-risk drinking on college campuses can seem insurmountable. Alcohol overconsumption and its consequences on campuses remains one of the foremost public health challenges in the United States. Traditionally, addressing problems related to high-risk drinking remained very much within those offices operating under the purview of student affairs. In addition, the problem was generally viewed as a university- or campus-based issue.

Yet, slowly but surely, things are changing, as many universities—big and small—are in the midst of reviewing this fairly intractable problem from a wider lens that takes into consideration both the academic and nonaca-demic consequences of overconsumption. In a time of shrinking resources and a perpetual shortage of time, our experiences suggest that investing in collaboration across campus divisions and beyond not only can facilitate dia-logue at multiple levels leading to problem solving, it can also help produce better information and resource sharing. Over time, these partnerships can lead the way toward creating a campus community that ensures the health and safety of all its members, thereby facilitating an environment that effec-tively fulfills the overall mission of a university, that of research, teaching, and learning.

References

American Medical Association (AMA). (2002). *Partner or foe? The alcohol industry, youth problems, and alcohol policy strategies*. Policy briefing paper. Retrieved May 19, 2006, from http://www.alcoholpolicysolutions.net/pdf/foe_final.pdf

Chaloupka, F., & Wechsler, H. (1995). *The impact of price, availability, and alcohol control policies on binge drinking in college*. Working paper 5319. National Bureau of Economic Research. Cambridge, MA.

Chaloupka, F., & Wechsler, H. (1996). Binge drinking in college: The impact of price, availability and alcohol control policies. *Contemporary Economic Policy, 14*, 112–124.

Coate, D., & Grossman, M. (1988). The effects of alcoholic beverage prices and legal drinking ages on youth alcohol use. *Journal of Law and Economics, 31*(1), 145–171.

College Alcohol Study (CAS). (2005). Summary of UW Madison findings of the College Alcohol Study 1993–2005. Retrieved May 19, 2006, from http://pace.uhs.wisc.edu/data_cas.php

DeJong, W., Vince-Whitman, C., Colthurst, T., Cretella, M., Gilbreath, M., & Rosati, M. (1998). *Environmental management: A comprehensive strategy for reduc-ing alcohol and other drug use on college campuses*. Newton, MA: Higher Education Center for Alcohol and Other Drug Prevention.

DiFulvio, G. (2005). *Annotated Bibliography of Alcohol, Other Drug, and Violence Prevention Resources 1995–2003*. A publication of the Higher Education Center for Alcohol and Other Drug Prevention. U.S. Department of Education.

Engs, R. C., & Hanson, D. J. (1993). Drinking games and problems related to drink-ing among moderate and heavy drinkers. *Psychological Reports, 73*, 115–120.

Erenberg, D. F., & Hacker, J. D. (1997). *Last call for high-risk bar promotions that target college students*. Center for Science in the Public Interest Alcohol Policies

Project. Retrieved May 19, 2006, from http://www.health.org/nongovpubs/lastcall/default.aspx

Fraser, A. G., Rosalki, S. B., Gamble, G. D., & Pounder, R. E. (1995). Inter-individual and intra-individual variability of ethanol concentration-time profiles: Comparison of ethanol ingestion before or after an evening meal. *British Journal of Clinical Pharmacology*, *40*, 387–392.

Grossman, M., Coate, D., &, Arluck, G. M. (1987). Price sensitivity of alcoholic beverages in the United States: Youth alcohol consumption. In H. Holder (Ed.), *Control issues in alcohol abuse prevention: Strategies for states and communities* (pp. 169–198). Greenwich, CT: JAI Press.

Gruenewald, P. J., Millar, A. B., & Treno, A. J., (1993). Alcohol availability and the ecology of drinking behavior. *Alcohol Health and Research World*, *17*, 39–45.

Higher Education Center for Alcohol and Other Drug Prevention (2003). *Alcohol, tobacco and other drugs prevention file.* Retrieved May 19, 2006, from http://pace.uhs.wisc.edu/docs/preventionfile 18-5.pdf

Hingson, R., Heeren, T., Winter, M., & Wechsler, H. (2005). Magnitude of alcohol-related mortality and morbidity among U.S. college students ages 18–24: Changes from 1998 to 2001. *Annual Review of Public Health*, *26*, 259–279.

Hingson R. W., Heeren, T., Zakocs, R. C., Kopstein, A., & Wechsler H. (2002). Magnitude of alcohol-related mortality and morbidity among U.S. college students ages 18–24. *Journal of Studies on Alcohol*, *63*(2), 136–144.

Hingson, R. W., & Howland, J. (2002). Comprehensive community interventions to promote health: Implications for college-age drinking problems. *Journal of Studies on Alcohol Supplement*, *14*, 226–240.

Institute of Medicine. (1989). *Prevention and treatment of alcohol problems: Research opportunities.* Washington, DC: National Academy Press. Retrieved January 20, 2004, from http://www.nap.edu/books/0309041821/html/

Kuo, M., Wechsler, H., Greenberg, P., & Lee, H. (2003). The marketing of alcohol to college students: The role of low prices and special promotions. *American Journal of Preventive Medicine*, *25*(3), 204–211.

Larimer, M. E., & Cronce, J. M. (2002). Identification, prevention, and treatment: A review of individual-focused strategies to reduce problematic alcohol consumption by college students. *Journal of Studies on Alcohol Supplement*, *14*, 148–163.

Maxwell, A., & Immergluck, D. (1997). *Liquor lining: Liquor store concentration and community development in lower-income Cook County (IL) neighborhoods.* Chicago IL: Woodstock Institute. Retrieved May 19, 2006, from http://woodstockinst.org/document/liquorlining.pdf

McKnight, J. A. (1993). Server intervention: Accomplishments and needs. *Alcohol Health and Research World*, *17*(1), 76–83.

McKnight, J. A., & Streff, F. M. (1994). The effect of enforcement upon service of alcohol to intoxicated patrons of bars and restaurants. *Accident Analysis and Prevention, 26*(1), 79–88.

National Institute on Alcohol Abuse and Alcoholism (NIAAA). (1997 January). *Alcohol alert: Alcohol metabolism. No. 35,* PH 371.

National Institutes of Health (NIH), National Institute on Alcohol Abuse and Alcoholism (2002). *A call to action: Changing the culture of drinking at US colleges. Final report of the Task Force on College Drinking* (NIH Publication No: 02-5010). Retrieved May 19, 2006, from http://media.shs.net/collegedrinking/Task ForceReport.pdf

Nelson, T. F., Naimi, T. S., Brewer, R. D., & Wechsler, H. (2005). The state sets the rate: The relationship of college binge drinking to state binge drinking rates and selected state alcohol control policies. *American Journal of Public Health, 95*(3), 441–446.

O'Hare, T. M. (1990). Drinking in college: Consumption patterns, problems, sex differences and legal drinking age. *Journal of Studies on Alcohol, 51*(6), 536–541.

Perkins, H. W. (2002). Social norms and the prevention of alcohol misuse in collegiate contexts. *Journal of Studies on Alcohol Supplement, 14,* 164–172.

Presley, C. A., Meilman, P. W., & Cashin, J. R. (1996). Alcohol and drugs on American college campuses: Use, consequences, and perceptions of the campus environment, vol. IV: 1992–1994. Carbondale, IL: Core Institute, Southern Illinois University.

Ryan, B. E., & DeJong, W. (1998). *Making the link: Faculty and prevention. A publication of the Higher Education Center for Alcohol and Other Drug Prevention.* The U.S. Department of Education. Retrieved May 19, 2006, from http://www .edc.org/hec/pubs/faculty-prevention.html

Schulenberg, J., Maggs, J. L., Long, S. W., Sher, K. J., Gotham, H. J., Baer, J. S., et al. (2001). The problem of college drinking: Insights from a developmental perspective. *Alcoholism: Clinical and Experimental Research, 25*(3), 473–477.

Scribner, R. A., MacKinnon, D. P., & Dwyer, J. H. (1995). The risk of assaultive violence and alcohol availability in Los Angeles County. *American Journal of Public Health, 85,* 335–340.

Singer, W. (2003). The role of the campus visit and the summer orientation program in the modification of student expectations about college. *The Journal of College Orientation and Transition, 10*(2), 52–57.

Steffain, G. (1999). Correction of normative misperception: An alcohol abuse prevention program. *Journal of Drug Education, 29,* 115–138.

Stevenson, R. J., Bronwyn, L., & Weatherburn, D. (1999). The relationship between alcohol sales and assault in New South Wales, Australia. *Addiction, 94*(3), 397–410.

Thombs, D. (2000). A test of the perceived norms model to explain drinking patterns among university student athletes. *Journal of the American College Health*, *497*, 5–84.

U.S. Department of Health and Human Services (USDHHS). (1999). *Preventing problems related to alcohol availability: Environmental approaches*. Washington, DC: Substance Abuse and Mental Health Services Administration, Center for Substance Abuse Prevention, Division of State and Community Systems Development.

Wechsler, H., Kuo, M., Lee, H., & Dowdall, G.W. (2000). Environmental correlates of underage alcohol use and related problems of college students. *American Journal of Preventive Medicine*, *19*(1), 24–29.

Wechsler, H., Lee, J. E., Hall, J., Wagenaar, A. C., & Lee, H. (2002a). Secondhand effects of student alcohol use reported by neighbors of colleges: The role of alcohol outlets. *Social Science and Medicine*, *55*(3), 425–435.

Wechsler, H., Lee, J. E., Kuo, M., Seibring, M., Nelson, T. F., & Lee, H. P. (2002b). Trends in college binge drinking during a period of increased prevention efforts: Findings from four Harvard School of Public Health study surveys, 1993–2001. *Journal of American College Health*, *50*(5), 203–217. Retrieved February 2, 2006, from http://www.hsph.harvard.edu/cas/Documents/trends/Trends.pdf

Weitzman, E. R., Nelson, T. F., Lee, H., & Wechsler, H. (2004). Reducing drinking and related harms in college: Evaluation of the "A Matter of Degree" program. *American Journal of Preventive Medicine*, *27*(3), 187–196.

Wolfson, M., Toomey, T. L., Forster, J. L., Murray, D. M., & Wagenaar, A. C. (1996a). Alcohol outlet policies and practices concerning sales to underage persons. *Addiction*, *91*(4), 589–602.

Wolfson, M., Toomey, T. L., Forster, J. L., Wagenaar, A. C., McGovern, P. G., & Perry, C. L. (1996b). Characteristics, policies and practices of alcohol outlets and sales to underage persons. *Journal of Studies on Alcohol*, *57*, 670–674.

3

VIOLENCE AND HATE CRIMES ON CAMPUS

Uncovering the Mystique

Darnell G. Cole, Meechai Orsuwan, and Anna Ah Sam

On August 9, 2006, Fullerton (California) police arrested Gaston Alejandro Gastelum, a 21-year-old student at California State University, Fullerton, because he incorrectly assumed that two young women were a lesbian couple and viciously attacked them.

On July 17, about 2 a.m., two women, ages 20 and 22, were walking through an alley near campus when they met Gastelum. He was walking with four friends, one man and three women. He laughed at the two victims, pointed at them, and yelled, "You look like boys. You must be lesbians! B****es! F***ing dykes!"

One of the victims asked him to show some manners, but Gastelum repeated his curses; punched her in the face, throat, and chest; and knocked her to the pavement. When the second woman wanted to protect her friend, Gastelum kept yelling, "What are you, her b****?" Then he slugged the second woman 12 to 15 times, forced her into a garage, and beat her, according to the police.

"The whole time he was beating us, he was yelling, 'B****es, dykes, lesbians,' and his male friend laughed during the attack. His female friends stood by and did nothing," the two victims said ("No class," 2006).

At a university in Maine, an African American student listened to an answering machine message left by three White students. The message was, "I wonder what you're gonna look like dead. Dead, I wonder if when you die you'll lose your color." The message continued, "Like the blood starts to leave your body and you're gonna . . . start deteriorating and blood starts to leave your skin. . . . You get the picture? You're **** dead" (Wessler & Moss, 2001, pp. 7–8).

On September 20, 1996, at the University of California at Irvine (UCI), a number of Asian American students received the following e-mail message written by former UCI student Richard Machado:

> Hey stupid f***, as you can see in the name, I hate Asians, including you. If it weren't of asias [sic] at UCI, it would be a much more popular campus. You are responsible for ALL the crimes that occur on campus. You are responsible for the campus being all dirt. YOU ARE RESPONSIBLE. That's why I want you and your stupid a** comrades to get the f*** out of UCI. If you don't, I will hunt all of you down and kill your stupid a**es. Do you hear me? I personally will make it my life career to find and kill everyone of you personally. OK?! That's how determined I am. Get the f*** out. (Lee, 2001, p. 67)

These incidents of hate crimes on college campuses, coupled with others such as the murders of Matthew Shepard and James Byrd Jr., are constant reminders that we still live in a violent country where discrimination is prevalent. Extreme violence in compulsory education, like the tragedy of Columbine, has sensitized our society to the constant threat of violence in what is assumed to be the safest place for students—school. While colleges and universities have not had the recent barrage of suicidal students wielding illegal handguns or the cross-burnings of the almost forgotten Klan, hate crimes and murderous fits of rage have ended in the deaths of people at the University of Northern Colorado, Penn State, and Indiana University, to name a few. Despite these events, empirical research examining the impact of violence, hate crimes, harassment, and discrimination on students is limited, although the topic has become fascinating to several scholars (Nora & Cabrera, 1996; Terenzini, Cabrera, Colbeck, Bjorklund, & Parente, 2001; Vogt, 1997).

This growing interest in research is probably due to the rapid increase in the number of traditionally underrepresented student populations such as non-Whites, women, and the economically disadvantaged across colleges and universities (Delucchi, 2003; Trower & Chait, 2002). Unfortunately, bias-motivated crimes on campus may occur because the mix of faculty, staff, and students possesses uniquely different values and backgrounds. In 1971, 42% of undergraduates were women, compared to 56% in 2001 (Trower & Chait, 2002). African American and Hispanic students in higher education accounted for 8.4% and 2.8%, respectively, in 1970, compared to 11% and 8% 30 years later. In 1976, Asian Americans comprised 1.8% of college students, compared to 6% in 2001. To make the campus climate more diverse, more international students attended institutions of higher education in the United States than any other country in the world. In 2001, 547,867 international students accounted for 3.9% of the total enrollment of higher education in the United States (Institute of International Education, 2003).

Consequently, concerns arise regarding these students' adjustment to the college environment because higher education was unfamiliar territory for them. The concerns are well understood because these students have to adjust to the institutional culture and the social culture of the predominant students (Burbach & Thompson, 1971). During the process of adjustment, minority students may or may not be accepted by the incumbent students, and many cases of racial tension, harassment, and discrimination occur on campus. These incidents may seem less violent, but they are a precursor to more extreme acts of violence such as those listed above. In fact, statistics show that bias-motivated crimes are based on race, ethnicity, and gender. This type of crime is also known as a hate crime. The Association of American Colleges and Universities (AAC&U) estimated that at least one hate crime occurs on a college campus every day, but most incidents are not reported to campus police or other agencies (Teraguchi, 2004). Hate crimes on campus tarnish the college experiences of students and hinder academic performance because the educational environment becomes unfriendly and uncomfortable (Schneider, Hitlan, & Radhakrishnan, 2000). And sometimes hate crimes are fatal, as in the case of Jeanne Clery and the case of Columbine.

This chapter discusses the nature of hate crimes in general as well as the intersection of violent crimes in general and hate crimes on college campuses; discusses hate crime cases on college campuses and profiles hate crime perpetrators and victims; and provides an empirical study on the effects of harassment and discrimination on students' satisfaction. Finally, discussions and implications for college administrators are included.

Intersection of Violent Crimes and Hate Crimes on College Campuses

Differentiating ordinary violent crimes and hate crimes on campus can be difficult, even in the eyes of witnesses. The World Health Organization defines violent crimes as "the intentional use of physical force or power, threatened or actual, against one's self, another person, or a group or community that either results in or has a high likelihood of resulting in injury, death, psychological harm, maldevelopment, or deprivation" (Krug, Dahlberg, Mercy, Zwi, & Lozano, 2002, p. 4). In an educational context, violent crimes on college campuses can be conceptually categorized into 13 subcategories: sexual violence, sexual assault, stalking, campus dating violence, hate crimes, hazing, celebratory violence, attempted suicide and suicide, murder/suicide, murder/non-negligent manslaughter, aggravated assault, arson, and attack on faculty or staff (Carr, 2005). By definition, a hate crime is a crime that is committed against a victim based on his or her group (i.e., race, religion, sexual orientation, ethnicity) (Federal Hate Crime Statistics Act, 1990). This definition subsequently included crimes motivated by gender (Hate Crimes Sentencing Enhancement Act, 1995). The key term is *motivation*; this seems to be the significant difference between ordinary violent crimes and hate crimes.

A crime on campus is an ordinary crime if it fits into one of the 13 subcategories above. That crime, however, becomes a hate crime if the perpetrator intentionally commits the crime against the victim because of the latter's membership in a group (i.e., race, ethnicity, gender, or sexual orientation) (Hate Crimes Sentencing Enhancement Act). It should be noted that a defamatory racial remark that is not acted on is considered hate speech, not a hate crime (Jost, 1993). Subsequently, if convicted under a hate crime law, the perpetrator receives at least three harsher levels of punishment than he or she would have received for an ordinary violent crime (Gerstenfeld, 2004). Because hate crimes are based entirely on the motive of the perpetrator, his or her words and speech are then considered in court (Lawrence, 1999). However, proving the perpetrator's motive is difficult because the prosecutor has to prove premeditation—that the perpetrator intentionally targeted the victim—by illustrating what the perpetrator said to the victim before committing the crime (Gerstenfeld, 2004). As a result, only 58 hate crime perpetrators have been tried in the United States under the auspices of the Hate Crimes Sentencing Enhancement Act (Chorba, 2001).

The term "hate crime" was formally defined sometime in the 1980s, when the first hate crime laws were enacted (Gerstenfeld, 2004). Before hate crime laws existed, the Civil Rights Acts were the tools used to punish perpetrators of hate crimes (Freeman, 1992). However, the Civil Rights Acts protect only people who are victimized based on their resident status, color, race, religion, or national origin (Freeman, 1992); they do not protect the victim of a crime that is based on his or her age, sexual orientation, disability, or gender. In addition to the federal government's efforts to enforce hate crime laws, state governments monitor such crimes as well.

Before hate crime laws were enacted, the states would arrest the hate crime perpetrators under laws prohibiting particular acts or activities (Freeman, 1992), which, for example, prohibited anyone from wearing masks in public places; damaging churches, cemeteries, and schools; and burning crosses (Gerstenfeld, 2004). These laws punish only some bias-motivated crimes, however. Alternatively, the states may punish bias-motivated crime perpetrators according to the crime they actually commit (Gerstenfeld, 2004). That is, if they assault gays and lesbians, they are charged with assault and battery, or if they burn a Buddhist temple, they are charged with arson. Many people strongly urge state governments to establish specific laws for hate crimes. Three reasons used to support specific laws for hate crimes are that hate crimes do more harm than ordinary crimes, their perpetrators need harsher punishments, and the government needs to send a strong message that bias-motivated crimes are intolerable in this country (Dillof, 1997; Gerstenfeld, 2004; Levin & McDevitt, 1995; Weisburd & Levin, 1994).

Currently, 42 states have hate crime laws (Jacobs & Potter, 1998). Some states do not have such laws partly due to the belief that hate crime laws are not necessary, and the existing laws are appropriate for punishing hate crime perpetrators. However, each state's hate crime laws are complex and diverse in terms of what they define as a hate crime or who is protected thereunder (Jacobs & Potter, 1998). Most states include at least race, religion, and ethnicity; however, only 23 include sexual orientation, 21 include gender, 23 include mental or physical disability, 4 include political affiliation, and 4 include age (Jacobs & Potter, 1998).

According to the Anti-Defamation League's website, Hawaii has institutional vandalism statutes, although not necessarily antibias, and harsher criminal penalties for vandalism aimed at houses of worship, cemeteries, schools, and community centers. The Anti-Defamation League's website also reports that California's hate crime legislation includes institutional vandalism; bias-motivated violence and intimidation; civil action as a result of hate crimes; criminal penalties as a result of hate crimes, race, religion, and ethnicity; interference with religious worship, sexual orientation, gender, and mental and physical disability; data collection; and training for law enforcement personnel (Anti-Defamation League). The establishment of hate crime laws is credited to the Anti-Defamation League of B'nai B'rith (ADL), which combats and keeps track of anti-Semitism and other forms of bigotry across the country and collects data to persuade states to pass hate crime laws (Anti-Defamation League [ADL], 1994).

The judiciary in state governments is responsible for holding criminal trials for hate crimes allegedly committed under that state's particular statutes regarding its legal definitions of such crimes (ADL, 1988, 1994). An example of a hate crime on a college campus that was prosecuted by a state government was the state of Maine convicting a college student for uttering antigay slurs and threats to another student while simultaneously strangling the victim, another student (Wessler & Moss, 2001). Another case involved three White students convicted by the state of Maine for leaving a life-threatening message for an African American student (Wessler & Moss, 2001). Even though state governments usually prosecute hate crimes, there are federal laws that allow the federal government to assist state governments in their hate crime trials.

Former President Bill Clinton asserted that the hate crime federal laws "allow federal prosecutors to pursue a hate crime case if local authorities declined to press charges" (CNN, 2000). The following case illustrates the role of the federal government in seeking justice for college students who were the targets of a hate crime involving a racist statement. James Samar was convicted for uttering anti-Semitic slurs and threats to two students and threatening to execute another student (Wessler & Moss, 2001). One of the victims received a photo as "a reminder of what happened to your relatives because they too made a mockery of Christianity" (p. 7). Another federal case involved sentencing Robert Allen Little, a Utah university student, to 12 years in prison and ordering him to pay a $12,000 fine. Little was convicted of bombing a dormitory room occupied by two African American students and planning to bomb another room occupied by another African American student (Wessler & Moss, 2001).

Hate Crimes on College Campuses

The previous section provides examples of how state and federal governments use the legal system to prosecute students involved in various hate crimes on college campuses. Across the state of California, for example, which has one of the most explicit state hate crime laws, 107 hate perpetrators were convicted under the state's hate crime laws in 1995, 87 in 1996, 223 in 1997, 131 in 1998, 174 in 1999, and 213 in 2000 (Gerstenfeld, 2004). Although these numbers include hate crimes conducted off college campuses, they do illustrate how more effective laws have the potential to convict hate crime perpetrators. In addition to state and federal governments' efforts to eradicate hate crimes, colleges and universities have campus codes prohibiting certain behaviors and activities (Gerstenfeld, 2004). Codes prohibiting hate speech, which encourage acts of violence and create an unwelcoming college atmosphere, are common, though these codes also have the potential to be viewed as a violation of the First Amendment—freedom of speech (Haiman, 1993; Heumann & Church, 1997).

Thanks largely to the Clery Act, updated information on institutional and government efforts is more available to college students. The Hate Crimes Statistics Acts of 1990, also known as the Clery Act, was initially enacted by Congress and later signed into law by President George H. W. Bush in 1990, after which it became the Crime Awareness and Campus Security Act of 1990 (Valentine, 1995). Howard and Connie Clery were strong advocates of this law after their daughter, Jeanne, was murdered at Lehigh University in 1986. The Jeanne Clery Disclosure of Campus Security Policy and Campus Crime Statistics Act, codified at 20 USC § 1092 (f) as a part of the Higher Education Act of 1965, requires colleges and universities to release information and statistics on campus crimes to their students on a timely basis (Gerstenfeld, 2004). All public and private postsecondary education institutions participating in federal student aid programs are subject to the act, and those who violate it can be fined up to $27,500 or face other enforcement action by the agency charged with the act's enforcement (Gerstenfeld, 2004).

While hate crime statistics are collected, they are generally flawed. According to former attorney general Janet Reno (U.S. Department of Justice [USDOJ], 1998), the most serious problem is that hate crimes are vastly underreported. In a survey distributed to students attending 12 institutions of higher education, only 25% of violent crime victims said they reported the incident to campus police or other agencies (Sloan, Fisher, & Cullen, 1997). There are several reasons why hate crimes are underreported. First, due to a lack of knowledge or sources of information, some victims may not know what a hate crime is (Levin, 1992–1993). If one needs to learn about hate crime statistics, however, information can be readily obtained only from three sources: the Federal Bureau of Investigation Uniform Crime Reports, the U.S. Department of Education Campus Security Statistics, and the International Association of College Law Enforcement Administrators' annual survey (Wessler & Moss, 2001).

Yet, the information and statistics these three agencies collect are incomplete. For example, the hate crimes included in the FBI's annual reports rely heavily on the data provided only by a certain number of colleges and universities. The statistics reported by the International Association of College Law Enforcement Administrators' annual survey do not categorize hate crimes based on gender separately (Wessler & Moss, 2001). There are also difficulties in recording information and determining the particular group of which the victim is a member (Gerstenfeld, 2004). For instance, when a hate crime victim reports that the crime is committed against him or her because of the victim's ethnicity, if the victim happens to be multiracial, it may be difficult for officers or agencies to record these crimes consistently.

Another reason hate crimes are underreported is that students, faculty, and staff are uneducated about reporting hate crimes (Wessler & Moss, 2001). That is, they lack information on how to report essential facts and detailed information about hate crimes, including the what, where, or when (Wessler & Moss, 2001). In addition, hate crimes are underreported because of the victims' fear of being victimized again and feelings of shame about being a victim of such a crime (California Attorney General, 2001; Center for Prevention of Hate Violence, 2001). Some lesbian, gay, bisexual, and transgender (LGBT) students simply do not report hate crime incidents to any agencies because they believe their states offer minimal or no legal protection to them (Center for Prevention of Hate Violence, 2001).

The Perpetrators and the Victims of Hate Crimes on Campus

The Perpetrators

Studies have attempted to profile the people who tend to commit hate crimes in hopes of increasing the awareness of students and the general public.

Unfortunately, the profiles of hate crime perpetrators are mixed and often surprising. Four types of people tend to commit the crimes: those who are *thrill-motivated, defensive, mission-oriented,* or *retaliatory* (Levin & McDevitt, 1995; McDevitt, Levin, & Bennett, 2002). *Thrill-motivated* perpetrators commit hate crimes for fun and enjoyment. Often the perpetrator might not be biased against the target victim, but may join his or her group's leader for acceptance or bragging rights. Two-thirds of hate crime perpetrators are thrill-motivated (McDevitt et al., 2002). Most thrill-motivated perpetrators said they were with their friends and wanted to impress them while committing these acts. They often perceive that hatred is "hip" or "cool" (Levin & McDevitt, 1995).

Defensive perpetrators view the outsiders as a threat and hence remove perceived outsiders from their lives by "getting rid of them." Usually, defensive perpetrators target victims who invade their perceived territory. An example of a hate crime committed by defensive perpetrators is the case of a Vietnamese teenager who was brutally executed by two Texas skinheads in 1990. Before being killed, the Vietnamese teenager pleaded for his life, saying, "Please stop. I'm sorry I ever came to your country. God forgive me!" (Southern Poverty Law Center [SPLC], 2000, p. 11). *Mission* perpetrators commit hate crimes to perpetuate their own supremacy. An example of a mission perpetrator is Marc Lepine, who walked into a classroom, allowed the male students to leave, and shot 14 female students at the University of Montreal on December 6, 1989. The suicide letter found after he took his own life reads:

> For seven years my life has brought me no joy, and being utterly weary of the world, I have decided to stop those shrews dead in their tracks . . . The feminists always have a talent for enraging me. They want to retain the advantages of being women . . . while trying to grab those of men . . . They are so opportunistic that they neglect to profit from the knowledge accumulated by men throughout the ages. They always try to misrepresent them every time they can. (Ramsland, 2005, p. 8)

Finally, *retaliatory* perpetrators attempt to get revenge for their group by committing hate crimes. An example of a hate crime conducted by retaliatory perpetrators is the case of Rodney King, who was beaten by Los Angeles police officers. Subsequently, this incident triggered a violent cycle of retaliatory incidents in south central Los Angeles and around the country (USDOJ, 1997).

Many researchers also have profiles of hate groups. Most surprising, current hate crimes are rarely committed by members of hate groups such as the Ku Klux Klan, racist skinheads, or the racist militia movement (Craig, 2002). It's not that these hate groups are harmless; in fact, the viewpoints these groups convey have tremendous impact on the people exposed to them. These people subsequently adopt the hatred and prejudiced viewpoints of hate groups, and some eventually commit violent hate crimes. Statistics are congruent with this finding, as authorities have found that hate crimes are mostly conducted by normal-looking people (Levin, 2002; Nolan, Akiyama, & Berhanu, 2002). Hate crime profilers often expect hate crime perpetrators to be young high school dropouts who live in fragile neighborhoods with divorced parents or family violence experience (Ezekial, 1995; Turpin-Petrosino, 2002). The bottom line, however, is that the profile of hate crime perpetrators is inconclusive. It is safe to say that anyone has the potential to commit hate crimes because violence motivated through everyday biases and prejudices can incite a hate crime. College campuses are vulnerable places for hate crimes since they comprise a diverse array of people who often have little experience with one another. It is not surprising that hate crimes on college campuses are severe and widespread (Gerstenfeld, 2004).

The Victims

Unlike hate crime perpetrators, the victims of hate crimes tend to be easier to profile. At the federal level alone, according to a 1998 report by the Federal Bureau of Investigation (FBI) Uniform Crime Reporting Program, 57% of hate crimes on college campuses are based on race/ethnicity. The Violent Victimization of College Students Report found that non-Hispanic Whites and African American students are more likely than other races to be assaulted (Baum & Klaus, 2005). This report of hate crimes on campus is consistent with data on hate crime victims reported by the FBI and California, Colorado, Illinois, and Texas (Wessler & Moss, 2001). Their statistics reveal that African Americans are by far the group most victimized by hate crime perpetrators in the United States (Gerstenfeld, 2004).

In 1998, 16% of hate crimes recorded by the FBI were based on sexual orientation (Wessler & Moss, 2001). Sexual orientation or gender identity caused 20% of faculty, staff, and students to fear for their well-being on campus (Rankin, 2003). Unlike hate crimes against other, more diverse groups, gays, lesbians, bisexuals, and transgenders usually are not protected by hate crime laws, and many LGBT people are even rejected by their own family members who believe that antigay sentiment is still widely acceptable. Hate crimes against victims based on ethnicity, such as Jews, or those of Japanese, Chinese, or Latino ancestry frequently occur even though the victims may have been in the United States for a long time (Gerstenfeld, 2004). Many perpetrators even consider their hate crimes against ethnic minorities to be patriotic. About 1,450 crimes and incidents against Muslims were reported to the authorities after the infamous September 11, 2001, attack (Council on American-Islamic Relations, 2002). Hate crimes based on gender occur widely, but many states do not have gender-based crime laws because the perpetrators do not really "hate" the victims, unlike hate crimes against African Americans and Jews (Gerstenfeld, 2004).

Victims of hate crimes are more psychologically harmed than are victims of other types of crimes (Sullaway, 2004). It takes longer for hate crime victims to recover (Herek, Gillis, & Cogan, 1999). Even after time has passed, victims of hate crimes are haunted by their horrendous experience (McDevitt, 1999). These victims experience a higher level of psychological damage because they blame themselves for being attacked or assaulted in a place they once believed to be safe (Janoff-Bulman, 1979). Some blame themselves because they are attacked or assaulted for who they are (Herek, Cogan, & Gillis, 2002; Herek et al., 1999). Consequently, a student who is a victim of a hate crime on campus may be troubled by the incident, withdraw from campus activities and feel isolated, vulnerable, and unprotected on campus, a supposedly safe place (Wessler & Moss, 2001).

Harassment and Discrimination at Minority-Serving Institutions

Bias incidents such as harassment and discrimination are "acts of prejudice that are not accompanied by violence, the threat of violence, property damage, or other illegal conduct" (Wessler & Moss, 2001, p. 5). Nevertheless, harassment and discrimination may breach institutional regulations. Under the Hate Crime Statistics Act of 1990, institutions must report harassment of and discrimination toward their students when these incidents occur (Clery & Clery, 2001; Wessler & Moss, 2001). Furthermore, harassment and discrimination are often viewed as the predecessors of more violent acts. Research in this area is scant due to the complexity of the issue and the lack of availability and low quality of data.

College campuses, as discussed previously, are often the site of diverse populations and are likely to be the place where hate crimes exist. Few studies, however, have explored the impact of harassment and discrimination on students. To expand literature in this area, this study examined the impact of discrimination and harassment on the educational satisfaction of students attending the University of Hawai'i, Mānoa (UHM). UHM, the flagship university in the state, is a minority-serving institution. Its student population is approximately 45% Asian American, 27% White, 10% Native Hawaiian and other Pacific Islander students, and 18% other ethnic minority students (University of Hawai'i, 2004). Hence, UHM presents a unique opportunity to study the experiences of various ethnic minority students' experience with and attitudes toward harassment and discrimination.

Research on harassment and discrimination, informed primarily through gender differences and minority college student experiences, has been linked to students' educational satisfaction. For instance, male and female students have different levels of satisfaction with respect to student-faculty contact, peer interactions, and experience with sexual harassment (Hearn, 1985; Neumann & Neumann, 1981). Researchers have also found that faculty members often treat female students differently in the classroom (Brooks, 1982; Follet, Andberg, & Hendel, 1982; Hall & Sandler, 1982; Whitt, 1999), while male students reportedly act more aggressively with female professors (Brooks, 1982). Women attending male-dominated institutions have insufficient faculty support and sometimes experience harassment (Hearn & Olzak, 1981).

Asian, Latina/o, and Native American students reported lower levels of satisfaction partly due to the greater prevalence of alienation, discrimination, and invisibility they experience compared to their White counterparts (Astin, 1977; Hune, 1998; Jones, Castellanos, & Cole, 2002). Cole and Jackson (2005), for instance, found that Asian students were more likely to be dissatisfied with their education if they did not have general kinds of contact with faculty (i.e., interacting with faculty outside classroom and discussing course work, research, grades, and career plans). Minority students, such as African Americans, tend to earn lower grades when they experience discrimination (Nettles, 1988; Prillerman, Myers, & Smedley, 1989; Smedley, Myers, & Harrell, 1993). According to Hurtado, Carter, and Spuler (1996), Nora and Cabrera (1996), and Bean (1990), students who perceived negative racial tension on campus were more likely to experience slow or poor adjustment to campus life and were more prone to drop out of college.

Although racial/ethnic discrimination disproportionately affects ethnic minority students, White students' sense of belonging (Gilliard, 1996) and educational satisfaction (Cole & Jackson, 2005) appear to suffer as a result of a deprived racial climate on campus. Overall, these studies suggest that discrimination could decrease educational satisfaction and the likelihood of success in college. The following research questions were examined in this study: (a) To what extent do students experience harassment and discrimination on campus? and (b) To what extent do harassment and discrimination impact students' educational satisfaction?

Methodology

The purpose of this study was to examine the impact of discrimination and harassment on the educational satisfaction of students' attending UHM, a minority-serving institution. Educational satisfaction typically refers to the positive feeling that students have toward their institution's instruction, curriculum, social life, and cultural activities (Delucchi, 2003). Earlier literature has identified differential college experiences across gender and racial/ethnic groups and their impact on educational satisfaction. This chapter provides separate models of educational satisfaction for Asian Americans, Pacific Islanders, and Whites, though each model used the same set of independent variables. Furthermore, the environmental variables used in this analysis were related to racial interaction, harassment, and discrimination.

Sample and Instrument

The data were obtained from a survey instrument based on the Assessment of Campus Climate for Underrepresented Groups used in the National Campus Climate for Diversity Project (Ah Sam, Agbayani, & Horikawa, 2005; Rankin, 2002). The original instrument was co-sponsored by the National Association of Student Personnel Administrators (NASPA) and the National Gay and Lesbian Task Force (NGLTF) and was administered on 10 college campuses in the continental United States (Ah Sam et al., 2005). The survey used in this study was edited to include additional ethnic categories, to identify groups specific to UHM, and to add items relating to student satisfaction with college (Ah Sam et al., 2005). Items encompassed the following areas: personal experience with diversity (e.g., harassment and discrimination); perceptions of campus climate (e.g., contact with people of different religions); institutional actions (e.g., diversity workshops/programs); and satisfaction with college. The original data collection included a form of stratified random sampling that was used to capture adequate numbers of underrepresented groups (e.g., African Americans, Filipinos, native Hawaiians, and Pacific Islanders) (Ah Sam et al., 2005). In the spring of 2003, a total of 356 surveys were returned for a response rate of 28%. Of that total, a usable sample of 226 students was included in this study. This sample consisted of Whites ($n = 45$), Asian Americans ($n = 120$), and Pacific Islanders ($n = 61$). There were a total of 226 students, 125 females and 101 males. The survey included 105 students who worked on campus.

Variables

The dependent variable was students' rating of educational satisfaction measured on a 4-point Likert scale (Excellent $= 4$, Poor $= 1$). There were seven independent variables, two of which were student background characteristics, which included gender (male $= 0$, female $= 1$) and years attending the institution ($1 = 1$ year, $4 = 4$ years or more). The five other independent variables were environmental, such as "observed/experienced harassment" ($0 = $ none, $1 = $ either of them, $2 = 2$ of them); "observed/experienced discrimination" ($0 = $ none, $1 = $ either of them, $2 = 2$ of them); "have contact with people of different religions" ($0 = $ none, $5 = $ very frequent); "attending diversity activities" ($0 = $ none, $5 = $ very frequent); and "having welcoming classroom climate for underrepresented groups" ($0 = $ none, $5 = $ very frequent).

Analysis

Statistical analysis included descriptive statistics and a multiple regression analysis. Ordinary least squares regression was used to examine this relationship and to identify significant predictors of educational satisfaction of American Asian, Pacific Islander, and White students. Separate multiple regression models were used for each group. The standardized coefficients employ the 5% level of significance test.

Findings

Although the target institution has a large number of American Asian and Pacific Islander students, descriptive statistics indicated that White students

(M = 2.91) gave the highest rating on educational satisfaction, followed by Asian American (M = 2.84) and Pacific Islander (M = 2.77) (see Table 3.1). From Table 3.2, men (M = 2.85) reported slightly higher levels of educational satisfaction than did women (M = 2.82), and Asian American, Pacific Islander, and White students rated their educational experiences at UHM as "good." Chi-square tests, however, showed no significant differences in educational satisfaction by racial/ethnic group or by gender.

As at other campuses, incidents of harassment and discrimination self-reported by respondents occurred at the University of Hawai'i at Mānoa. Students reported that harassment based on ethnicity (51 cases) was the most frequent incident they experienced. Other forms of harassment often encountered by students were based on gender (42 cases), race (31 cases), sexual orientation (28 cases), and physical characteristics (26 cases), respectively. Only students who worked for the university (n = 105) were asked about discrimination. Obviously, fewer cases of discrimination were reported,

TABLE 3.1
Means of Rating on Educational Experience by Ethnicity
(1 = poor, 4 = excellent)

Variable	Asian (n = 120) M (S.D.)	Pacific Islander (n = 61) M (S.D.)	White (n = 45) M (S.D.)
How would you evaluate your educational experiences at the institution?	2.84 (.78)	2.77 (.72)	2.91 (.76)

TABLE 3.2
Means of Rating on Educational Experience by Gender
(1 = poor, 4 = excellent)

Variable	Women (n = 125) M (S.D.)	Men (n = 101) M (S.D.)
How would you evaluate your educational experiences at the institution?	2.82 (.76)	2.85 (.81)

compared to cases of harassment. Similar to harassment, incidents of discrimination occurred more frequently based on gender (9 cases) and ethnicity (7 cases).

Table 3.3 reveals how student satisfaction for each group was affected by harassment. The means of student satisfaction for those Asian American students who have not experienced or observed harassment ($M = 2.91$) was higher than for those who have experienced or observed harassment ($M = 2.67$). Pacific Islander students who have experienced or observed discrimination rated their educational experience ($M = 2.58$) lower than those who have not experienced or observed harassment ($M = 2.89$). Similarly, the satisfaction of White students who have not experienced or observed harassment ($M = 3.15$) was much higher than it was for those who have experienced or observed harassment ($M = 2.55$).

Harassment, Discrimination, and Their Effect on Student Satisfaction

Separate multiple regression models were used for Asian American, Pacific Islander, and White students. For each model, the dependent variable—rating of educational experiences on campus—was regressed on the seven independent variables simultaneously. For Asian American students, the results indicated that the seven independent variables explain 43.4% ($R^2 = .434$, adjust $R^2 = .42$) of the students' educational satisfaction. Most estimated parameters have the expected directional sign. Six of seven independent variables were statistically significant in explaining the students' level of educational satisfaction (see Table 3-4).

TABLE 3.3
Ratings of Satisfaction of Those Who Did or Did Not Observe and Experience Harassment, by Ethnicity

Variable	Asian (N = 120)		Pacific Islander (N = 61)		White (N = 45)	
	M (S.D.)	n	M (S.D.)	n	M (S.D.)	n
Have observed or experienced harassment	2.67 (.76)	73	2.58 (.65)	30	2.55 (.60)	24
Have *not* observed or experienced harassment	2.91 (.82)	47	2.89 (.74)	31	3.15 (.85)	21

On the one hand, "having contact with students of different religions" (β = 2.16, p < .01), "having a welcoming classroom climate for underrepresented groups" (β = .13, p < .05), and "attending the institution for a longer time" (β = .19, p < .05) had a significantly positive impact on Asian American students' educational satisfaction. On the other hand, being a female (β = −.15, p < .05), "observed/experienced harassment" (β = −.18, p < .05), and "having attended diversity activities" (β = −1.25, p < .05) had a negative impact on students' educational satisfaction. The statistical significance of "observed/experienced harassment" indicated that students' educational satisfaction is hampered when they observe and/or experience campus harassment. It was surprising that the variable, "observed/experienced discrimination," had no significant effect on Asian American students' satisfaction.

For Pacific Islander students, the results indicated that the seven independent variables explain 37% (R^2 = .37, adjusted R^2 = .36) of students' educational satisfaction. However, only three of seven independent variables were statistically significant in explaining the level of students' educational satisfaction (see Table 3.4). For Pacific Islander students, "having contact with students with different religions" (β = 1.98, p < .05) and "attending the institution for a longer time" (β = .16, p < .05) had a significantly positive impact on their satisfaction. As was the case with Asian American students, "observed/experienced harassment" (β = −.16, p < .05) had a significantly negative effect, but "observed/experienced discrimination" had no significant effect on their educational satisfaction.

For White students, the results indicated that the seven independent variables explain 39% (R^2 = .382, adjusted R^2 = .38) of their educational satisfaction. Only two of seven independent variables were statistically significant in explaining the level of students' educational satisfaction (see Table 3.4). Both "having contact with students with different religions" (β = 2.08, p < .01), and "having a welcoming classroom climate for underrepresented groups" (β = .14, p < .05) had a significantly positive impact on their educational satisfaction. For White students, "observed/experienced harassment" and "observed/experienced discrimination" had no significant effect on their educational satisfaction.

Because only students who worked on campus were asked about discrimination, it was interesting to see whether discrimination had any effect on their satisfaction. Using the same set of independent variables, the results indicated that all of the independent variables in the model explain 40% (R^2

TABLE 3.4
Student Characteristics and Environmental Variables Regressed onto Educational Satisfaction

Independent Variable	Asian (n = 120)	Pacific Islander (n = 61)	White (n = 45)	Campus-employed students (n = 105)
Student Characteristics:				
Gender	−.15*	−0.97	−0.85	−0.66
Years attending the institution	.19*	.16*	.16	1.56*
College Experience Variables:				
Observed or experienced harassment	−.18*	−.16*	−0.21	.17*
Observed or experienced discrimination	−0.01	−0.002	−0.02	.15*
Having welcoming classroom climate for underrepresented groups	.13*	.06	.14*	.08
Having contact with students of different religions	2.16**	1.98*	2.08**	1.67
Attending diversity activities	−1.25*	.33	.42	.06
R^2	.43	.37	.39	.40
Adjusted R^2	.42	.36	.38	.39

Note: $* p < .05$, $** p < .01$. Coefficients are standardized.

$= .40$, adjusted $R^2 = .39$) of campus-employed students' satisfaction. Most important, for campus-employed students, both "observed/experienced harassment" ($\beta = .17$, $p < .05$) and "observed/experienced discrimination" ($\beta = .15$, $p < .05$) had a significantly negative impact on these students' educational satisfaction.

Implications for Institutions and Student Affairs

This chapter reviewed the general nature of hate crimes and the reasons why such crimes are underreported and focused on the role of the judiciary at both the state and federal levels in trying hate crime cases. To illustrate how hate crimes are judged by each of these levels of government, example cases were presented and summarized. These hate crime cases often include a violence incident. Such crimes are opposed to the mission of any educational institution and are unacceptable on any college campus. Furthermore, colleges and universities risk litigation by their own students if they fail to protect them. As such, hate crime cases are extremely complex and often impossible to resolve without the help of a sophisticated criminal court system at both the state and federal levels. Universities and colleges should be reassured by the knowledge that their campuses are required to make available information to forewarn their students of any hate crimes. In addition, campus policies and guidelines regarding hate speech and hate crimes have the potential to affect campus culture and student behavior.

The empirical analyses revealed that, based on the research results, despite attending a minority-serving institution, harassment lowered the quality of students' educational experience. Regardless of their racial/ethnic background, White, Asian American, and Pacific Islander students who experienced and/or observed incidents of harassment had a lower level of satisfaction than did those who did not. Even though the discrimination variable had no significant impact on student satisfaction across groups, it lowered students' level of educational satisfaction. College and university administrators must be proactive in minimizing acts of violence motivated by prejudice and intolerance, not only for the sake of student satisfaction, but also for the sake of creating an educational environment that reflects the ideals of tolerance and civil rights advocated throughout our democracy.

In doing so, college and university officials must have and report accurate, clear information about these incidents (e.g., by intersections of racial/ethnic groups and combinations of various categories, such as gender, religion, sexual orientation, etc.); make readily available information about how to identify and where to report such crimes; and act decisively to condemn the behavior while swiftly reprimanding the perpetrators. In other words, college and university officials must be intolerant of hate crimes. Without a resolute and unrelenting stance on hate crimes, ineffective or slow action, or inaction, by institutional officers will likely do little to alter future hate crime behaviors.

References

Ah Sam, A., Agbayani, A., & Horikawa, R. (2005). Campus climate for diversity: A study of undergraduate students' perspectives at the University of Hawai'i at Mānoa. Honolulu, HI: University of Hawai'i at Mānoa, Office of Student Equity, Excellence and Diversity.

Anti-Defamation League, The (ADL). (1988). *Hate crimes: Policies and procedures for law enforcement agencies.* New York: Author.

Anti-Defamation League, The (ADL). (1994). *Hate crime laws: A comprehensive guide.* New York: Author.

Astin, A. W. (1977). *Four critical years: Effects of college on beliefs, attitudes, and knowledge.* San Francisco: Jossey-Bass.

Baum, K., & Klaus, P. (2005, January). *Violent victimization of college students, 1995–2002.* (NCJ Publication No. 206836). Washington, DC: U.S. Department of Justice, Office of Justice Programs, Bureau of Justice Statistics.

Bean, J. P. (1990). *Why students leave: Insights from research.* In D. Hossler, J. P. Bean, and associates (Eds.), *The strategic management of college enrollments* (pp. 147–169). San Francisco: Jossey-Bass.

Brooks, V. R. (1982). Sex differences in student dominance behavior in female and male professors' classrooms. *Sex Roles, 8*(7), 683–690.

Burbach, H. J., & Thompson, M. A., III. (1971). Alienation among college freshmen: A comparison of Puerto Rican, Black and White students. *Journal of College Student Personnel, 16,* 53–56.

California Attorney General. (2001). *Reporting hate crimes.* Retrieved February 16, 2003, from http://caag.state.ca.us

Carr, J. L. (2005, February). *American college health association campus violence white paper.* Baltimore, MD: American College Health Association.

Center for Prevention of Hate Violence. (2001). Retrieved October 11, 2005, from http://www.cphv.usm.maine.edu

Chorba, C. (2001). The danger of federalizing hate crimes: Congressional misconceptions and the unintended consequences of the Hate Crimes Prevention Act. *Virginia Law Review, 87,* 319–379.

Clery, H., & Clery, J. (2001). *What Jeanne didn't know.* Retrieved April 10, 2006, from http://www.securityoncampus.org/

CNN. (2000). *Clinton: Hate crimes bill "profoundly important."* Retrieved October 10, 2005, from http://www.cnn.com/2000/ALLPOLITICS/stories/04/25/hate.crimes/index.html

Cole, D., & Jackson, J. F. L. (2005). The impact of interracial interactions and campus-based diversity functions on students' educational satisfaction in higher education. In D. N. Byrne & J. Williams, *Thurgood Marshall Scholarship Fund: Brown v. Board of Education: Its impact on public education* (pp. 249–269). Brooklyn, NY: Word For Word Publishing Co.

Council on American-Islamic Relations. (2002). Article retrieved September 23, 2005, from http://en.wikipedia.org/wiki/Council_on_American-Islamic_Relations

Craig, K. M. (2002). Examining hate-motivated aggression: A review of the social psychological literature on hate crimes as a distinct form of aggression. *Aggression and Violent Behavior, 7,* 85–101.

Delucchi, M. (2003). *Student satisfaction with higher education during the 1970's: A decade of social change.* Lewiston, NY: E. Mellen Press.

Dillof, A. M. (1997). Punishing bias: An examination of the theoretical foundation of bias crime statutes. *Northwestern University Law Review, 91,* 1015–1081.

Ezekial, R. (1995). *The racist mind: Portraits of American neo-Nazis and Klansmen.* New York: Viking Penguin.

Federal Hate Crime Statistics Act, The. 28 U.S.C. § 534 (1990).

Follet, C. V., Andberg, W. L., & Hendel, D. D. (1982). Perceptions of the college environment by women and men students. *Journal of College Student Personnel, 23,* 525–31.

Freeman, S. T. (1992). Hate crime laws: Punishment which fits the crime. *Annual Survey of American Law, 4,* 581–585.

Gerstenfeld, P. B. (2004). *Hate crime: Causes, controls, and controversies.* Thousand Oaks, CA: Sage Publications.

Gilliard, M. D. (1996). *Racial climate and institutional support factors affecting success in predominantly White institutions: An examination of African American and White student experiences.* Unpublished Ph.D. dissertation, University of Michigan Ann Arbor.

Haiman, F. S. (1993). *"Speech acts" and the First Amendment.* Carbondale: Southern Illinois University Press.

Hall, R. M., & Sandler, B. R. (1982). *The classroom climate: A chilly one for women. Project on the status and education of women.* Washington, DC: Association of American Colleges.

Hate Crime Sentencing Enhancement Act, The, 28 U.S.C. § 994 (1995).

Hearn, J. (1985). Determinants of college students' overall evaluations of their academic programs. *Research in Higher Education, 23*(4), 413–437.

Hearn, J. C., & Olzak, S. (1981). The role of college major department in the reproduction of sexual inequality. *Sociology of Education, 54,* 195–205.

Herek, G. M., Cogan, J. C., & Gillis, J. R. (2002). Victim experiences in hate crimes based on sexual orientation. *Journal of Social Issues, 58,* 319–339.

Herek, G. M., Gillis, R., & Cogan, J. C. (1999). Psychological sequelae of hate crime victimization among lesbian, gay, and bisexual adults. *Journal of Consulting and Clinical Psychology, 67,* 945–951.

Heumann, M., & Church, T. W. (Eds.). (1997). *Hate speech on campus: Cases, case studies, and commentary.* Boston: Northeastern University Press.

Hune, S. (1998). *Asian Pacific American women in higher education: Claiming visibility and voice and executive summary.* Washington, DC: Association of American Colleges and Universities.

Hurtado, S., Carter, D. F., & Spuler, A. (1996). Latino student transition to college:

Assessing difficulties and factors in successful college adjustment. *Research in Higher Education, 37*(2), 135–157.

Institute of International Education. (2003). *Open doors: Statistics on international student mobility.* New York: Author.

Jacobs, J. B., & Potter, K. (1998). *Hate crimes: Criminal law and identity polities.* New York: Oxford University Press.

Janoff-Bulman, R. (1979). Characterological versus behavioral self-blame: Inquiries into depression and rape. *Journal of Personality and Social Psychology, 37,* 1798–1809.

Jones, L., Castellanos, J., & Cole, D. (2002). Examining the ethnic minority student experience at predominantly White institutions: A case study. *Journal of Hispanic Higher Education, 1*(1), 19–39.

Jost, K. (1993, January). Hate crimes. *CQ Researcher, 3* 19.

Krug, E. G., Dahlberg, L. L., Mercy, J. A., Zwi, A. B., & Lozano, R. (Eds.). (2002). *World report on violence and health.* Geneva, Switzerland: World Health Organization.

Lawrence, F. M. (1999). *Punishing hate: Bias crimes under American law.* Cambridge, MA: Harvard University Press.

Lee, M. K. (2001). Hate crime on the internet: The University of California, Irvine case. In P. W. Hall & V. M. Hwang (Eds.), *Anti-Asian violence in North America: Asian American and Asian Canadian reflections on hate, healing, and resistance* (pp. 67–76). Walnut Creek, CA: Rowman & Littlefield.

Levin, B. (1992–1993). Bias crimes: A theoretical and practical overview. *Stanford Law and Policy Review, Winter,* 165–180.

Levin, J. (2002). *The violence of hate: Confronting racism, anti-Semitism, and other forms of bigotry.* Boston: Allyn & Bacon.

Levin, J., & McDevitt, J. (1995, August 4). The research needed to understand hate crime. *The Chronicle of Higher Education, 41,* B1–B2.

McDevitt, J. (1999). *Plenary keynote address.* Paper presented at the Meeting of Hate Crimes: Research, Policy and Action, Los Angeles, CA.

McDevitt, J., Levin, J., & Bennett, S. (2002). Hate crime offenders: An expanded typology. *Journal of Social Issues, 58,* pp. 303–318.

Nettles, M. T. (Ed.). (1988). *Toward Black undergraduate student equality in American higher education.* New York: Greenwood.

Neumann, Y., & Neumann, L. (1981). Determinants of students' satisfaction with course work. *Research in Higher Education, 14,* 321–333.

No class: Student faces prison after anti-gay attack. (2006). *OC Weekly.* Retrieved September 14, 2006, from http://www.ocweekly.com/news/news/no-class/25758/

Nolan, J. J., Akiyama, Y., & Berhanu, S. (2002). The Hate Crime Statistics Act of

1990: Developing a method for measuring the occurrence of hate violence. *American Behavioral Scientist, 46,* 136–153.

Nora, A., & Cabrera, A. F. (1996). The role of perceptions in prejudice and discrimination and the adjustment of minority students to college. *Journal of Higher Education, 67*(2), 119–148.

Prillerman, S. L., Myers, H. F., & Smedley, B. D. (1989). Stress, well-being, and academic achievement in college. In G. L. Berry & J. K. Asamen (Eds.), *Black students: Psychosocial issues and academic achievement* (pp. 198–217). London: Sage.

Ramsland, K. (2005). *Gendercide: The Montreal massacre.* Retrieved April 3, 2006, from http://www.crimelibrary.com/notorious_murders/mass/marc_lepine/index.html

Rankin, S. R. (2002). Transformational tapestry model. Retrieved August 15, 2006, from http://www.rankin-consulting.com

Rankin, S. R. (2003). *Campus climate for gay, lesbian, bisexual, and transgender people: A national perspective.* New York: The National Gay and Lesbian Task Force Policy Institute.

Schneider K. T., Hitlan, R. T., & Radhakrishnan, P. (2000). An examination of the nature and correlates of ethnic harassment in multiple contexts. *Journal of Applied Psychology, 85,* 3–12.

Sloan, J. J., Fisher, B. S., & Cullen, F. T. (1997). Assessing the Student Right-to-Know and Campus Security Act of 1990: An analysis of the victim reporting practices of college and university students. *Crime & Delinquency, 43*(2), 148–168.

Smedley, B. D., Myers, H. F., & Harrell, S. P. (1993). Minority-status stresses and the college adjustment of ethnic minority freshmen. *Journal of Higher Education, 64*(4), 435–452.

Southern Poverty Law Center (SPLC). (2000, Winter). The year in hate. *Intelligence Report,* 97.

Sullaway, M. (2004). Psychological perspectives on hate crime laws. *Psychology, Public Policy, and Law,* 1–33.

Teraguchi, D. H. (2004). *A systematic plan to fight hate on campuses.* Retrieved February, 2, 2006, from http://www.aacu-edu.org/bildner/Resources/Hate_Crimes.cfm

Terenzini, P. T., Cabrera, A. F., Colbeck, C. L., Bjorklund, S. A., & Parente, J. M. (2001). Racial and ethnic diversity in the classroom: Does it promote student learning? *Journal of Higher Education, 72*(5), 509–531.

Trower, C., & Chait, R. (2002). Faculty diversity: Too little for too long. *Harvard Magazine, 10*(4), 33–37, 98.

Turpin-Petrosino, C. (2002). Hateful sirens . . . who hears their song? An examination of student attitudes toward hate groups and affiliation potential. *Journal of Social Issues, 58,* 281–301.

University of Hawai'i. (2004). *University of Hawaii institutional research report.* Retrieved January 10, 2006, from http://www.hawaii.edu/iro/

U.S. Department of Justice, Federal Bureau of Investigation, Criminal Justice Information Service (CJIS). (1997). *Division, uniform crime reports: Hate crimes, 1997.* Washington, DC: Author.

U.S. Department of Justice, Federal Bureau of Investigation Hate Crime Statistics. (1998). Retrieved March 6, 2006, from http://www.usdoj.gov/opa/pr/1998/January/004.htm

Valentine, B. (1995). *Gang intelligence manual. Identifying and understanding modern-day violent gangs in the United States.* Boulder, CO: Paladin.

Vogt, P. V. (1997). *Tolerance and education: Learning to live with diversity and difference.* London: Sage.

Weisburd, S. B., & Levin, B. (1994). "On the basis of sex": Recognizing gender-based bias crimes. *Stanford Law and Policy Review, 5,* 21–43.

Wessler, S., & Moss, M. (2001). *Hate crimes on campus: The problem and efforts to confront it.* Washington, DC: U.S. Department of Justice, Office of Justice Programs, Bureau of Justice Assistance.

Whitt, E. (1999). Women's perceptions of a chilly climate and cognitive outcomes in college: Additional evidence. *Journal of College Student Development, 40,* 163.

4

WHY STUDENTS BEAT EACH OTHER

A Developmental Perspective for a Detrimental Crime

Walter M. Kimbrough

O ne of the more interesting phenomena on college campuses today is the continued practice of students beating each other as part of some ritual required to be associated with a group. Sometimes the beating is a part of a formal process, while other times it is something that happens as students search for new and inventive ways to make their peers earn their place in a group. In either case, this dangerous practice continues to make headlines every year, and every year students are injured and even killed because of these activities.

There is generally no way to predict which students are most likely to engage in these practices. Physical hazing occurs at Ivy League schools as well as at open admission colleges. Students with high aspirations and a lot to lose also engage in these activities as much as do students who are content with college life. While historically physical beatings have been the province of men, we are now seeing a dangerous trend of more of these activities occurring with young women. The highly publicized high school hazing in Illinois, as shown on the *Oprah Winfrey Show*, demonstrated that suburban girls at "good schools" could also display the viciousness that causes bruises and broken bones.

This chapter provides a context for why this physical abuse, which has existed almost since the inception of American higher education, continues to proliferate today, and is now seen even in high schools. A developmental theory provides a powerful frame of reference to understand this phenomenon, and I offer several recommendations to help address the problem.

What this chapter does not do is provide "the" solution for this problem. In reviewing years of literature and best practices in higher education, it is hard to say that we have made insignificant change in this culture. Students today are probably more knowledgeable about hazing issues than were students 20 years ago, and continued education is clearly a part of the strategy. However, we have not yet found the message that will convince students not to participate in these dangerous activities. More students appear to be distancing themselves from groups that engage in these activities, which serves as some protection. However, the benefits from associating with such groups continue to serve as a huge draw for students in need of affiliation and identity formation. It is because of this tremendous force that we continue to struggle with this issue.

A Short History of Hazing

Author Hank Nuwer has been the foremost expert on hazing and has done an excellent job of chronicling its rise in American higher education. I do not attempt to rehash the work of Nuwer, but rather offer a short overview. For a detailed analysis, please refer to Nuwer's *Wrongs of Passage: Fraternities, Sororities, Hazing and Binge Drinking* (1999) as well as his edited work, *The Hazing Reader* (2004). Hazing rituals can traced to European higher education in the 1400s, when German students conducted a process known as *pennalism*. Freshmen were required to carry with them pen cases and were subjected to physical hazing in the form of beatings by upperclassmen around the clock, for an entire academic term (Kimbrough, 2003). British students in the 1700s altered the activity and referred to it as "fagging," where underclassmen performed menial servitude for upperclassmen. Nuwer (1999) writes, "The 'fag' fetched tea and food for his young 'master,' serving as a valet and submitting to a brutal kick or a hard rap if he tarried or failed to obey an order" (p. 99).

Hazing in the United States, according to Nuwer (2004) dates back to Harvard in 1657. He writes, "Many early college presidents, preferring absolute order to the flourishing of individual identities encouraged hazing. They saw it as a way to teach precedence, build school loyalty, and assimilate students from all economic classes" (pp. xiv–xv). The methods used to haze students varied during this period. Students were pelted with garbage, beaten, and even had their heads' scalped. By the 1920s, deaths had been associated with campus hazing, which led campus administrators to abolish hazing (Kimbrough, 2003; Nuwer, 2004).

Since the gradual phasing out of freshman hazing through the 1970s, the culture of hazing essentially moved from the macro-university or college level to the micro-level, confined primarily to fraternities and sororities, athletic teams, social clubs, and even marching bands. The beating of a Florida A&M University student in the marching band received national media coverage as he reported being paddled more than 70 times before being initiated into the clarinet section.

Even with the tremendous amount of education about hazing since the 1990s, physical abuse and even deaths occur every year. The 1994 death of Michael Davis at Southeast Missouri State University still serves as the most prominent and painfully clear evidence that savage beatings occur on campus in the quest for membership in special groups and organizations. The death of Davis, who sustained tears to his liver, lung, kidneys, spleen, and brain, garnered national attention through many media outlets, including *Dateline NBC*. Yet, severe physical hazing continues at an active rate, with at least five cases reported each year (Kimbrough, 2003).

Recent Cases of Abuse

Despite numerous attempts to educate students about hazing and physical violence, there continue to be many high-profile incidents that make the headlines every year. Most of the time, these incidents revolve around hazing new members, be they students who are still in the process of joining, or those who have officially joined and still seek group validation. The vast majority of physical hazing tends to be associated with African American fraternal organizations (Kimbrough, 2003). The cases discussed below provide an idea of the kind of abuse that goes on.

In December 2004, a St. John's University student testified against members of Phi Beta Sigma fraternity for hazing that allegedly took place in 2003. The student, Brian Chambers, testified that he was paddled more than 50 times during the summer of 2003. He spent two weeks in the hospital after suffering kidney failure (Lowe, 2004a). Three men were charged with second-degree assault, and, if convicted, would have faced up to seven years in prison. However, the three were found not guilty, as the court was not convinced the men charged had committed the crime (Lowe, 2004b).

In April 2004, Raymond McCoy sent a 14-page letter to various media outlets describing the hazing he alleged took place when he attempted to join the Kappa Alpha Psi fraternity. He included nine photographs of his body to show the scars and bruises on his back, chest, and buttocks. His roommate appeared to validate the claims and asked him why he allowed the abuse to continue (Stahl, 2004).

In February 2005, McCoy filed a lawsuit against Kappa Alpha Psi for alleged hazing abuses he suffered during the spring of 2003. He alleged, as a result of the incident, that he suffered brain damage and emotional injuries, which caused him to drop out of school (Jones, 2005). The fraternity chapter was placed on cease and desist orders from the national office, which meant they could no longer function in the name of the organization.

In January 2005, a student at Southern University in Louisiana accused members of the Omega Psi Phi fraternity of hazing him. In an interview with the *Southern University Digest*, the campus newspaper, the accuser said he was instructed to meet a member of the fraternity at a location, then was blindfolded and joined by two other men. Subsequently, the students were allegedly beaten—and paddled—by fraternity members. The accuser claimed that he went to the hospital and began throwing up blood due to internal injuries (Dorn, 2005).

Initially, a student judiciary body comprised of members from other fraternities and sororities found the chapter not guilty. However, the university, through the dean of student life, suspended the fraternity for three years after a hearing where the university was presented with pictures of the student's injuries. In addition, the fraternity had not been approved to begin meeting with prospective members and was in violation of related university policies. The dean believed the evidence was overwhelming, which warranted the decision to suspend (Tate, 2005).

In a rare story involving women, members of Frostburg State University's field hockey team hazed new members in April 2005. The incident involved alcohol, which required one student to be hospitalized with a blood alcohol content four times the legal limit. The new members were assaulted with flour, ice, and eggs and were made to sit in their own vomit and urine. Six current and former students were given a 60-day suspended sentence, one year of unsupervised probation, and ordered to pay a $300 fine (Dish-neau, 2005; Dorfman, 2005).

Finally, in September 2005, an Asian fraternity held a members versus pledges football game where the pledges were outnumbered five to one. The ritual was to be the final stage of a nine-week pledge program. In the end, 19-year-old Kenny Luong, a student at Cal Poly Pomona, died of head injuries from the contest. One member of the Lambda Phi Epsilon fraternity described it as hazing disguised as a football game (Reyes & Reza, 2005).

These examples provide an idea of the range of physical abuses on college campuses each year. While some may seem unbelievable, there have been many more that were egregious as well as deadly. Campus leaders should assume that students are engaging in hazing activities, and that many of those activities include physical abuse from simple calisthenics to severe beatings.

Why Students Beat Each Other: A Developmental Explanation

Numerous theories have been established since the mid 1960s to describe the change students undergo in their own development. Some focus more on the psychosocial development of students (e.g., Josselson, 1990), while others focus on the cognitive aspects of development (e.g., Perry, 1998). In addition, new theories have been established to examine specific subgroups of students, including women and students of color (e.g., Cross, 1992).

One of the seminal theories of student development was initially developed by Arthur Chickering in 1969 as published in *Education and Identity*. In essence, Chickering established seven vectors through which students move in their search for identity. Almost 25 years later, Chickering and Reiser completely updated *Education and Identity* to take advantage of the research published since the volume first appeared. It is through this model of student development that some sense can be gained about why students beat each other.

The first of the vectors appears to be the key to the continued existence of physical violence in student groups for the past 600 years. This vector, entitled *developing competence*, has three main elements: (a) intellectual competence, (b) physical and manual skills, and (c) interpersonal competence. Chickering and Reiser (1993) summarized intellectual competence as "skill using one's mind. It involves mastering content, gaining intellectual and aesthetic sophistication, and, most important, building a repertoire of skills to comprehend, analyze, and synthesize" (p. 45).

The second component, physical and manual competence,

> Involve[s] athletic and artistic achievement, designing and making tangible products, and gaining strength, fitness, and self-discipline . . . [to] bring emotions to the surface since our performance and our projects are on display for others' approval or criticism. (Chickering & Reiser, 1993, p. 46)

The third element of this vector, interpersonal competence,

> Entails not only the skills of listening, cooperating, and communicating effectively, but also the more complex abilities to tune in to another person and respond appropriately, to align personal agendas with the goals of the group, and to choose from a variety of strategies to help a relationship flourish or a group function. (Chickering & Reiser, 1993, p. 46)

If we analyze each element, we are able to understand better how this violence is perpetuated via student groups, most notably, fraternal organizations (especially African American and Latino) and athletic teams. On the surface, the first element, intellectual competence, would seem not to fit in with physical hazing and violence in student groups. Yet, this is often the catalyst for the physical abuse that takes place within these groups.

A key part of the collegiate experience is for students to transition successfully from high school and to experience success in the classroom by passing their courses. Students are generally motivated by the prospect of a degree that will lead to graduate studies or employment, but initial sources of motivation may include a desire to please family and friends or to avoid a sense of shame from going away to college and failing. Generally, the goal is not to learn for the "sake of learning," but to achieve some professional goal that provides monetary rewards. This trend is supported with the increasing numbers of students who have left the liberal arts and sought the "practical arts," such as business or preprofessional fields (Bok, 2005).

For some student organizations, intellectual competence is used as a test of worthiness for aspiring members of the group. Full-fledged members often use a series of questions or mind games as a part of the process of becoming members. In this game, aspirants are motivated by their desire to gain approval and avoid punishment. For some student groups, this punishment takes the form of physical abuse (e.g., paddling, slapping, and calisthenics).

On the simplest level, aspirants are often questioned regarding basic historical facts and tenets of the organization in which they are seeking membership. Within the fraternal world, pledges are normally required to memorize the names of all the founders of the group, sometimes the names of local founders, and significant dates in the life of the organization. During some of the pledge sessions, now known as "sets" in the African American context, aspirants are asked to repeat these names and dates. An error often results in physical abuse, as mentioned above.

In some instances, aspirants are asked to master the basic information about the group in which they are seeking membership. Pledges have been (and probably still are) asked to memorize factoids about every other pledge: hometown, major, mother's name, father's name, siblings, etc. The idea is to foster some form of sisterhood or brotherhood among aspirants. However, many have argued that these kinds of activities do more to create a sense of unity among the aspirants (in this case, an oppressed group) than to create a unity throughout the entire organization. While this argument has been made successfully for decades, it has yet to be a factor in curtailing this kind of activity.

Other intellectual challenges are more involved. For example, a fraternity orders its aspirants to obtain an item that can only be found several states away. The group has to decide how to accomplish this task. In many cases, the group would drive all night long and drive back to attempt to meet the deadline. However, based on how the question was asked, they simply could have gotten a picture of the item and submitted it to show their understanding of the game.

These kinds of mind games are common among student groups and provide easy ways to use physical abuse when the aspirants do not figure out the game properly. Unfortunately, popular culture provides numerous examples of how these kinds of tests are used through reality shows, which undoubtedly provide ideas for students. Instead of firing an apprentice candidate for not figuring out how to sell a product, or penalizing members of a band after walking miles for cheesecake, some student groups use pure physical force to show their displeasure and ultimately reinforce their position of power in the relationship.

The second element, physical and manual competence, plays an interesting role when examining why students beat each other on campus. For student-athletes, their participation in athletics should provide the mechanism by which students can achieve this level of competence. Chickering and Reiser (1993) clearly indicate:

> Athletics offers a context in which concrete, unequivocal, and public performance provides clear evidence of achievement and of developmental progress. In this arena, students' attitudes toward personal abilities and potentials are starkly revealed, and competence or the lack of it must be faced squarely. If the competence is there, it is publicly acclaimed and the sense of competence is likely to soar. Disappointed or indifferent observers may have the opposite effect. (p. 65)

It is because of this fact that we normally see a different type of physical violence among athletic groups. Very rarely do reports indicate that students are paddled or punched in their quest for full membership, partially because, in the case of student athletes, they were already selected for the team by the coaches based on their ability. The secondary hazing they experience is to achieve a level of respect from their peers, but has no real bearing on whether they will actually play.

However, the notion of physical competence has become, in itself, a driving force for the continued pledging and hazing prevalent in Black fraternal organizations, and part of the culture of many Latino fraternal organizations as well. Two key core values of undergraduate members of these groups are that: (a) you must earn membership, and (b) it is hard to gain membership. This has been very easy to detect over the years, through both slogans (i.e., "We pledge all night, we pledge night and day") and physical artifacts.

Recalling my experience as a fraternity pledge, we learned how to step as a part of the pledge program. Stepping is the most visible and exciting form of the Black fraternal experience; it is how students display mastery of physical and manual competence. Good steppers are treated with respect and admiration because they may entertain hundreds while performing complex routines and sequences. And just as those who show proficiency in this display of physical and manual competence, those who participate in a show and have trouble with their moves, miss cues, or show no rhythm, are ridiculed to a degree that either prevents them from wanting to perform again, or causes the group to prevent them from participating. Stepping is a good vehicle for achieving this level of competence.

However, for Black fraternity and sorority pledges, especially before 1990, the chants learned along with the steps reinforced the importance of physical competence, in this case, the ability to endure a long, brutal, pledge program to earn your letters. Take the words from this Alpha Phi Alpha fraternity chant: "It's the price you've got to pay, pledging night and day/Because you just can't skate into A Phi A." The term *skate* in this chant means that one cannot simply sign up for membership and become duly initiated. Those who "skate" did not display any physical or manual competence to deserve membership and are viewed as lesser members. All Black fraternal organizations have these kinds of phrases in their chants and songs that continue to suggest and reinforce the role of physical force in the life of the organization at the undergraduate level.

However, the real clues to how ingrained the culture of physical force and violence are can be found in the language of Black fraternal organizations, for example, in the concept of "bloody chapters." Used more commonly with fraternities, and even more often for chapters with a "Beta" designation, it reinforces the notion of chapters that conduct difficult (and physical) pledge programs. Often, the chapter name (for example, Beta Delta), is sewn on the jacket of a member, or on a chapter website's home page, in red letters. One of the more creative websites had an animated chapter designation in red and dripping blood.

Another, more ominous concept is the *death chapter*. More prevalent in Midwestern schools, this designation refers to chapters in a state that have been determined to pledge the hardest. Not as visible as the bloody chapter designation, you can find "death chapter" written on a jacket or a website as well. For example, all chapters at Indiana State University are "death chapters." This becomes an easy cue for administrators at those campuses that a chapter or chapters engage in physical violence.

As athletic prowess assists in self-esteem, the ability of students to handle physical hazing also seems to be tied to self-esteem and self-confidence. In the postpledging era of Black fraternalism, students have found new and creative ways to show their ability to handle physical abuse. Particularly on campuses where Black and Latino groups co-exist, students might host an event, known as a "viewing." During a viewing, a group invites members of other organizations to watch them pledge their aspirants, which essentially means to watch them physically challenge the newcomers. This provides proof that the students who are joining the Black groups have "earned" their membership.

Chickering and Reiser (1993) also suggest that "participation in intercollegiate and intramural athletics also can foster increased awareness of emotions and increased ability to manage them . . . Rage and delight are expected reactions; their expression in voice, gesture, and action are part of the game" (p. 66). Aspirants are also taught to manage their emotions during the frenzy of physical abuse that may take place during a pledge session. In fact, they may be viewed as weak if they break down and cry, and once they show any signs of weakness, they may in fact be encouraged to quit their quest for membership.

The final element of the quest for competence is the development of interpersonal competence. Chickering and Reiser indicate that these are complex and discrete skills, "like listening, asking questions, self-disclosing, giving feedback, and participating in dialogues that bring insight and enjoyment" (1993, p. 72). This facet of competence is the key component in that it is generally the reason why students allow the physical abuse to occur. Interpersonal competence allows students to develop the brotherhood or sisterhood they are seeking through membership in an exclusive club or organization.

The rhetoric for fraternal groups in particular involves the concept of brotherhood or sisterhood being the ultimate goal of the relationship. These concepts, which imply close relationships made stronger through interpersonal communication, make fraternal organizations good vehicles to achieve this kind of competence. It is doubtful that students consciously attempt to develop this kind of competence, but the desire to have meaningful relationships is attractive to all students.

Chickering and Reiser (1993) sum up the idea of competence and make several points concerning how students socialize each other, even when creating a strong subculture that values behaviors, and in the face of activities that the larger culture of higher education knows to be dangerous and negative.

> Once a student identifies with a particular group, it becomes both an anchor and a reference point . . . When the subculture becomes important, individuals try to fit in . . . If a pledge must prove endurance or grace under pressure, poise and discipline begin to emerge. (p. 394)

Once students decide that a particular subgroup is desired, and they begin the process of joining, they work to fit in, which in some cases means enduring (often risky) physical abuse to join the group.

This desire to fit in, to gain competence, is the reason why physical violence continues to plague student groups. The lingering question is why these behaviors are especially prevalent among African American and Latino fraternal organizations. As mentioned earlier, while there is some physical hazing in athletic teams, there are generally few reports of paddling or punching within these groups. For predominantly White fraternities, the hazing overwhelmingly involves the use and abuse of alcohol, which does have potentially dangerous physical ramifications. The fewest hazing reports are associated with predominantly White sororities, and the few incidents documented in these groups involve either alcohol or emotional abuse.

It is unclear why physical abuse, especially paddling and punching, is found in Black and Latino groups overwhelmingly. There are probably numerous theories explaining the phenomenon, from African rites of passage, to a subliminal effect of slavery on African people. The goal here is not to offer new theories of why physical abuse is prevalent in these groups. This is where these behaviors are seen the most, and those who advise these groups must be aware of this fact and begin to address this behavior.

Strategies

Physical hazing has been documented in the United States since the mid-1800s. Certainly, the behavior has moved from the accepted uniform hazing of college freshmen to the illegal, secretive hazing of specific subgroups on campus. This move was facilitated by institutions beginning in the 1920s. What once was something that could have been described as organized chaos now takes place in a very clandestine manner, the vast majority of the time without the institution's concrete knowledge. The fact that hazing is prevalent among groups of students of color that are often neglected in the larger campus culture facilitates the physical abuse.

Colleges and universities can take some practical steps to address the continued hazing, especially physical hazing. The big-picture answer is for higher education to declare a state of emergency with regard to hazing on campus. The major professional associations should create an interorganizational group to study the problem and begin to seek long-term solutions. To date, there has been no such effort, and while smaller organizations continue to address the issue, there has been no outcry about the seriousness of the issue. This tacit response to the physical abuse on campus has sent the message that it is an acceptable practice.

This is not acceptable. Effective strategies must be developed to combat physical violence on campus. Students spend countless hours developing complex, covert schemes to conceal hazing activities. They are successful over 95% of the time, as few reports of hazing surface. Yet, we know that physical hazing is prevalent, not only from the anecdotal information, but now from empirical data as well.

In his thesis, Anthony Crenshaw (2003) surveyed undergraduate members of historically Black fraternal organizations attending a leadership conference. His purpose was to determine how many of the activities associated with the former pledge process were still prevalent in an unsanctioned form. With a surprising degree of honesty that mirrors the anecdotal information that many student affairs professionals gather, students verified the prevalence of physical violence occurring on campuses today. Over 70% responded that they had participated in a "set," a structured event where aspirants may be quizzed on history, required to perform skits or songs, or participate in other activities with the knowledge that making mistakes would result in physical punishment. More important, 49.5% of those surveyed said they "received wood," as a part of their process, which means they were paddled (Crenshaw, 2003). With roughly half of the students indicating they were physically hazed, many decades after hazing was banned and almost 15 years after the Black fraternal organizations formally ended the process of pledging to gain membership, it is clear that students still value hazing as a part of this subculture.

With that in mind, several strategies may be used to make students think twice before engaging in physical hazing. At this point, these strategies are unlikely to eradicate hazing from higher education; educational and developmental activities alone cannot be effective. What we need is some form of "tough love" to address these behaviors and help students make better decisions.

Continuously Educate!

For colleges and universities, a generation of students is generally around five years. In that time, a group that has entered will have graduated, left school, or is so focused on finishing that its members are removed from the day-to-day life of the institution. The generation is even shorter for a fraternal group, and among Black fraternal organizations—which normally require sophomore standing for membership—most students will spend less than three years as active members on campus.

While one hopes that valuable information is passed down through the organization, practical wisdom says that students do a poor job of relating the policies and procedures of the institution to newer members. As a former Greek advisor, I have worked with chapters that changed officers every semester, and the new officers needed to be given all the information that was shared with the previous ones because it was not passed on.

Therefore, hazing education must be done every year. Students hate hazing programs, because they are required to attend the meetings, and many speakers have not found creative ways of imparting information. Many students also hate the programs because they know what the rules are (even if just the ones for their organization), and they have consciously decided to violate those rules. To sit for an hour to hear someone tell you what not to do and why it is wrong is not a great way to spend an evening for many students.

However, as a result of these presentations, there are always some who finally understand the seriousness of the issue, even if it is the potential consequences for their own lives. While doing a book tour in the spring of 2004, on several separate occasions, I encountered students who wanted to speak with me after the presentation to acknowledge that their group was hazing, and to ask my advice about how to avoid any potential sanctions or liability. While students have an allegiance to their group, self-preservation still trumps group affiliation in most instances.

Educational programs are an important means to challenge the strong organizational norms that permit physical hazing to occur. Many campuses use mandatory programs to guarantee they reach a maximum number of students. This often creates a problem for the speaker in dealing with an audience that is not receptive, but colleges and universities can counter this by finding a skilled lecturer who can engage the audience despite its unwillingness to hear the message.

In addition, schools should attempt to register the attendance of those participating in the sessions. This is a risk prevention strategy for the institution in the event of a serious injury or death. It proves that the institution did provide regular, comprehensive education that required attendance, and the presence or absence of the students involved in the incident could bolster the school's defense. While it may seem unsavory to discuss risk management strategies for schools, the fact is that as the deepest pocket in hazing injury cases, schools must do a better job of showing that they offer comprehensive training and education.

Aggressively Sanction Violations of the Student Conduct Code

Hazing expert Hank Nuwer eloquently summed up the problem with campus judicial systems in *Broken Pledges* (Nuwer, 1990):

> Educators make lousy law-enforcement officers and judges. Serious offenses that violate state law should not be tried by university groups in place of state courts . . . When illegal acts have been committed, law-enforcement authorities must take over and try the cases in state courts. (pp. 207–208)

As a former hearing officer and Greek life coordinator, I have had firsthand experience with the difficulties associated with these cases. Unless you have savvy, even crafty, administrators who quickly gather information, separate witnesses to prevent rehearsing a single story, and skillfully convince students to cooperate or even confess, it becomes difficult to prove wrongdoing. Most student affairs professionals, based on the natural personality of most drawn to this profession, are not interested in these kinds of confrontations, which are often unpleasant and on occasion have elicited verbal and actual threats.

Because college codes can operate separately from those of local law enforcement, both should continue to exist. However, colleges and universities should move quickly to involve local law enforcement in investigation of crimes so that evidence can be discovered promptly. Students generally lack respect for college policies, especially when so few students are expelled for physical hazing. Colleges must dramatically increase sanctions and begin automatic expulsions in response to physical beatings. However, when local law enforcement is involved, students immediately understand the seriousness of their actions.

Hazing Must Be Viewed as a Crisis

Hazing education programs come and go. National fraternities and sororities issue statement after statement condemning the practice and implement new policies. Athletic associations are now creating conferences to address the topic. What has not happened is a coordinated attack against this menace that has been an active part of education for centuries. While the problem seems to be spreading (as evidenced by more high school hazing reports), our actions have not been of the magnitude to effect change.

College presidents and administrators, fraternal organizations, and athletic leaders in higher education must come together to begin to eradicate hazing. This revolutionary act would be unprecedented in the history of higher education, but it is the kind of act that is needed to dissuade students who, though knowledgeable about hazing, participate in it anyway because the perceived benefit outweighs the risk. Simply put, we have not made the consequences greater than the perceived benefit ("perceived" because there are no data to suggest that any real benefits, such as bonding, are achieved by physical hazing).

This revolutionary stance would let students know that hazing must end, and we are going to engage in a "war" against this culture. Facets of this attack on hazing should include:

1. Immediate expulsion of students found guilty of physical hazing, with no exceptions. All campuses must have a no-tolerance policy, and expulsion must be the maximum sentence allowable. In addition, because campuses' burden of proof is generally less than that of the courts, it would be possible to expel students who physically haze as a part of the range of sanctions.

2. Lobbying Congress to pass tougher laws to address these crimes, either by increasing hazing penalties or by treating these cases not as hazing but as assaults that carry tougher penalties. If states refuse to increase hazing penalties, efforts should be made to eliminate those laws so assault charges would be the only option available.

3. Greek letter organizations must begin permanently revoking entire chapters for physical hazing crimes. It is the responsibility of undergraduates to keep the college experience alive; if they refuse to stop physical hazing, the undergraduate experience will end for them. Specifically for Black fraternal organizations, the termination of undergraduate chapters must be considered if the organizations are to continue to exist (Kimbrough, 2005).

Hazing has been with us far too long. The strength of it can be seen once we look at Chickering's model of student development, as it provides a clear understanding of why students continue this practice, especially those who willfully submit to beatings that have proven in some cases to be injurious and deadly. Within that context, higher education has failed to provide a strong enough enforcement that prevents students from carrying out these crimes. Therefore, a vigorous attack on the culture of hazing must be made if we are serious about ending it.

As I was writing this chapter, I received notice of another physical hazing attack involving a fraternity. This victim needs surgery, possibly due to paddling. An extensive recovery is anticipated, and a lawsuit is also imminent. This is just another reminder that not enough has been done and that we must step up our efforts dramatically to end the beatings on campuses.

References

Bok, D. (2005). *Our underachieving colleges.* Princeton, NJ: Princeton University Press.

Chickering, A., & Reisser, L. (1993). *Education and identity* (2nd ed.). San Francisco: Jossey-Bass Publishers.

Crenshaw, A. (2003). *Undergraduate member perceptions of the current membership intake process among selected Black Greek-lettered organizations.* Blacksburg, VA: Virginia Tech.

Cross, W. (1992). *Shades of black: Diversity in African-American identity.* Philadelphia: Temple University Press.

Dishneau, D. (2005, September 12). Six Frostburg female athletes plead guilty in near-fatal hazing. Associated Press. Retrieved October 31, 2006, from http://www.zwire.com/site/news.cfm?newsid=15198964&BRD=2212&PAG=461&dept_id+465812&rfi=6

Dorfman, S. (2005, October 5). A wake-up call to end hazing. *The Newark Star-Ledger,* 64.

Dorn, N. (2005, March 1). Alleged Omega victim talks. *The Southern Digest Online.* Retrieved March 1, 2005, from http://www.southerndigest.com/vnews/display.v?TARGET=printable&article_id=4224928e32c99

Jones, A. (2005, February 8). Former student sues Emory frat, claiming hazing. *The Atlanta Journal-Constitution,* B5.

Josselson, R. (1990). *Finding herself: Pathways to identity in women.* San Francisco: Jossey-Bass.

Kimbrough, W. (2003). *Black Greek 101*. Madison, NJ: Fairleigh Dickinson University Press.

Kimbrough, W. (2005). Should Black fraternities and sororities abolish undergraduate chapters? *About Campus, 10*(4), 27–29.

Lowe, H. (2004a, December 12). St. John's hazing judge urges jury to push through deadlock. *Newsday*, A14.

Lowe, H. (2004b, December 13). Not guilty verdict in hazing case. *Newsday*, A16.

Nuwer, H. (1990). *Broken pledges: The deadly rite of hazing*. New York: Longstreet Press.

Nuwer, H. (1999). *Wrongs of passage: Fraternities, sororities, hazing and binge drinking*. Bloomington: Indiana University Press.

Nuwer, H. (Ed.). (2004). *The hazing reader*. Bloomington: Indiana University Press.

Perry, W. (1998). *Forms of ethical and intellectual development in the college years: A scheme*. San Francisco: Jossey-Bass.

Reyes, D., & Reza, H. G. (2005, September 1). Fraternity held edge at fatal ballgame. *Los Angeles Times*, B1.

Stahl, J. (2004, April 15). Scholar alleges hazing by fraternity brothers. *The Emory Wheel*. Retrieved February 18, 2005, from http://www.emorywheel.com/vnews/display.v/ART/2004/04/15/407eb3ad609b9

Tate, J. (2005, February 22). Omega Psi Phi suspended at Southern U. *Black College Wire*. Retrieved February 22, 2005, from http://www.blackcollegewire.org/news/050221_southern-omegas/printable/

5

SAFE CAMPUSES FOR STUDENTS

Systemic Transformation Through
Re(A)wakened Senior Leaders

Susan R. Rankin, Elizabeth A. Roosa Millar, and Christian Matheis

I n the fall semester, members of the LGBTQA[1] student community held a silent demonstration aimed at educating attendees of the Community Fund dinner and reception about the recipient of the Fund's 2005 "Person of the Year," Mid-State women's basketball Coach Smith, and her two-decade-old reputation for discrimination against lesbian athletes or those she perceived as such. They stood in silent support of one courageous student-athlete who spoke out against the coach's "policies" and for many other student-athletes who were silenced for fear of retribution. In 1986, Coach Smith was quoted in a national newspaper saying that she did not allow lesbians to play on her team, citing her "no drugs, no alcohol, no lesbians"

---

[1] A note on language: In this chapter, the authors use the terms, *lesbian, gay,* and *bisexual,* when referring to sexual orientation or identity. We also use the terms, *women, men,* and *transgender people,* when describing gender identities, with the understanding that most transgender people also identify as *men* or *women.* Similarly, we use the term, *lesbian, gay, bisexual, and transgender people* or *LGBTQA people,* to describe individuals who share related experiences based on sexual orientation, gender identity, or gender expression. However, this language is used with the understanding that many individuals who identify as LGBTQA may choose to use other self-identifying terms or none at all. Recent research (Rankin, 2003) made clear that not all respondents wanted to place themselves in these boxes. Many would prefer choices, such as *same-gender loving, gender-queer, pansexual, queer, woman-loving-woman,* etc. Some considered the *gay, lesbian, bisexual,* and *transgender* categories to be predominately White social constructs of identity and, therefore, not relevant to their personal experiences. The authors recognize the personal and political import of language and the need to recognize a broad range of self-identity choices.

policy. In 1991, one player suggested that pressures from Coach Smith led her to change her appearance to fit a more "feminine" social construct. Despite Coach Smith's claim that she now adheres to the university's nondiscrimination policy, which since 1991 has included sexual orientation, there are serious rumors that she maintains and exhibits discriminatory beliefs and behaviors based on offensive stereotypes due to one's perceived sexual orientation. The students suggested in their demonstration that Coach Smith is only a symptom of a much larger problem, a systemic problem within intercollegiate athletics and Mid-State around issues of sexual orientation, gender identity, and gender expression.

As a community of scholars, what is our response? Around the nation, senior administrators struggle with understanding how to establish and sustain commitments to students who are lesbian, gay, bisexual, transgender, queer, and ally (LGBTQA) in ways that effectively contribute to their education. Often, this struggle is exaggerated by tensions among the following: desire to support students, general lack of knowledge about students who are LGBTQA, and long-standing traditions through which academic institutions maintain unique cultural identities. Given heterosexist values underlying higher education, the work involved in proactively addressing "safety issues" among students who are LGBTQA and building an inclusive and nurturing campus community is often controversial and demanding. Advocates and allies do not have an easy task. The problems are unique to individuals, yet they are also systemic throughout institutions. Systematically examining and publicizing the extent of problems and thoughtfully developing comprehensive intervention strategies are necessary steps to build support for change.

Acknowledging these struggles, we offer administrators an initial framework for bringing attention positively and proactively to the ways in which senior leadership can improve campus climates for students who are LGBTQA. Following a brief overview of historical contexts in which campuses have or have not met the safety needs of students who are LGBTQA, we present the challenges to transformational change at both the organizational and administrative levels, then we describe emerging practices for creating and sustaining communities in which LGBTQA students' dignity and humanity are affirmed. Further, we engage our readers that they may consider the facets of deep *personal* introspection necessary for moving toward systemic change. Through this discussion of emerging practices, we share a starting point from which senior administrators may envision unique aspects of their own (re)awakening.

Preparing for Transformation: Uncovering the Challenges

It has long been understood—an understanding that has been well supported by research-based evidence—that institutional climate has a profound effect on any academic community's ability to carry out its tripartite mission of teaching, research, and service (Bauer, 1998; Boyer, 1990; Peterson & Spencer, 1990; Rankin, 1994, 1998; Tierney & Dilley, 1996). With the acknowledgment that institutions differ in the level of attention and emphasis on issues of diversity and campus climate, it is safe to say that a campus climate offering equitable learning opportunities for all students, academic freedom for all faculty, and fairness in employment for all staff and administrators is one of the primary responsibilities of institutions of higher education. In other words, colleges and universities must model an environment free from arbitrary discrimination. Indeed, the well-established educational value of diversity supports policies such as affirmative action, a "difference-conscious" policy whose legitimacy was enhanced by the U.S. Supreme Court's decisive ruling in favor of the University of Michigan Law School's admissions policy (Gurin, Dey, Hurtado, & Gurin, 2002; Milem, 2003; Schmidt, 2003).

Current Campus Climate for Students Who Are LGBTQA

For the purposes of our work, campus climate is defined as current attitudes, behaviors, and standards of employees and students concerning the level of respect for individual needs, abilities, and potential (Rankin, 2003). Campus climate is operationalized through personal experiences of people who are LGBTQA on campus, perceptions of both LGBTQA and heterosexual campus community members regarding the climate for people who are LGBTQA, and institutional efforts to address needs and concerns brought to light by those who are LGBTQA.

In a recent national study of campus climate for underrepresented groups with more than 17,000 participants (Rankin, 2001[2]), respondents indicated that of all the underrepresented groups on campus, the climate was

---

[2] This unpublished manuscript is available upon request.

"least accepting" of people who are LGBTQA. Further, 42% of lesbian, gay, and bisexual (LGB) respondents indicated they were the target of harassment based on their sexual orientation, compared to 30% of persons of color who reported harassment based on their race and 28% of women who reported harassment based on their gender.

Previous studies have documented the perceptions of campus quality of life for people who are LGBTQA and those who work and study with them (Brown, Clarke, Gortmaker, & Robinson-Keilig, 2004; Evans & Broido, 2002; Garber, 2002; Malaney, Williams, & Geller, 1997; Waldo, 1998). Other studies have documented experiences of harassment and violence (D'Augelli, 1992; Herek, 1993; Waldo, Hesson-McInnis, & D'Augelli, 1998); related consequences of harassment and violence (D'Augelli, 1992; Herek, 1994, 1995; Hershberger & D'Augelli, 1995; Norris & Kaniasty, 1991; Savin-Williams & Cohen, 1996; Slater, 1993); or examined the success of and best practices for programs to improve campus climate (Draughn, Elkins, & Roy, 2002; Little & Marx, 2002; Louvaas, Baroudi, & Collins, 2002; Sausa, 2002; Yep, 2002).

Much of the academic writing about people who are LGBTQA is not empirical, but, rather, takes the form of advice or personal reflections based on lived experiences; this is particularly true for minorities who also identify with LGBTQA communities, such as people with disabilities, transgender people, and people of color (Draughn et al., 2002; Ferguson & Howard-Hamilton, 2000; Louvaas et al., 2002; Schreier, 1995). While these scholarly contributions are valuable, because they both provide testable hypotheses and indicate issues only some administrators and LGBTQA service professionals are aware of, they do not provide systematic documentation of existing problems or solutions. The few existing empirical studies generally include small participant numbers, from 10 for the smallest qualitative study, which only included lesbian and bisexual women, to almost 2,000 for an extensive study of one university, which included both heterosexual and LGBTQA students (Stevens, 2004; Waldo, 1998). Further, none of these studies is national in scope; most include one or two campuses and thus are geographically nongeneralizable. Although these studies reveal that victimization appears to be decreasing and the openness of heterosexual people on campus to LGBTQA issues is improving, it is difficult to conclude that this is a widespread phenomenon as there is no consistent measurement of these concepts, nor are there longitudinal studies of change over time.

To address many of these limitations, a national study to investigate the campus climate for people who are LGBTQA was undertaken (Rankin, 2003). This national study was the first to examine a full range of experiences of campus life for people who are LGBTQA. It was also the first to include a significant number of people of color and persons who are transgender: 237 identified as persons of color and 67 identified as transgender.

Although similar to other LGBTQA campus climate research, the study used snowball sampling to obtain a sufficient number of respondents, a significant improvement in generalizabilty due to the number and types of campuses it included. The study included 1,669 respondents from 14 geographically dispersed campuses.

The study was designed to address (a) respondents' personal campus experiences; (b) their perception of the campus climate; and (c) their perceptions of institutional responses to issues specific to people who are LGBTQA. The results provided several important insights about campus climate experienced by people who are LGBTQA. One-third of students and one-quarter of employees in the sample reported having experienced some form of harassment, and 11 respondents indicated they had experienced physical violence enacted on the basis of perceived or actual sexual orientation. Other findings noted that both LGBTQA-identified students and employees reported the overall campus climate as homophobic and indicated that they hid their sexual orientation to avoid discrimination and harassment.

The results also indicated that LGBTQA-identified students were threatened with physical assault much more than were employees. In addition, students and employees reported that they were uninformed about procedures for enacting institutional responses and actions on their own behalf. Most respondents were unaware of rapid response systems intended to address anti-LGBTQA acts of intolerance on their campus, and few agreed that their colleges addressed issues related to sexuality and gender identity. Many felt there was a lack of visible leadership regarding LGBTQA issues and concerns. Finally, respondents suggested that educational programming should be more inclusive of LGBTQA issues and that LGBTQA content should be integrated into the curriculum.

The study's findings also suggested that the existence of LGBTQA centers, support services, and educational programming does not necessarily lead to positive ratings of campus climate. Although individual programs or interventions, such as LGBTQA centers, are important because they provide needed services to people who are LGBTQA and they demonstrate institutional support, the "paradigm shift" called for by Schreier (1995) demands more than individual programs or enforced tolerance of people who are LGBTQA. Simply adding programs does not transform heterosexist institutions into ones that nurture and embrace people who are LGBTQA. As we move forward, it is clear from this study that even institutions that have begun to create LGBTQA-inclusive policies and LGBTQA-specific programs will need to continue and expand efforts to ensure full participation of LGBTQA individuals in the campus community. We argue that this systemic transformation will only occur through positive and proactive senior leaders who act as catalysts for organizational change.

Institutional Challenges: Building Communities of Difference

Organizational change within colleges and universities is neither easy nor immediate. Higher education researchers and scholars who study institutional change do not agree on the "best" approach to creating such grand transformations; however, they do agree that change is possible, necessary, and can be accomplished strategically (Simsek & Seashore Louis, 1994). The following section presents the theoretical foundations of organizational change as it relates to higher education. It concludes with a framework for institutional leaders to analyze and initiate change—foremost, by (re)awakening their commitment to social justice, inclusiveness, and a safe campus for *all* students.

Organizational Change Theory

Early systems theories of organizational change explored the process by which educational institutions evolve (Simsek & Seashore Louis, 1994). Organizations were originally viewed as adaptive organisms that responded to changing environmental conditions, primarily internal. Growing from this research, the processes of organizational change expanded to include the following characteristics of change within educational institutions: slowly adapting when dramatic environmental change was absent; the "loosely coupled" nature of these institutions, which inhibits large-scale shifts; and unpredictability in universities (i.e., "organized anarchies") due to the random, politicized nature of various stakeholders with conflicting interests (Cohen &

March, 1974; Weick, 1976). These notions of organizational change shared the perspective that change is possible, albeit limited, especially that which is rapid and strategically designed to achieve particular outcomes. Kuhn's (1970) analysis of scientific progress provided an alternative theory for the Simsek and Seashore Louis model described below. Although their theories are similar in their emphasis on shared beliefs, values, and norms within an organizational culture, Kuhn focuses primarily on the need for radical change to maintain vitality and progress, rather than on earlier arguments that claimed radical change was unlikely.

Simsek and Seashore Louis (1994) offer a model of organizational change as a paradigm shift. Organizational paradigm is defined as "a world view, a frame of reference, or a set of assumptions, usually implicit, about what sorts of things make up the world" (p. 672). This concept goes beyond a set of beliefs that precipitate action, or cultural frames, which involves shared beliefs, values, and norms of behavior. The organizational paradigm shift model assumes that organizations are defined by prevailing worldviews, "under a particular dominant paradigm, structure, strategy, culture, leadership, and individual role accomplishments are defined . . . radical change in organizations may be construed as a discontinuous shift in this socially constructed reality" (p. 671).

More recent organizational scholars (e.g., Peters & Waterman, 1982; Feldman, 1990; Hofstede, Neuijen, Ohayv, & Sanders, 1990) approached the possibility of substantive change within university cultures viewing change as anticipatory adaptation rather than transformations. The paradigm shift model considers the importance of altering institutional worldviews and is the crux of what we term *transformative* change. Transformative change involves the reconstruction of previous social constructs of bigotry toward a positive perception of difference, where differences are valued rather than being tolerated, assimilated, or merely allowed. The unique cultural identities and traditions through which academic institutions maintain these paradigms must be challenged, uprooted, and transformed to build and sustain communities of difference.

> However strong an organization's culture and ideology may be, there are times when such cultural strength breeds insularity. We must constantly remind ourselves that previous ideas of community often based themselves on notions that absented women, people of color, and others from the

community. A postmodern version of organizational culture demands a comparative awareness of other institutional cultures—their structures, interactions, and ideologies. (Tierney, 1993, p. 548)

Today's colleges and universities must cast the net of inclusion beyond traditionally marginalized social groups and transform their organizational paradigms to build an authentic community of difference, where cultural pluralism is the intended outcome and students who are LGBTQA are no longer ignored, devalued, and unsafe.

We argue that to transform organizational reality, the dominant paradigm of institutional leadership must also change. What we do not debate is that such change in leadership precedes, follows, or occurs alongside organizational change; the chicken or egg metaphor applies to this issue: which comes first, organizational change or leadership transformation? Whether the *process* of achieving a safe campus for lesbian, gay, bisexual, transgender, queer, and ally students is linear is not as important to us as creating a safe campus by any means necessary. Therefore, what follows is a suggested framework for understanding leadership transformation within a diverse campus climate.

Judith Palmer's (1989) pivotal work eloquently presents competing leadership paradigms related to diversity that often operate within institutional cultures. From these disparate perspectives of how change leaders view diversity, Palmer suggests that organizational leaders become aware of the various perspectives—including their own—and those operating from dominant positions within an organization. We believe that once diversity change leaders are aware of existing systemic inequities, they can begin the difficult and necessary work to transform themselves, others, and the institutional climate for LGBTQA students who may feel unsafe.

Palmer's Paradigms

Palmer's (1989) work addresses conflicting paradigmatic orientations of organizational change leaders as they relate to diversity at the individual level; we offer these paradigms as a framework to comprehend the complexities of leadership transformation that may ultimately lead to institutional-level change. Because organizations tend to operate within a dominant paradigm, which determines institutional structures, strategies, culture, leadership, individual roles, accomplishments, and rewards, changing a university's dominant paradigm requires understanding what paradigms exist and how movement toward new and different paradigms would create desired results. In this chapter, the desired outcome is a community of difference (i.e., diversity) where students who are LGBTQA feel safe and valued.

Paradigm I. Palmer (1989) labels Paradigm I "The Golden Rule," which, as its name implies, treats diversity as a moral issue; thus, creating equitable opportunities for all students is right, just, and fair (Esty, Griffin, & Schorr Hirsch, 1995). This worldview focuses on similarities rather than differences and is characterized by statements such as, "I treat everyone the same"; "I don't see color or gender"; and "I'm not a racist, sexist, or heterosexist." According to Paradigm I perspectives, oppression stems from only those few "bad" individuals and occurs in isolated incidents; it is not viewed as a systemic problem requiring institution-wide change.

A university operating with this as a dominant paradigm provides an environment where all students and personnel are accounted for *regardless of* their differences; thus, a pleasant, conflict-free work atmosphere is promoted (Palmer, 1989). Programs that focus on social groups, such as awareness training or affirmative admissions and hiring policies, are not readily accepted and often come under scrutiny for being unfair to members of the university who share certain, and most often unearned, societal privileges. Paradigm I institutions appear homogenous from the outside, and those who differ from the majority, who are expected to sublimate differences from which they derive value and uniqueness, may not perceive institutional environments as welcoming, nurturing, or safe.

Paradigm II. Contrary to Paradigm I, Paradigm II ("Right the Wrongs") focuses on group differences and disadvantages related to social group membership, rather than on similarities and individual-level responsibilities for existing injustices (Palmer, 1989). Rectifying systemic manifestations of past injustices through difference-conscious policies to improve recruitment, retention, development, and reward of "target" groups becomes the primary focus of universities where this is the dominant paradigm. Majority members are expected to learn about the experiences of those within particular target groups, thus stressing processes of uprooting prejudices and internalized biases. This often results in conflict, tension, and struggle between majority and target groups. Such organizational characteristics convey an "us versus them" reality to outsiders, although university leaders may believe they are working to produce a "we/you" dialogue with sincerity. The intended outcome of Paradigm II organizations is equality of participation, opportunity, respect, and reward for those whose current social mobility has been partially determined by systematic disadvantages and historical injustices.

Paradigm III. Much like Tierney (1993), Palmer's (1989) third paradigm, labeled "Value the Differences," presents an organizational worldview whose groups and individuals are sought out for their differences, and members of such an institution have learned to continually relate to one another in community, acting around and toward this tenet. Unlike Paradigm I, Paradigm III expects everyone to understand and value heritages, cultures, and belief systems of all groups, in addition to being open to uniqueness of individuals within the organization and beyond. Assimilation and "treating everyone the same" are not goals of Paradigm III change leaders, who recognize that their own potential and uniqueness depends on recognizing and affirming differences. Thus, students and employees are expected to reach beyond their own experiences and learn to value and work effectively with a wide array of community members who are often very different from themselves.

Throughout Paradigm III organizations, diversity of perspectives encourages creative problem solving and an appreciation of variance from a majority, which may result in previously inconceivable solutions to often-difficult problems. To create such a community of difference, change leaders integrate unique, often nontraditional, values into hiring, development, assessment, and reward systems. "Difference-conscious" policies are used to ensure heterogeneity at all levels of the campus community.

Organizational Change Through Valuing Multiple and Different Paradigms

Much like Palmer (1989), we do not wish to imply that any one of these paradigms is ultimately right or more desirable to create and sustain a safe campus climate for people who are LGBTQA. All of these paradigms contribute to healthy institutional cultures and can co-exist in an organization in which people value and actively pursue building communities of difference. However, these paradigms, which are often applied in competitive ways operating within highly politicized organizations such as colleges and universities, require thoughtful choreography to meet the shared outcome of a safe campus climate for those who are LGBTQA.

A precursor to successful transformation of an organization is an overarching commitment to a single unified aspiration, such as building a safe campus environment for previously marginalized students. If senior leaders do not agree that campus climate should be a focus of institutional initiatives, some groundwork must be laid before attempting to invoke change of this magnitude. Once such a shared vision exists among influential university leaders, challenges take new forms in negotiating processes of institutional change toward specific outcomes. Put differently, as institutional leaders reach consensus regarding specific outcomes, new and more complex challenges emerge regarding the specific methods through which such outcomes will be achieved.

The gateway to transforming an organizational climate for LGBTQA communities is awareness. (Re)Awakening such awareness can be done through a careful analysis of the current campus climate, the multiple diversity paradigms among leaders, and, most important, the paradigm(s) from which you operate in different situations: how do you see the world, and how do you affect change as a result of your paradigm(s)? Your worldview and those of other senior leaders are often in conflict because they are based on/substantiated by strongly held personal belief systems (e.g., values) that most often remain unquestioned or unexplored. Navigating these differences is not easy, but once certain levels of awareness are realized, action toward achieving shared goals becomes plausible.

Working for institutional change, Palmer's (1989) framework can be used as an analytic tool by you as an individual leader to assess your effectiveness within organizations and offer insights into how you may be called upon to negotiate among different paradigms, or transform your own paradigmatic orientation to achieve desired outcomes. If thoughtfully carried out through personal reflection and analysis, other individuals with whom you share time, space, and energy within an organization may be influenced to engage actively in these processes with you, thus leading an institution toward a shared vision of a safe campus for all community members. However, a note of caution is in order. It is often the case that leaders identify themselves too quickly as operating from Paradigm III perspectives, though this is often untrue.

Vision and values espoused by Paradigm III are often *accurately* interpreted to represent little blame and *inaccurately* interpreted to hold no expectations for individuals to acknowledge current systemic inequities based on historical injustices. In fact, many people who believe they use Paradigm III approaches are actually operating from deep-seated Paradigm I perspectives, even while their motives for creating change are extremely valuable. Rest assured that students, staff, administrators, and faculty who identify with historically underrepresented groups through Paradigm II worldviews can generally detect whether institutional leaders have made this mistake. Yet, leaders who operate from such motives often remain unaware that their actions and inactions maintain an unjust status quo as long as they resist opportunities to overcome their lack of critical information and dismiss relatively undervalued evidence that could be impetus for change. Such evidence often comes in unfamiliar forms; specifically, we refer to forms of evidence adopted and valued by people from underrepresented communities.

At different times in our personal and professional lives, we act on/react to resistance to change and growth. Sometimes our reactions are thoughtfully planned, while other times our reactions emerge without full awareness of why and from what sources we learned to resist. Yet, despite familiar and comfortable pathways on which we have made ourselves into leaders, a great deal more than comfort and familiarity is what communities need from us. Meeting such needs requires deep and personal honesty. Coming to awareness of how institutional climate affects those "different" from "us" demands that we *choose* to come to terms with discomfort and unfamiliar realms of thought. Acknowledging that each of us fails to understand differences from time to time—as with any learning process, there are successes and failures from which we grow—we argue that individuals who manifest resistance to understanding difference in deep empathic ways likely prevent communities of difference from forming within organizations.

The *trappings of blame* must also be dealt with to lead organizational cultures successfully in which many will cope with similar feelings. While approaches such as Paradigm II (right the wrongs) contribute immensely in educational settings by fostering a thorough critique of oppressive institutional systems, it is often the case that some community members apply newly found knowledge while motivated to assess blame on majority groups, the members of which often operate from Paradigm I perspectives. From our perspectives, blame has no place in creating and sustaining safe institutional cultures. Rather, we emphasize accountability paired with willingness to acknowledge how individuals and groups have unfairly inherited benefits or disadvantages on the basis of historical injustices. Leaders who truly wish to create and sustain communities of difference recognize that blame can be sidestepped and dismantled in favor of (re)awakening to thoughtfully planned creative action.

Administrator Challenges: Re(A)wakening Self

Thus far, we have reviewed research supporting our claim that institutional transformation is vital to the future of higher education. Creating and sustaining communities of difference requires commitment to establishing safe environments. From such environments, educational missions and values can be realized in ways that are currently not possible, due in part to climates of fear, hostility, intolerance, and apathy.

We have also explained ways in which awareness of at least three different paradigms allows for new interpretations of individual and group motives, desired outcomes, and methods for achieving desired outcomes. Moving from justification provided by existing research, through means of paradigmatic interpretation, we describe at least one application of Palmer's paradigms to bring motives, outcomes, and methods into alignment. Paradigm I can contribute motives for change, Paradigm II can contribute critical information regarding changes to institutional systems, and Paradigm III can provide methods through which those with Paradigm I motives become willing to both learn and create communities of difference. We suggest it is possible to use *methods* that correspond to Paradigm III perspectives to empower and affirm *motives* held by majority cultures that operate from primarily Paradigm I perspectives such that they can seek information delineating *outcomes* informed by Paradigm II perspectives. What does this mean for you as a leader within your institution? What first steps must you be willing to take?

Each of the paradigms described by Palmer can be observed in institutions of higher education. However, it is most often the case that hierarchical power structures privilege certain paradigms in certain situations. Individual senior leaders tend to affirm paradigmatic approaches that they consider most likely to bring about desired results. Thus, which paradigms become or remain dominant in a given institutional culture often depends on the actions of those with institutional power to affirm, reward, or reject the status quo. Thus, as a senior administrator, your worldview and your actions can foster or stifle positive change. Consider how you may be able to operate from a different paradigm—one in which you use your institutional authority to affirm and reward many different worldviews to create a climate where community members are empowered to facilitate change. Specifically, for the purposes of this chapter, imagine how your institutional authority can become invigorated through new paradigmatic approaches to create and sustain safe environments for LGBTQA communities.

Through the Lens of Roper

In "The Role of Senior Student Affairs Officers in Supporting LGBT Students: Exploring the Landscape of One's Life," Roper (2005) suggests that institutional administrators must undergo a "re-awakening" to ensure safety for students who are LGBTQA. Such processes require people in administrative roles to consider specific attitudes, behaviors, and values one must hold to fulfill the mission(s) of his or her institution of higher education. For Roper, working to "affirm the dignity and humanity of all students" represents a necessary core value underlying and legitimizing administrators' work (p. 81). However, as he points out, most undergraduate and graduate course work from which current senior leaders gained knowledge about the world likely did not include affirmative discussions about people who are LGBTQA. Roper explains how he began work in higher education "ill prepared to lead an institution toward the meaningful inclusion of LGBT students into the life of an educational community. Moreover," he states, "I lacked the awareness, skills or commitment sufficient to be seen as a legitimate supporter of LGBT issues" (p. 82). Therefore, developing such a knowledge base is a process many begin later in their careers.

Writing from the perspective of a senior student affairs officer, Roper identifies the need for administrators located anywhere within institutions of higher education to support students who are LGBTQA, even when those in positions of authority are not generally prepared by traditional educational and professional experiences. Thus, Roper asserts, one must be prepared to develop leadership philosophies of service capable of affirming all students. Further, this requires developing personal capacities to support students who are LGBTQA; ultimately, this is done by demonstrating commitments to leadership and community building. Roper poses the following questions regarding three dimensions of personal being administrators should consider; these are "weight, depth and breadth" (2005, p. 85). Each administrator, aware of his or her desire to uphold the mission of his or her institution, must be prepared to ask the following:

Regarding the weight of one's being:
- What is the heaviness or lightness I bring to relationships?
- How much psychic or emotional weight am I carrying?
- What challenges might others encounter trying to be in a relationship with me?

Regarding the depth of one's being:
- Who am I capable of wrapping my arms around?
- What is the range of people with whom I am capable of being in community?

Regarding the breadth of one's being:
- How far am I able to invite others into my life (through sharing my personal experiences)?
- How deeply am I able to explore the life and experiences of others?
- How deeply am I able to feel for others? (Roper, 2005, pp. 85–86)

Roper (2005) concludes:

[L]eadership will be a key factor in promoting the growth of our institutions as we attempt to cultivate positive, living-learning environments for students who are LGBTQA. That long and challenging journey to institutional transformation will be enhanced by leaders who are personally invested in student success and possess the qualities necessary to support the needs of students who are LGBTQA and the mission of the institution concurrently. (p. 88)

The work of building community through individual leadership requires that senior leaders *awaken* to understand the impact of their own values. By critically considering personal capacities to create and sustain community within an institution, administrators take initial steps toward securing safety for all students.

The questions posed above are meant for you, as a senior administrator, to answer—but this is only one of many possible ways to create or discover your capacity for leading change. It is imperative that you pay close attention to how seriously you take these questions and how honestly your answers reflect the truth of your experiences. Moreover, it is crucial that you consider the implications your unique answers hold for those who are different from you; how does the truth of your experiences influence the truth of experiences held by those who are different from you? Introspection necessary for (re)awakening differs from person-to-person. However, evidence of whether (re)awakening has taken place—and continues to take place—can be observed in the ways you choose to act or not to act to build communities of difference.

(Re)Awakening to create safe campuses for people who are LGBTQA cannot occur as a result of a purely theoretical exercise regarding individually held perspectives. Once again, much more is required for such growth. Just as teachers learn more deeply and thoroughly about their students through processes of teaching, it is true that senior leaders within institutions genuinely learn about institutional climate and positive organizational change by taking action toward these ends. In this case, we refer specifically to actions meant to sustain communities in which human differences are affirmed, and through which institutional cultures, structures, and processes are systematically transformed. Simply speaking of abstract "transformation" and "change" is insufficient; it is imperative for improving campus climate that senior leaders decide:

1. Toward which outcomes should change and transformation seek to move organizations?
2. How broadly traditional and nontraditional forms of evidence will be used to determine success or failures of change/transformation.
3. How, and by what practices of reward, will members of university communities affirm broad and nontraditional forms of leadership? That is, how will agents of change be rewarded for demonstrating leadership as a result of (re)awakening?

Potential Best Practices

The beginning of this chapter includes a case study that we return to here in an attempt to apply the ideas presented in the chapter via a context particular to communities of people who are LGBTQA. We suggest that senior leaders acknowledge systems of institutional inequity, express individual commitments, welcome activist energies, reward innovation, be authentic, and decide what matters most.

Acknowledge Systems of Institutional Inequity

Students involved in planning campus-wide responses to the homophobic and heterosexist environment in the women's basketball program at Mid-State are educated about systems of institutionalized inequities. Through their academic, co-curricular, and personal life experiences, students who are involved in engaging administrators view and experience this situation as one incident among many in a system that has long sustained a hostile campus climate. Administrators who arbitrarily reject and/or consistently refuse to acknowledge systemic factors help to sustain environments in which students feel and actually are unsafe. Conversely, administrators who acknowledge institutional systems of inequity are those who openly, publicly, and consistently take a vital step toward creating and sustaining communities of difference. Whether, as a senior administrator, you consider yourself educated about such systems, or you find yourself at a disadvantage, you have capacities to learn during challenging moments such as these that undoubtedly will occur in your career.

Come Out About Your Commitments

Acknowledging systemic inequities does not mean administrators are obligated to take positions identical to those of students or of any polarized constituent group in particular. Rather, it is advantageous for administrators to affirm many different paradigmatic perspectives by openly and consistently asserting their commitment to all community members. Institutions of higher education have statements of nondiscrimination, vision, and mission for a purpose: to be used as a consistent frame of reference when processes of change strain community relationships. This does not mean senior leaders would not position themselves *against* those who commit unjust acts. Rather, it is more important that administrators position themselves *toward* substantial commitments; substantial commitments are those by which we recognize the kind of beliefs, values, and actions consistent with communities of difference. Thus, individuals who behave with overt and covert homophobia, in this case Coach Smith, are viewed as acting against the whole community.

Therefore, using these commitments, we act to protect overarching educational missions of the institution.

Welcome Activist Energies

Many believe that institutions function best when in equilibrium, that is, without shifts of energy and changes in process most tend to view as "disruption." Yet, as with all historically beneficial growth and innovation, disruptions in equilibrium are opportunities to interrupt and transform oppressive status quo. LGBTQA students in this case study, who organized protests and demonstrations in response to the alleged homophobic actions of Coach Smith, felt that some "administrators" attempted to *control* them. In some part, this was due to the unfortunate conflation of *actions* with *energies* and *motives*. Rather than engaging student activist *energies* as positive and genuine forces for change and innovation, some senior leaders chose to focus on actions, which they perceived as a threat to equilibrium commonly found in sustaining the status quo (which also sustains homophobic and heterosexist systems of oppression).

The actions of student activists who truly care about their educational community may or may not ultimately be informed, legal, or respectful. However, the energies student activists mean to contribute are valuable and usually based on motives consistent with creating and sustaining communities of difference. Thus, student activists will not respect, trust, or seek to support senior leaders who are unwilling to experience the discomfort and dynamic tension that comes with changes to institutional systems. Rather, students need to know that their senior leaders welcome their energies and motives as gifts from which important innovations in higher education can be affirmed. From this place, senior leaders have the capacity to enter into valuable partnerships as change agents with students who hold many different perspectives and who operate from many different paradigms.

Reward Innovation

Each member of your community demonstrates commitment to the shared institution in different ways. For some, gifts of energy and commitment take the form of maintaining important and valuable traditions. For others, gifts and commitment emerge as innovation. Sometimes innovation is inextricable from challenges to status quo through activism. Sometimes, to innovate, community members take activist approaches. For many senior leaders on campus, creating and sustaining space in which activist energies contribute to the mission of the institution can be a great challenge, particularly for those who have built their personal and professional careers around values more closely aligned with sustaining tradition than with empowering innovation. We suggest that once senior leaders choose not to control forces of change using dominant means it is possible to discover how change agents can be rewarded.

Where some senior leaders in this case study suggested threats of consequences for students, staff, faculty, and administrators who took public stands against homophobia and heterosexism, others suggested alternatives that were in the interest of developing a community of difference. Displacing the tendency to rely exclusively on threats of police intervention, conduct and judicial processes, loss of employment, and other institutional sanctions is a necessary step toward affirming and rewarding agents of change, thus also toward (re)awakening. When such tactics are no longer an easy means of intimidation, reserved only as responses to cases of severe abuse of position and personal power, senior leaders open their minds to the possibilities available beyond dominance and intimidation. We open our minds, hearts, and vision to our capacity for using our institutional authority to protect agents of change, thus protecting the integrity of the institution and forging new potential for communities of difference to flourish.

Be Authentic

Sometimes it appears that administrative cultures have their own languages and scripts for "appropriate" behavior. It seems these rules rarely permit, encourage, or allow administrators to be authentic. By "authentic," we mean safely experiencing oneself as fully participating in human interactions with the weight of our hopes, fears, strengths, flaws, wisdom, and ignorance. When we look, as Roper suggests, at the landscape of our professional lives, we will probably find that there are few places in which we have truly been authentic, and few places in which we felt safe exposing our true and dynamic selves. Yet, (re)awakening to create a safe climate for students who are LGBTQ means that we have to become vigilant about our own authenticity.

As community members at Mid-State struggled to make sense of administrative and legal processes through which charges were brought against Coach Smith, many administrators appeared to affirm traditionally "appropriate" norms. However, we suggest that what was needed to sustain the community truly required authentic engagement with those who saw individuals in heterosexist systems steal opportunities from young and promising athletes. Administrators began to lobby students, staff, and faculty with traditional language, instantiating traditional status quo on which is built the very concept of "appropriate" administrative behavior. Thus, such actions may suppress and eradicate the creativity and innovation from which educational missions and values are realized. On what basis can we expect students who already feel, and are, unsafe to trust traditional behavior when these traditions sustain old and familiar patterns of injustice?

Administrators who (re)awaken to affirm communities of difference will regularly challenge themselves to be authentic. Each individual will look carefully at the impact of his or her respective language and behavior for the sake of engaging the energies and motives vital to innovation and change. Students who are LGBTQA need each of us to demonstrate our hopes, fears, wisdom, and flaws. Your authenticity will indicate your commitment, as well as your capacity to persevere in maintaining your commitments, even if/when you make mistakes. Some community members may never meet you with similar trust and esteem, but your authenticity will allow you to see yourself with consistent integrity.

Decide What Matters Most

There are many different motives for creating safe campuses for students who are LGBTQA. Some argue that industry and corporations need diverse people to "keep up" with changing national demographics. There are those who suggest we are becoming part of a "global marketplace" in which future generations will need to know how to interact positively with those who are different. Many seem to associate financial profit with the ability of institutions to cater to a wider spectrum of customers in previously untapped markets. Others suggest that there exists an incontrovertible moral imperative to bring about "social justice." Senior leaders can come to (re)awakening from many different motives and through many different ways of seeing the world. From which motives do you act to create safe campuses? How do your motives empower or impede the motives, behaviors, and desired outcomes of those from whom you differ?

Paradigms Differ

At least one axiom endures across all of these motives and binds different paradigmatic perspectives. Foremost, breadth and depth of individual potential depends on experiencing oneself as a unique human being in relationship with other unique human beings (Buber, 1992; Burke, 2002; Royce, 2003). Students, staff, faculty, and administrators at Mid-State suffocate their own potential talents in vacuums of homogeneity. As some at Mid-State worked to constrain to a narrow list the qualities of who could contribute to the women's basketball program, they worked against their own dignity and capacities. The formation of knowledge and innovation we use to become better scholars, athletes, and community members depends on our willingness to bring our uniqueness into relationship with the uniqueness of others, expounding on our differences and our similarities as beautiful and immutable.

Conclusion

Communities of difference, thus safe campus climates, are places where we embrace the *whole community* as an epistemology (Matheis, 2004, 2005). That is, we know ourselves as unique and worthy of dignity by knowing one another as unique and worthy of dignity. Our power, institutional and personal, is best applied when it empowers those who are, institutionally and personally, least advantaged by structures and processes (Rawls, 1990). Students who are LGBTQA need our unique authenticity; they need us to reward their innovations and activist energies. As administrators who are also community members, these students call for us to (re)awaken our capacities to change systems as actors within those systems, by coming out with our commitments and staying out as people who choose to transform higher education.

References

Bauer, K. (1998). Campus climate: Understanding the critical components of today's colleges and universities. *New Directions for Institutional Research, 98*. San Francisco: Jossey-Bass.

Boyer, E. (1990). *Campus life: In search of community*. Princeton, NJ: The Carnegie Foundation for the Advancement of Teaching.

Brown, R., Clarke, B., Gortmaker, V., & Robinson-Keilig, R. (2004). Assessing the campus climate for gay, lesbian, bisexual and transgender (LGBT) students using a multiple perspectives approach. *Journal of College Student Development, 45*(1), 8–26.

Buber, M. (1992). Community as the basic social framework of human creativity. In S. N. Eisenstadt (Ed.), *Martin Buber on intersubjectivity and cultural creativity* (pp. 93–107). Chicago: University of Chicago Press.

Burke, J. F. (2002). *Mestizo democracy: The politics of crossing borders.* College Station: Texas A&M University Press.

Cohen, M., & March, J. (1974). *Leadership and ambiguity: The American college president.* New York: McGraw-Hill.

D'Augelli, A. (1992). Lesbian and gay male undergraduates' experiences of harassment and fear on campus. *Journal of Interpersonal Violence, 7*(3), 383–395.

Draughn, T., Elkins, B., & Roy, R. (2002). Allies in the struggle: Eradicating homophobia and heterosexism on campus. *Journal of Lesbian Studies, 6*(3/4), 9–20.

Esty, K., Griffin, R., & Schorr Hirsch, M. (1995). *Workplace diversity: A manager's guide to solving problems and turning diversity into a competitive advantage.* Holbrook, MA: Adams Media Corporation.

Evans, N., & Broido, E. (2002). The experiences of lesbian and bisexual women in college residence halls: Implications for addressing homophobia and heterosexism. *Journal of Lesbian Studies, 6*(3/4), 29–40.

Feldman, S. P. (1990). Stories as culture creativity: On the relation between symbolism and politics in organizational change. *Human Relations, 43,* 809–828.

Ferguson, A., & Howard-Hamilton, M. (2000). Addressing issues of multiple identities for women of color on college campuses. In N. Evans, V. Wall, & N. Lanham (Eds.), *Toward acceptance* (pp. 288–314). Baltimore, MD: University Press of America.

Garber, L. (2002). Weaving a wide net: The benefits of integrating campus projects to combat homophobia. *Journal of Lesbian Studies, 6*(3/4), 21–28.

Gurin, P., Dey, E. L., Hurtado, S., & Gurin, G. (2002). Diversity and higher education: Theory and impact on educational outcomes. *Harvard Educational Review, 72*(3), 330–366.

Herek, G. (1993). Documenting prejudice against lesbians and gay men: The Yale sexual orientation study. *Journal of Homosexuality, 25*(4), 15–30.

Herek, G. (1994). Heterosexism, hate crimes, and the law. In M. Costanzo & S. Oskamp (Eds.), *Violence and the law* (pp. 89–112). Newberry Park, CA: Sage Publications.

Herek, G. (1995). Psychological heterosexism in the United States. In A. R. D'Augelli and C. J. Paterson (Eds.), *Lesbian, gay and bisexual identities across the lifespan* (pp. 321–346). New York: Oxford University Press.

Hershberger, S. L., & D'Augelli, A. R. (1995). The impact of victimization on the mental health and suicidality of lesbian, gay and bisexual youth. *Developmental Psychology, 31,* 65–74.

Hofstede, G., Neuijen, B., Ohayv, D. D., & Sanders, G. (1990). Measuring organizational cultures: A qualitative and quantitative study across twenty cases. *Administrative Science Quarterly, 35,* 286–316.

Kuhn, T. S. (1970). *The structure of scientific revolutions* (2nd ed.). Chicago: University of Chicago Press.

Little, P., & Marx, M. (2002). Teaching about heterosexism and creating an empathic experience of homophobia. *Journal of Lesbian Studies, 6*(3/4), 205–218.

Louvaas, K., Baroudi, L., & Collins, S. (2002). Transcending heteronormativity in the classroom: Using queer and critical pedagogies to alleviate trans-anxieties. *Journal of Lesbian Studies, 6*(3/4), 177–189.

Malaney, G., Williams, E., & Geller, W. (1997). Assessing campus climate for gays, lesbians and bisexuals at two institutions. *Journal of College Student Development, 38*(4), 356–375.

Matheis, C. G. (2004). *Creating and sustaining a whole community in hierarchical institutions.* Unpublished master's thesis, Oregon State University, Corvallis, OR.

Matheis, C. G. (2005). *Critical theory, intersubjectivity and community.* Unpublished manuscript. Oregon State University, Corvallis, OR.

Milem, J. F. (2003). The educational benefits of diversity: Evidence from multiple sectors. In Mitchell Chang, Daria Witt, James Jones, & Kenji Hakuta (Eds.), *Compelling interest: Examining the evidence on racial dynamics in higher education* (pp. 87–106). Report of the AERA Panel on Racial Dynamics in Colleges and Universities. Palo Alto, CA: Stanford University Press.

Norris, F. H., & Kaniasty, K. (1991). The psychological experience of crime: A test of the mediating role of beliefs in explaining the distress of victims. *Journal of Social and Clinical Psychology, 10,* 239–261.

Palmer, J. (1989, March). Diversity: Three paradigms for change leaders. *The Journal of the O.D. Network,* 1–5.

Peters, T. J., & Waterman, R. H. (1982). *In search of excellence.* New York: Harper & Row.

Peterson, M., & Spencer, M. (1990). Understanding academic culture and climate. In W. Tierney (Ed.), *Assessing academic climates and cultures* (pp. 1–21). San Francisco: Jossey-Bass, Inc.

Rankin, S. (1994). *The perceptions of heterosexual faculty and administrators toward gay men and lesbians.* Unpublished master's thesis, The Pennsylvania State University, University Park.

Rankin, S. (1998) Campus climate for lesbian, gay, bisexual and transgendered students, faculty, and staff: Assessment and strategies for change. In R. Sanlo (Ed.), *Working with lesbian, gay and bisexual college students: A guide for administrators and faculty* (pp. 277–284). Westport, CT: Greenwood Publishing Company.

Rankin, S. (2001). *Campus climate for underrepresented groups.* Unpublished manuscript.

Rankin, S. (2003). *Campus climate for lesbian, gay, bisexual, and transgender people: A national perspective.* New York: New York: NGLTF Policy Institute.

Rawls, J. (1990). A theory of justice. In S. Cahn, & P. Markie, (Eds.), *Ethics: History, theory, and contemporary issues* (pp. 541–563). New York: Oxford University Press.

Roper, L. (2005). The role of senior student affairs officers in supporting LGBT students: Exploring the landscape of one's life. In R. Sanlo (Ed.), *Gender identity and sexual orientation: Research, policy, and personal perspectives* (pp. 81–88). *New Directions for Student Services, 111*. San Francisco, CA: Jossey-Bass.

Royce, J. (2003). The moral insight. In L. Roberts (Ed.), *PHL 205 Class Notes* (pp. 9–10). Corvallis: Oregon State University Printing & Mailing Services.

Sausa, L. (2002). Updating college and university campus policies: Meeting the needs of trans students, staff and faculty. *Journal of Lesbian Studies, 6*(3/4), 43–55.

Savin-Williams, R. C., & Cohen, M. N. (1996). *The lives of lesbians, gays and bisexuals: Children to adults*. Fort Worth, TX: Harcourt Brace.

Schmidt, P. (2003). The Michigan rulings: Affirmative action survives, and so does the debate. *The Chronicle of Higher Education, 49*(43), 10.

Schreier, B. (1995). Moving beyond tolerance: A new paradigm for programming about homophobia/biphobia and heterosexism. *Journal of College Student Development, 36*(1), 19–26.

Simsek, H., & Seashore Louis, K. (1994). Organizational change as paradigm shift: Analysis of the change process in a large, public university. *The Journal of Higher Education, 65*(6), 670–695.

Slater, B. (1993). Violence against lesbians and gay male college students. *Journal of College Student Psychotherapy, 8*(1/2), 177–202.

Stevens, R. (2004). Understanding gay identity development within the college environment. *Journal of College Student Development, 45*(2), 185–206.

Tierney, W. G. (1993). *Building communities of difference: Higher education in the twenty-first century*. Westport, CT: Bergin & Garvey.

Tierney, W. G., & Dilley, P. (1996). Constructing knowledge: Educational research and gay and lesbian studies. In W. Pinar (Ed.), *Queer theory in education* (pp. 24–32). Mahwah, NJ: Lawrence Erlbaum Publishing.

Waldo, C. (1998). Out on campus: Sexual orientation and academic climate in a university context. *American Journal of Community Psychology, 26*(5), 745–774.

Waldo, C., Hesson-McInnis, M., & D'Augelli, A. (1998). Antecedents and consequences of victimization of lesbian, gay and bisexual young people: A structural model comparing rural university and urban samples. *American Journal of Community Psychology, 26*(2), 307–334.

Weick, K. (1976). Educational organizations as loosely coupled systems. *Administrative Quarterly, 25*, 1–19.

Yep, G. (2002). From homophobia and heterosexism to heteronormativity: Toward the development of a model of queer interventions in the university classroom. *Journal of Lesbian Studies, 6*(3/4), 163–176.

6

A GROWING CONCERN
Sexual Violence Against Women on College Campuses

Elizabeth M. O'Callaghan

E very year as the month of December approaches, many in the academic community are reminded of the massacre at l'Ecole Polytechnique in Toronto, Canada. On December 6, 1989, Marc Lepine entered an engineering classroom. Wielding a gun, he separated the female from the male students and proceeded to execute 13 female students and one female staff member before taking his own life. Witnesses reported that before the shootings, Lepine shouted, "Feminists have ruined my life." The women did nothing to provoke the attack. In fact, Lepine was not even an enrolled student at the university. (For more detail, see Green, 2005; for an analysis of femicide, see Caputi & Russell, 1992). This event, while admittedly an extreme example, nonetheless reminds us of the dangers facing women on college and university campuses. Regardless of the details surrounding the planned attack, the reality is that Lepine targeted students, and the violence was directed explicitly at women. While this attack occurred in Canada, violent perpetrators do not respect national borders, and American colleges and universities could find themselves host to a similar tragic event.

This chapter deals specifically with sexual violence against women on college and university campuses. Research has documented that during the past decade overall violent crime rates have fallen (Catalano, 2005), and, in particular, female students ages 18–24 experience proportionally less violent crime than do their nonstudent peers (Baum & Klaus, 2005; Hart, 2003). While statistics reveal that female students are overall less likely to be victims of robbery, aggravated assault, simple assault, and serious violent crime than their male student, female nonstudent, or male nonstudent peers (Baum & Klaus, 2005; Hart, 2003), of critical importance to campus administrators and personnel is the exception to this statistic: sexual violence (i.e., rape, sexual assault).

The rates of sexual violence against women do not differ significantly between students and nonstudents and affect all women, regardless of social position (Baum & Klaus, 2005; Hart, 2003). Research has documented that women on campus are in danger of being sexually victimized (Fisher, Sloan, Cullen, & Lu, 1998; Fisher, Cullen, & Turner, 2000; Karjane, Fisher, & Cullen, 2002; Koss, Gidycz, & Wisniewski, 1987; National Advisory Council on Violence Against Women [NACVAW], 2004).

National reports have indicated that one-quarter of college-age women report having been raped, and approximately 20% of female students are raped during their collegiate years (Fisher et al., 2000; Koss et al., 1987). In addition, the vast majority of rapes and sexual assaults are committed against women. Females were the victims in 94% of all completed rapes, 91% of all attempted rapes, and 89% of all completed and attempted sexual assaults (Rennison, 2002). Women also comprised 85% of the victims of intimate partner violence (Rennison, 2003). Among college students, nonstrangers accounted for approximately three-fourths of the offenders in reports of rape and sexual assault (Hart, 2003).

Approximately two-thirds of all sexual assaults and completed and attempted rapes go unreported to the police (Rennison, 2002). Three-fourths of sexual assaults and more than 75% of attempted and completed rapes are unreported when the offender is a current or former husband or boyfriend (Rennison, 2002). Other research indicates that the rates of under- and nonreporting are even higher, with more than 80% of sexual assaults not reported to police (Fisher, Sloan, & Cullen, 1995; NACVAW, 2004). These alarming statistics, coupled with the reality that women are enrolling at colleges and universities at unprecedented rates, should be of great concern to administrative personnel; as these statistics intimate, sexual violence is more prevalent on college campuses than is known or understood.

Adding to the problem is the increased enrollment and employment of women in higher education. Beginning in 1978, the total number of women enrolled in higher education exceeded the number of men (Wirt et al., 2004). During the decades that followed, women's enrollment increased at a greater rate than that of men, and the trend is expected to continue. By 2001, more than 7 million women were enrolled in degree-granting institutions and accounted for approximately 56% of total student enrollment (Wirt et al., 2004). By 2013, women are projected to increase their representation on college and university campuses to almost 58% of all students (Wirt et al., 2004). Women also account for over half (53%) of all employees at degree-granting institutions (Knapp et al., 2005). The fact that women comprise an increasing majority of students on college campuses and the majority of campus personnel, along with the fact that the majority of violence on campus is directed at women (Cortina, Swan, Fitzgerald, & Waldo, 1998; Fitzgerald et al., 1988; Hall & Sandler, 1986; Koss et al., 1987), means that violence against women is a pressing and critical issue for student affairs administrators, public safety personnel, and students alike.

This chapter analyzes the impact of sexual harassment, sexual assault, rape, stalking, and courtship/dating/domestic violence on women's collegiate and workplace experiences. Violence against women, especially sexual violence, can have a devastating effect on a woman's life, educational aspirations, and career goals. By focusing on understanding how violence affects women, administrators and university personnel may be able to initiate programs and policies aimed at decreasing sexual violence on college campuses. This chapter also assists college and university administrators in determining how to provide adequate support to the campus community to decrease the victimization of women on campus.

Perspectives on Sexual Violence on College Campuses

There are various perspectives from which to view the reality of crime on campus, including crime as an academic problem, as a national problem, as a public health crisis, and as a women's issue. In addition, there are multiple difficulties with reporting crime, including underreporting incidents and identifying characteristics of crime victims without engaging in victim blaming.

College is a time for academic growth and social exploration; unfortunately, however, the campus environment can be dangerous for female students and staff (Gross, Winslett, Roberts, & Gohm, 2006). Specifically, women on college campuses are at a greater risk than are their male peers for sexual assault, rape, stalking, and courtship/dating/domestic violence (Carr, 2005; Fisher et al., 1995; Sampson, 2002).

Other national studies and surveys report that anywhere from 20 to 50% of students experience dating violence by the end of their college career (Makepeace, 1981). Consistent with this finding, the Bureau of Justice Statistics (Rennison & Welchans, 2000) reports that the age of the victim matters, with the highest rate of intimate partner violence occurring among women ages 16–24. Similarly, according to the Office of Violence Against Women (Tjaden & Thoennes, 1998), more than 50% of all stalking victims are between 18 and 29 years old. At one particular institution, 11% of women experienced a completed rape while an undergraduate at the university, and 3% reported experiencing an attempted or completed rape while in graduate school (Cortina et al., 1998).

Violence and sexual victimization is a serious academic problem because it affects the learning environment and learning experiences of women and is a pervasive problem on college campuses (DeKeseredy & Schwartz, 1998; Fisher et al., 2000; Fisher et al., 1998; Fitzgerald et al., 1988; Koss et al., 1987; NACVAW, 2004; Paludi, 1996; White & Koss, 1991). Highlighting the seriousness of this problem are studies showing that assault outcomes for women include negative academic consequences, diminished feelings of respect and acceptance on campus, and a negative climate for women and gender issues (Cortina et al., 1998; Krug, Dahlberg, Mercy, Zwi, & Lozano, 2002).

Women who experience harassment and/or assault often choose not to return to campus for fear they may face their attacker again, and they often have negative evaluations of instructor interactions, lowered feelings of acceptance on campus, and decreased academic self-confidence. These women also perceived receiving less respect and poorer treatment as women on campus (Cortina et al., 1998). These experiences are especially true for women who experience more severe forms of sexual violence. For instance, acquaintance rape victims often suffer from shock, humiliation, anxiety, depression, substance abuse, suicidal thoughts, loss of self-esteem, social isolation, anger, distrust of others, fear of AIDS, guilt, and sexual dysfunction (Sampson, 2002; Yeater & O'Donohue, 1999).

Campus crime has been recognized as a national problem by the federal government since the early 1990s. In 1991, President George H. W. Bush declared the first week of September as National Campus Crime and Security Awareness Week. This time was set aside to recognize safety and security issues on campus and to recognize the student victims of violent crime (H. J.

Res. 142). In addition, national statistics prepared by the U.S. Department of Education reveal that 2,392 sex offenses occurred on college campuses in 2002 (Keels, 2004).

Campus crime may also be thought of as a public health issue. The American College Health Association (Carr, 2005) makes this case quite clearly. For example, in a description of a public health approach to campus violence prevention, a former dean of students from the University of Wisconsin-Madison is quoted as saying:

> The essence of [an] environmental management approach is for adminis-trators, faculty, and staff, working in concert with the local community, to change those campus and community policies, practices and infrastructure, and culture which promote violence and tolerance for it. (p. 8)

This approach differs from others in that it seeks to shift the focus from individual perpetrators and survivors toward the community and campus structures in which acts of violence and aggression occur, and a concurrent emphasis on proactive educational outreach for violence awareness and prevention.

Campus-based violence can also be characterized as a women's issue as women are disproportionately the victims in sexually based incidents. Sexual assault and rape are the two most common violent crimes committed on college campuses in the United States (Finn, 1995; Fisher et al., 1995; Sampson, 2002), and researchers have documented that anywhere from 27 to 33% of undergraduate women report surviving a sexual assault while in college (Koss et al., 1987; Lott, Reilly, & Howard, 1982; Miller & Marshall, 1987; Wilson & Durrenberger, 1982). A joint research project by the National Institute of Justice and the Bureau of Justice Statistics remains the most comprehensive survey of sexual violence and victimization on college campuses to date (Fisher et al., 2000). Through a national telephone survey, researchers found that during the seven months before the study, 1.7% of college women in their sample had experienced a completed rape, 1.1% had experienced an attempted rape, and 13% reported they had been stalked during that same seven-month period (Fisher et al., 2000). The data, extrapolated over a five-year college career, suggest that the proportion of women who experience a completed or attempted rape may climb to 20–25%.

How violence and sexual aggression is described or defined, analyzed, and reported affects crime statistics, which can create contradictory information for college administrators, faculty, and students. The difference in the prevalence of rape and other forms of sexual violence may appear confusing and contradictory at first. However, many of these differences have more to do with discrepancies in the methodology, semantics, instruments, and interview protocol for independent research projects and less to do with the violence women experience on campus. For example, the Cortina et al. (1998) study revealed that while approximately one of two college-age women reported experiencing some form of harassment during their collegiate years, only 20–25% of the victims labeled the experiences as sexually harassing. The underreporting of crime has been attributed to embarrassment, not understanding legal definitions of crime, not wanting to identify the perpetrator as a rapist, self-blame, shame, and fear of repercussions or not identifying certain situations as sexual harassment (Brooks & Perot, 1991; Goodwin, Roscoe, Rose, & Repp, 1989; Pitts & Schwartz, 1993). Regardless of the precise statistics, women still experience violence on campus—a reality that must be changed.

The circumstances surrounding violence against women on campuses have been researched and documented by campus administrators, researchers, and campus police forces. The vast majority of sexual violence against women on college campuses occurs when they are alone with a man they know in the privacy of a residence (i.e., no witnesses) and between the hours of 6 p.m. and 6 a.m. (Fisher et al., 2000; Waryold, 1996). In essence, this means that women are most vulnerable to attacks perpetrated by acquaintances, friends, and colleagues. Other identified risk factors for female college students include: (a) having been on campus for only a short period (i.e., the first few weeks of the first and second years of college); (b) living on campus; (c) being unmarried/single; (d) engaging in frequent and/or excessive drinking; (e) using drugs; (f) having experienced prior sexual victimization; (g) miscommunication about sex and desire; and (h) having liberal attitudes toward sexual relations (Fisher et al., 2000; Sampson, 2002). However, given this information, we must be careful not to engage in victim blaming. While it is important to recognize the risk factors associated with violence against women, it is not the woman's fault that she is attacked or violated. That responsibility lies with the perpetrator and with a society that tacitly condones violence against women.

A significant problem is exploring the myriad causes of violence on college and university campuses. Research has indicated that there is no single cause of violence against women on campus (Langford, 2004). Since the causes of violent behavior on college campuses are varied, often no one factor is identified as the proximate cause for particular types of incidents. Attributes of campus and community environments, the individual characteristics of the victim, and the individual characteristics of the perpetrator have all been explored (Langford, 2004). However, there is no consensus on what creates an atmosphere in which sexual violence and aggression may occur on campus.

Last, how key decision makers on campus respond to allegations and complaints and the level of sensitivity shown to victims and survivors is of critical importance. A comprehensive understanding of college and university response mechanisms to campus crime against women is important to monitor the implementation of effective techniques, programs, policies, and procedures (Karjane et al., 2002).

The next section deals specifically with some of the challenges associated with defining campus-based crime. In addition, particular descriptions of campus crime are provided. By paying special attention to those crimes that disproportionately affect women, other forms of violence, such as arson, homicide, suicide, hazing, and bias or hate crimes, should not be minimized. However, due to this chapter's focus, only acquaintance rape, sexual harassment, stalking, and courtship/dating/domestic violence are highlighted.

Defining Crimes Against Women

The main categories of sexual violence against women on college campuses include acquaintance rape, sexual harassment, stalking, and courtship/dating/domestic violence. However, providing definitions for campus-based violence against women is more challenging than it may first appear. Crime on campus bridges the legal, criminal, social science, and public policy arenas, and, as noted previously, there are multiple lenses through which to view college-based violence (Fitzgerald et al., 1988). Often colleges and universities rely on disparate sources of information for their antiviolence policies and adjudication and/or disciplinary processes and procedures on campus.

The lack of uniformity in defining sexually based crimes against women from campus to campus, or between the criminal justice system in a community and the local educational institution, is likely a result of the campus police/security force relying on statutory definitions of criminal activity and administrators deferring to institutional definitions during their adjudication procedures (Karjane et al., 2002; Langford, 2004). For example, there are definitions and legal standards specific to criminal investigations and legal proceedings surrounding the prosecution of particular crimes. Colleges and universities do not conduct criminal or legal proceedings; however, they do investigate violations of codes of conduct and initiate disciplinary hearings. During campus-based adjudication processes, colleges and universities may rely on their own definitions of sexual violence embedded in codes of conduct—the documents that govern the adjudication of disciplinary proceedings.

Social scientists often rely on an entirely different set of definitions in their attempts to measure experiences of college women (e.g., National Crime Victims Survey; Sexual Experiences Questionnaire). These studies are often more general in their description of certain crimes or violent acts. Underlying this approach is the fact that individual survivors of violence do not think of their experiences in terms of legal standards or criminal definitions. For example, The National Crime Victims Survey (U.S. Department of Justice [USDOJ], 2006) defines rape as:

> Forced sexual intercourse including both psychological coercion as well as physical force. Forced sexual intercourse means vaginal, anal, or oral penetration by the offender(s). This category also includes incidents where the penetration is from a foreign object such as a bottle. Includes attempted rapes, male as well as female victims, and both heterosexual and homosexual rape. (p. 141)

On a global scale, some definitions exceed the national and international constructs of various forms of violence (i.e., rape as a war crime). The World Health Organization defines sexual violence in part as "any sexual act [or] attempt to obtain a sexual act [and] unwanted sexual comments or advances" (Krug et al., 2002, p. 149). This definition of sexual violence includes rape, which is further defined as "physically forced or otherwise coerced penetration—even if slight—of the vulva or anus, using a penis, other body parts or an object."

National-level legislation is one place to look for unifying definitions on which to base campus programs and policies. For example, the Clery Act has emerged as the preeminent source for definitions of campus crime. The act divides violence into multiple categories, which include murder, sex offenses, robbery, aggravated assault, burglary, motor vehicle theft, manslaughter, arson, and other violations related to alcohol, drugs, and weapons. The definitions that appear in this act are drawn from the Uniform Crime Reporting (UCR) program of the Federal Bureau of Investigation (USDOJ, 2002). For the sake of comparison with the definitions above, the UCR definition of forcible rape is: "The carnal knowledge of a female forcibly and against her will. Rapes by force and attempts or assaults to rape regardless of the age of the victim are included."

While each of these definitions resembles the other, there are subtle differences between them that have far-reaching implications for discussing, documenting, and researching campus based violence against women. The inclusion of the imprecise and seemingly outmoded term, *carnal knowledge*, highlights the definitional challenges inherent in capturing a complete portrait of sexual violence on college campuses. While this issue will not be resolved easily, college and university administrators should be mindful of these definitional challenges when reading and interpreting campus-based crime statistics. In an effort to provide more information on the different forms of sexual violence that occur on campus, acquaintance rape, sexual harassment, stalking, and courtship/dating/domestic violence are described in more detail below.

Acquaintance Rape

The majority of women who are raped know their assailant, which should be of primary concern for campus administrators. Researchers have noted that 90% of college women who were victims of rape or attempted rape knew their assailant (Fisher et al., 2000). This means that colleges and universities have both perpetrators and victims among their student body. By acknowledging this fact, colleges and universities can begin to develop programs and policies that address this unique form of violence against women. Acquaintance rape is readily defined as rape that is committed by an assailant whom the victim knows and with whom the victim is familiar. Acquaintance rape can take many forms, including party rape, date rape, rape in nonparty or nondate situations (e.g., rape while studying or working with another individual), or rape by a previous or current intimate partner (Sampson, 2002).

While alcohol is not the sole factor contributing to acquaintance rapes, it is frequently associated with these incidents. Research has documented that in more than 75% of acquaintance rapes, the victim, the perpetrator, or both had been drinking (Hanson & Gidycz, 1993; Sampson, 2002). Alcohol not only reduces motor function, it has also been shown to reduce a person's ability to analyze complex social situations appropriately, and thus may lead either the victim or perpetrator to misunderstand or ignore certain sexual cues (Sampson, 2002). College athletics and Greek organizations are also frequently discussed in the context of acquaintance rape. A disproportionate number of college athletes are reported to college and university administrators for acquaintance rape (Koss & Cleveland, 1996; Sampson, 2002), and a disproportionate number of reported gang rapes involve fraternities (Bohmer & Parrot, 1993; Sampson, 2002).

Sexual Harassment

The problem of how to define certain acts, behaviors, and attitudes as violence toward women becomes most pronounced when working with sexual harassment incidents (Dey, Korn, & Sax, 1996). Not withstanding this challenge, over time, two distinct types of harassing behavior have been crystallized: (a) quid pro quo and (b) hostile environment (Dey et al., 1996; Paludi & Barickman, 1991; Paludi & DeFour, 1989). Quid pro quo harassment includes, but is not limited to, sexual acts or behaviors that are performed in exchange for a particular outcome. One of the most common examples is when a student agrees to have sexual relations with a faculty member in exchange for a particular grade in a course. Hostile environment harassment is created when sexual conduct is severe, persistent, or so pervasive that it affects a student's ability to participate in or benefit from an educational program or activity. This includes creating an intimidating, threatening, or abusive educational environment. An alternative way of viewing sexual harassment incorporates a continuum perspective where different sexually harassment behaviors are located among different levels depending on their frequency. They may range from one-time/rare assaults to pervasive/frequent harassment (Carroll & Bristor, 1993; Paludi & Barickman, 1991). Figure 6.1 captures the breadth and frequency of actions that constitute sexual harassment.

FIGURE 6.1
Actions that constitute sexual harassment.

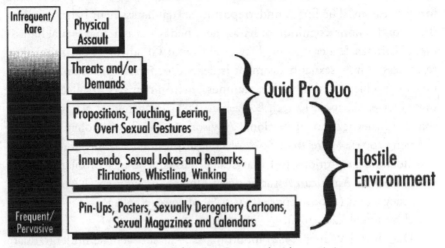

© 1993 The American Council on Education. Reprinted with permission.

Long before sexual harassment was a recognized problem on the college campus, it was a problem facing many employers. Turning to the employment arena for guidance, the Equal Employment Opportunity Commission (EEOC) (1980) defines sexual harassment as unwelcome sexual advances, requests for sexual favors, and other verbal or physical conduct of a sexual nature. Sexual harassment occurs when one of the following qualifications is met: (a) submission to such conduct is made either explicitly or implicitly a term or condition of an individual's employment; (b) submission to or rejection of such conduct is used as the basis for employment decisions affecting that individual; or (c) such conduct has the purpose or effect of unreasonably interfering with an individual's work performance or creating an intimidating, hostile, or offensive working environment.

It is important to note that while the EEOC guidelines outline what constitutes sexual harassment under federal law for employment purposes, it is Title IX of the Educational Amendments of 1972 that prohibits discrimination on the basis of sex at educational institutions that receive federal funding. Title IX is also the federal legislation that provides the legal framework for addressing sexual harassment in institutions of higher education.

Difficulties in defining sexual harassment often go hand in hand with difficulties identifying and reporting sexual harassment. Reporting sexual harassment acts, behaviors, and attitudes on college campuses is problematic for two reasons. The first is underreporting sexual harassment behaviors, and the second is nonrecognition of harassment behaviors as actual sexual harassment. (Brooks & Perot, 1991; Dey et al., 1996; Goodwin et al., 1989). Yet, regardless of how sexual harassment is defined or reported, it remains a significant problem within college campus environments (Carroll & Bristor, 1993; Dey et al., 1996; Dziech & Weiner, 1984; Fitzgerald et al., 1988; Hobson & Guziewicz, 2002; National Advisory Council on Violence Against Women, 2004). More than 60% of college presidents from large research and doctoral institutions feel that sexual harassment is a problem (Boyer, 1990), and the American Association of University Women (AAUW) Legal Advocacy Fund (2000) reports that 75% of female college students are affected by sexual harassment.

Dziech and Weiner (1984) found that 20–30% of female undergraduate students reported experiencing some form of sexual harassment by at least one faculty member during their undergraduate years. This is consistent with a study by Roscoe, Goodwin, Repp, and Rose (1987) that found that approximately 25% of female university students experience sexual harassment by either a professor or a work supervisor. At one particularly troublesome university, the problem was much worse. At that university, Cortina et al. (1998) found that as many as 49% of female undergraduate and 53% of female graduate students reported experiencing at least one harassing behavior from an instructor or professor. While the risk factors for sexual harassment have not been studied exhaustively (nor have the characteristics and traits of the perpetrators), these include being a woman of color, being a graduate student, and receiving financial aid (Sandler & Shoop, 1997). These factors are shared to highlight the populations of students most vulnerable to this type of violence.

The effects of sexual harassment on undergraduate and graduate students' experiences are profound (Cortina et al., 1998; Schneider, Swan, & Fitzgerald, 1997). The impact on female students is great and can take a variety of forms, such as physical, psychological, or behavioral effects (Hobson & Guziewicz, 2002). Experiencing sexual harassment has been shown to lead to negative perceptions of campus climate and the belief that women and gender issues on campus are not taken seriously. Incidents of sexual harassment can lead to an increase in fear for personal safety on campus in undergraduate students and, for survivors, increased levels of self-doubt regarding their own academic competence. Survivors are often less apt to return to the university (Cortina et al., 1998). Sexual harassment may also cause lowered levels of self-confidence, impaired ability to concentrate, and social and emotional withdrawal from school. Survivors of sexual harassment may experience ulcers, sleep disorders, eating disorders, high blood pressure, impaired immune system functioning, stress and anxiety, depression, guilt, shame, low self-esteem, inability to concentrate, decreased motivation, suicidal thoughts, increased tardiness and absenteeism, lower grades, higher incidence of class withdrawal, and a greater likelihood of quitting school (Cortina et al., 1998; Hobson & Guziewicz, 2002; Schneider et al., 1997).

Sexual harassment affects not only students, but female faculty and staff as well. A national survey of faculty revealed that 15.1% of female faculty nationwide reported being harassed at their present institution (Dey et al., 1996). Elite Ivy League institutions are no exception. Sandler (1986) reported that 32% of tenured female faculty and 49% of nontenured female faculty had experienced sexual harassment during their employment at Harvard University. Other studies have also documented high rates of sexual harassment within particular institutions (Goodwin et al., 1989; Williams, Lam, & Shively, 1992). At other universities, the proportion of women reporting experiences with some form of sexual harassment during their careers was recorded as 50–76% (Fitzgerald et al., 1988).

Sexual harassment of faculty members also extends beyond peer-to-peer incidents. McKinney (1990) found that 13.8% of female faculty reported being harassed by their male colleagues, and 22% reported being harassed by their students. Additionally, it seems that the disciplines in which faculty members are employed influence experiences of sexual harassment. More than 25% of faculty who taught women's studies courses and 20% of those who had done research on women's and gender issues reported being harassed (Dey et al., 1996). Women who are especially susceptible to sexual harassment are those in nontraditional fields, in graduate school, minority women, and women who are vulnerable because of youth, inexperience, or unassertiveness (Hughes & Sandler, 1986). Beyond sexual harassment, Moses (1989) documented the "double jeopardy" faced by African American females in academia—race and sex discrimination (Hughes & Sandler, 1986; Tangri, Burt, & Johnson, 1982). Not only do African American women risk being victimized for being women, but they also risk harassment for their racial identity.

Similar to the effect of sexual harassment on female students, the effects of sexual harassment on female faculty can be devastating and can cause cognitive, affective, and behavioral changes (Terpstra & Baker, 1986). Research has also demonstrated that harassment can fundamentally alter the way female faculty view their institutional climate (Dey et al., 1996). Some specific outcomes of harassment for female faculty include worse emotional and physical health (i.e., increased stress levels), negative feelings about work, decreases in job satisfaction, and a decreased ability to work with others (Tangri et al., 1982; Terpstra & Baker, 1986).

Stalking

As with sexual harassment, it can be difficult to come up with a precise definition of stalking. While the legal definitions of stalking differ from state to state (Kirkland, 2002; USDOJ, Federal Bureau of Investigation [FBI], 2002); these definitions are commonly guided by two distinct features of the crime: (a) the repeated victimization of one individual, and (b) the impact of stalking on the victim (USDOJ, FBI, 2002). Since isolated incidents are usually not considered stalking behavior, the behavior typically forms a recognizable pattern. In regard to the impact, the repeated actions of the perpetrator are usually those that would cause a reasonable person to have fear (i.e., of bodily injury or death).

The National Center for Victims of Crime (2004) provides a "working" definition of stalking that is applicable to campus-based incidents. Stalking is defined as "a course of conduct directed at a specific person that would cause a reasonable person to feel fear" (p. 1). The Montana Coalition Against Domestic and Sexual Violence (2000) takes the definition of stalking a step further and actually identifies the methods by which stalking commonly occurs. In addition to defining stalking as a pattern of repeated, unwanted attention, harassment, and contact, the definition includes:

> Repeated unwanted, intrusive, and frightening communications from the perpetrator by phone, mail, and/or e-mail, harassment through the Internet, known as cyberstalking, online stalking, or Internet stalking and securing personal information about the victim by using Internet search services. (Montana Coalition Against Domestic and Sexual Violence, 2000, ¶ 1)

Due to the prevalence of technology available to most campus communities, this high-tech stalking, or cyberstalking, is an important dimension of harassing and violent behavior that must be considered by campus officials. Approximately 25% of all stalking cases among college women are reported as cyberstalking (USDOJ, 1999). Cyberstalking typically involves offensive or threatening language via the Internet, e-mail, chat rooms or instant messages or other electronic communication tools (e.g., cell phones, pagers, and PDAs [personal digital assistants]) (Kirkland, 2002). Cyberstalking is notoriously difficult to track, since perpetrators are able to disguise their identities and easily adopt false ones (Kirkland, 2002).

The University of Texas maintains a website, http://www.stalkinghelp .org, that provides information about stalking behaviors, campus policies, and resources for individuals who believe themselves to be victims of stalking behaviors. This website defines stalking as "an abnormal or long-term pattern of threat or harassment that: is directed repeatedly toward a specific individual, is experienced as unwelcome or intrusive, and is reported to trigger fear or concern" (http://www.stalkinghelp.org). While this definition does not specifically identify the methods by which individuals may be victimized, it does not preclude Internet or cyberstalking.

Women are the victims in 78% of stalking cases, making this crime of primary concern for female college students (Tjaden & Thoennes, 1998; USDOJ, FBI, 2002). Researchers have reported rates as high as 13% of college women being stalked on campus, and, of these incidents, 80% of campus stalking victims knew their stalkers (Fisher et al., 2000); however, 83% of stalking incidents are not reported to police or campus law enforcement (Fisher & Cullen, 2000). As many as 3 in 10 college women have reported being injured emotionally or psychologically by being stalked (Fisher et al., 2000). High levels of stress and anxiety and feelings of vulnerability, fear, paranoia, guilt, self-blame, shame, isolation, low self-esteem, anger, rage, and depression are also correlated with being the victim of stalking (USDOJ, FBI, 2002). Dietary changes, sleep disturbances, difficulty concentrating on course work, and other academic responsibilities also accompany victimization (Kirkland, 2002).

Courtship/Dating/Domestic Violence

Stalking is also highly correlated with dating and domestic abuse. Similar to stalking, the majority of victims of domestic abuse are female. According to

Bureau of Justice statistics, drawn from data in the National Crime Victimization Survey, approximately 85% of victimizations by intimate partners were against women in 2001 (Rennison, 2003). The Bureau of Justice Statistics also reported that the highest rate of intimate partner violence occurs among women ages 16–24 (Rennison, 2003). As this age range covers traditional, residential college students, it is clear that courtship, dating, and domestic violence are cause for concern on college campuses today. Many colleges and universities are recognizing this fact and creating administrative positions within their institutions to work on this problem. For example, the University of Wisconsin-Madison, a large public university, employs a relationship violence prevention counselor in its health services office. In support of the institutional mission of raising awareness of domestic violence on campus, the violence prevention counselor assisted a student at the university in creating a publication that included eight anonymous biographies of female students who lived with domestic abuse during their time in college. Each woman described how the abuse affected her experiences on campus and her education, including causing feelings of isolation, low course grades, and fear of physical harm (Perry, 2002).

Power and control wheel. Physical and sexual assaults, or threats to commit them, are the most apparent forms of domestic violence and are usually the actions that allow others to become aware of the problem. However, it must be understood that battering behavior extends far beyond physical harm into an entire system of abuse and control. Physical assaults may occur only once or occasionally; however, they instill fear of future violent attacks and allow the abuser to take control of the partner's life. The power and control wheel is a particularly helpful tool in understanding the overall pattern of violent behaviors experienced within the context of abusive relationships. Often, batterers use these behaviors to establish and maintain control over their partners, and each violent incident usually is accompanied by an array of other types of abuse. While these ancillary types of abuse are more difficult to identify, and in isolation may not actually appear abusive (i.e., male privilege), when pieced together, they establish a pattern of intimidation in the relationship that is used to control the actions, behaviors, and emotions of the other partner. The image reproduced in Figure 6.2 demonstrates how power and control are used by abusive partners. The wheel also contains concrete examples of how one partner establishes control over another.

FIGURE 6.2
How power and control are used by abusive partners.

© Domestic Abuse Intervention Project, Minnesota Program Development Inc. Reprinted with permission.

Legislative History Regarding Sexual Violence on College Campuses[1]

The history of legislation covering sexual violence and sexual harassment specifically can be traced to the Title VII of the Civil Rights Act (1964). The act broadly prohibits sex discrimination and specifically identifies sexual harassment as unlawful. The act identifies sexual harassment as practices ranging from direct requests for sexual favors (quid pro quo) to uncomfortable workplace conditions (hostile environment). The Civil Rights Act of 1991 greatly

---

[1] More detail on the information in this section is available from http://thomas.loc.gov/home/thomas.html, a service of the Library of Congress.

expanded the scope of Title VII claims concerning sexual harassment. Plaintiffs were granted the right to a trial by a jury of their peers and could be awarded compensatory and punitive damages.

Title IX of the Education Amendments (1972) is the federal statute prohibiting sex discrimination in education. The law provides that:

> No person in the United States shall, on the basis of sex, be excluded from participation in, be denied the benefits of, or be subjected to discrimination under any educational program or activity receiving federal financial assistance.

This act extends to all matters as they relate to admissions, housing and residence halls, course work and other educational endeavors, career guidance and counseling services, financial aid, health and insurance benefits, and scholastic, intercollegiate, club, or intramural athletics. The act's regulations require recipients of federal education aid to evaluate current policies and practices to ensure compliance with Title IX, including the adoption, publication, and dissemination of grievance procedures and a policy against sex discrimination. The act also requires the appointment of at least one employee to coordinate compliance efforts on campus.

Title II of the 1990 Student-Right-to-Know and Campus Security Act is referred to as the Crime Awareness and Campus Security Act of 1990 (also known as the Clery Act) and amends the Higher Education Act of 1965. This act requires all higher education institutions receiving federal monies to prepare, publish, and distribute an annual report of campus crime statistics and security policies to all current and prospective students and current employees.

The Campus Sexual Assault Victims' Bill of Rights is part of a 1992 amendment to the federal Crime Awareness and Campus Security Act that requires each educational institution receiving Title IV federal aid to include a statement of policy regarding the rights of victims of sexual assault in its disclosure of campus security policy and campus crime statistics. Furthermore, it requires each institution of higher education to establish and implement a written policy establishing a campus sexual assault victims' bill of rights that provides that specified rights shall be accorded to such victims by all campus officers, administrators, and employees of such institutions.

As part of the 1998 reauthorization of the Higher Education Act, there was an amendment to the Student Right-to-Know and Campus Security Act, called the Jeanne Clery Disclosure of Campus Security Policy and Campus Crime Statistics Act. This amendment is one of the most far-reaching pieces of legislation affecting campus crime. This act requires eligible institutions to collect campus crime statistics and campus security policies and prepare, publish, and distribute them to all current students, applicants, and employees annually. The report must contain the following items: (a) a statement of current campus policies regarding how criminal actions and other emergencies occurring on campus should be reported and are adjudicated; (b) a statement of current campus security policies; (c) a statement of current law enforcement policies; (d) a description of educational programs that inform students and employees about campus security procedures and practices and crime prevention strategies and initiatives; (e) statistics concerning the occurrence of murder, sex offenses (forcible or nonforcible), robbery, aggravated assault, burglary, motor vehicle theft, manslaughter, arson, and alcohol, drug, or weapons violations that occur on- or off-campus, during the most recent calendar year and during the two preceding calendar years for which data are available; and (f) a host of other statements regarding off-campus criminal activity, drug use, and underage alcohol use. In addition, the act lists other statements that are to be distributed to campus and university communities, including information on crime prevention programs, possible sanctions for criminal activity that affects the campus community, and the procedures that should be followed when offenses and violations of college or university policy occur.

National legislation lays the groundwork for campus administrators in their aims to protect students and staff. Other women-centered forms of assistance include campus-based resource centers such as campus women's centers, educational outreach programs, and national awareness campaigns. Each of these is discussed in more detail with an emphasis on the manner in which they help provide a safe campus.

Women-Centered Antiviolence Programs and Initiatives

Campus Women's Centers

There is little current research documenting the status and programming of campus-based women's centers (Davie, 2001; Kasper, 2004), much less their role in creating a campus climate that is intolerant of violence. At best, there

is a strand in the literature that focuses on the theory and pedagogical con-
nections among women's studies, political activism, and campus-based
women's centers (Martell & Avitable, 1988; Parker & Freedman, 1999). Yet,
campus women's centers appear to play an integral role in the political, activist, and social justice movements on college campuses through their unique
programming. Often they are the only center on campus that is dedicated
exclusively to serving the needs of female faculty, staff, and students. This is
usually most apparent in the support group services that centers provide to
female students, faculty, and staff. The issues dealt with through support
groups often include eating disorders, depression/anxiety, girls who like girls,
sexual assault, single parenting, and body image. Campus women's centers
also provide a very concrete "theory into practice" link between the academic endeavors of women's studies programs and the practice of feminist
politics. From a student affairs and service learning perspective, one benefit
to the presence of women's centers on college campuses is that students have
a unique opportunity to advance their knowledge of organizing and their
administrative, group process, public relations, and community education
skills. From a social policy and public health perspective, campus women's
centers provide the campus community with a safe place for women to find
support and services when dealing with issues of violence.

In addition to serving the emotional, psychological, and social needs of
women, campus women's centers are often the host or co-host of women-
centered antiviolence initiatives and campaigns on campus. These are usually
annual events, whose purpose is to publicize how violence against women
affects students, faculty, staff, and the campus community. Some popular
initiatives that have a presence on numerous college campuses include the
"Take Back the Night" march, the Silent Witness initiative, the Clothesline
Project, the Handprint Project, Domestic Violence Awareness Month, and
Sexual Assault Awareness Month.

"Take Back the Night." Take Back the Night marches in the United
States appear to have started in the late 1970s in California as a response to
the sexism and violence experienced by all women through the perpetuation
of pornography. More than 5,000 women from 30 states attended the event.
The first documented march in the United States was organized as a part of a
larger conference focused on feminism and pornography, entitled "Feminist
Perspectives on Pornography" (Lederer, 1980). During the intervening years,

these marches have started to take place all over the United States and numerous international locations as well. The focus of these marches has shifted to combating violence against women in their communities and actively encouraging male participation and support. While there is a great debate about male participation on many campuses, most organizers and marchers agree that male support is crucial in changing a society that condones violence against women.

Silent Witness National Initiative. The goal of the silent witness initiative is to promote healthy, nonviolent relationships and have zero domestic murders of women or children by the year 2010. All 50 states and 20 countries are involved with this initiative, which seeks to visually represent a "silent witness" to domestic violence. This artistic display takes the form of freestanding, life-size red wooden figures representing the individuals whose lives ended violently at the hands of a husband, ex-husband, partner, or acquaintance. An additional figure is always added to the group to represent those uncounted women whose murders went unsolved or were erroneously ruled accidental. This anonymous figure is called the "silent witness" (http://www.silentwitness.net). There is a silent witness college program that offers information on how to bring the program to a college or university campus, and more than 40 institutions have participated and helped to raise awareness of violence against women on their campuses. The national initiative provides educational materials, ideas for implementation, a list of past collegiate participants, and photographs from various colleges and universities that have participated in the initiative.

The Clothesline Project. The Clothesline Project began in 1990 in Massachusetts as a project of the Cape Cod Women's Agenda. A powerful visual representation of how violence affects communities and relationships, this project provides an important avenue for survivors of sexual violence to break their silence and help with the healing process for people who have lost a loved one or are survivors of violence themselves. This project uses a visual display of T-shirts to portray the impact of domestic and sexual violence. Each shirt is decorated to represent a particular person's experience and is made by the survivor or someone who cares about them. The T-shirts are then hung on a clothesline and displayed to the public to educate, document, and raise awareness of the extent of domestic and sexual violence (University of New Hampshire Sexual Harassment and Rape Prevention Program).

The Handprint Project. This project, used by such organizations as Amnesty International and the International Federation of the Red Cross, allows men to participate in antiviolence campaigns. Typically, a handprint campaign is initiated by males offering to help stop violence against women. Men sign a pledge stating that they will not commit or condone violence against women. Then they make a handprint, which is displayed in a prominent location on campus. This is a powerful, visual way for men to show their support of efforts to stop violence on campus (The Feminist Majority Foundation, 2005).

Domestic Violence Awareness Month. Domestic violence awareness started on a national level in the late 1980s with National Domestic Violence Awareness Day, organized by the National Coalition Against Domestic Violence. By 1987, the event had become so popular that October was declared Domestic Violence Awareness Month. Congress recognized this designation in 1989. Purple ribbons are distributed and worn during October as a sign of support for survivors of domestic violence and in honor and memory of those who have lost their lives as a result of domestic violence (Domestic Violence Awareness Month, n.d.).

Sexual Assault Awareness Month. The National Coalition Against Sexual Assault (NCASA) declared April to be sexual assault awareness month in response to the growing social outrage at this type of violence. Originally, sexual assault was recognized alongside domestic violence in October. However, as events and activities surrounding domestic violence became more prominent, sexual assault awareness needed its own time and space for recognition. In 1989, NCASA declared April as Sexual Assault Awareness Month (Kansas Coalition Against Sexual and Domestic Violence, 2001).

Role of Student Affairs Administrators

The complexity of violence on campus requires an approach to reducing violence that embraces multiple, mutually supportive methods, initiatives, and programs (Langford, 2004). A comprehensive approach to violence prevention requires a focus not only on adjudication and conflict resolution, but also on the prevention of violence and provision of educational campaigns designed to empower students and staff alike.

While creating initiatives, programs, and task forces to address problems on campus can be overwhelming, Langford (2004) offers multiple principles to help guide such actions. He advised that administrative interventions should be both prevention- and response-focused and should be comprehensive in addressing on- and off-campus violence. Programs and initiatives should be planned and subsequently evaluated for effectiveness. They should be strategic and targeted in their approach and research-based. The programs should have multiple components and involve multiple methods of delivery, yet also be coordinated and synergistic with other campus-based crime prevention initiatives. Efforts should also be multisectoral and collaborative by drawing on the resources across campuses and supported by institutional commitments and systems designed to reduce violence within the college or university community.

It has also been suggested that creating a safe and supportive campus community requires that administrators focus on (a) enhancing women's safety and well-being on campus; (b) developing effective campus adjudication processes; (c) expanding services for victims of sexual assault, dating and domestic violence, and stalking; and (d) engaging fraternities and athletic departments in efforts to end violence against women (NACVAW, 2004). When applying these principles to a comprehensive violence prevention program, campus administrators may want to refer to recommendations by the National Advisory Council on Violence Against Women (2004). This group recommends taking the following concrete steps toward elimination of campus violence: (a) institutionalize a campus-wide response to violence against women; (b) create an interdisciplinary task force to address violence against women; (c) establish a fair campus adjudication process; (d) administer sanctions for perpetrators that convey the seriousness of the offense; (e) invest in comprehensive and accessible on-campus and community services to victims; (f) provide training on violence against women for all campus law enforcement; (g) form partnerships with local victim service programs and criminal justice agencies; (h) highlight men's ability and responsibility to prevent violence against women; (i) enlist men in education efforts; and (j) participate in full disclosure of campus crime data reports.

It is widely agreed that each educational institution, if not each department, program, center, and office on campus, should have a highly publicized, clearly worded, and widely disseminated policy against harassment and violence on campus (American Council on Education Office of Women in Higher Education, 1992; Carroll & Bristor, 1993; Hobson & Guziewicz,

2002; Riggs, Murrell, & Cutting, 1993). Policies designed to encourage educational and training programs should be included in the curriculum, extracurricular activities, campus-sponsored events, residence hall programs, and faculty and staff professional development activities (American Council on Education Office of Women in Higher Education, 1992; Hobson & Guziewicz, 2002; Riggs et al., 1993). There should also be provisions for counseling/therapy services for victims (Dey et al., 1996; Paludi & Barickman, 1991). In addition, clear grievance or complaint procedures should be available to all students, staff, and faculty on campus (American Council on Education Office of Women in Higher Education, 1992; Carroll & Bristor, 1993; Hobson & Guziewicz, 2002). It is recommended that this information also include formal and informal resolution mechanisms available to individuals on campus (Riggs et al., 1993).

Student affairs administrators often adopt multiple roles when dealing with crime on their campuses. These include providing support for antiviolence initiatives on campus; creating educational programs around alcohol and other drugs; developing sexual violence prevention strategies; providing counseling or referral services for victims and perpetrators of sexual violence; implementing the adjudication of violations of campus codes of conduct; serving as a liaison among the administration, staff, and campus security force; and lastly, serving as a campus representative in all efforts to draft and implement campus crime prevention efforts and campus antiharassment policies and adjudication procedures. Each of these roles is discussed in more detail next.

Provide fiscal and/or material support. The student affairs professional should strive to provide other administrators and campus personnel with adequate levels of funding, space, staffing, and other assistance to create, implement, and sustain violence prevention programming. In addition, support for antiviolence programs may be demonstrated through strategic alliances and administrative support. For example, programs may be housed in particular units or divisions to give them credibility in the campus community or additional access to extramural resources.

Support educational programming. Educational efforts can substantially increase awareness of university programs and policies as well as the illegal nature of certain actions (e.g., sexual harassment). More specifically, educational programming has been linked to declines in reports of sexual violence, including sexual harassment, on campuses (Williams et al., 1992).

Make counseling/referral services available. Student affairs administrators have the professional responsibility for student health and well-being on campus. When a student approaches the administrator to talk about an incident of sexual violence, counseling services should be made available to that student immediately.

Manage adjudication processes. The mediation, adjudication, and arbitration processes at colleges at universities are typically informed by good student affairs principles and rooted in the educational goals of the institution. Colleges and universities have lower standards of review and rules of evidence than do criminal processes, which allows them to take immediate action in response to allegations of misconduct. While critics of student disciplinary proceedings argue that investigatory and hearing procedures outside of the legal process fail to afford accused students their due process rights (Tenerowicz, 2001), colleges and universities often ensure fair, timely, and just processes for all parties involved.

Yet, depending on the nature of the violation and the victims' feelings regarding the incident, students who engage in misconduct on campus may be subject to both the criminal and the student disciplinary processes. A student may also be subject to additional disciplinary proceedings if the misconduct occurred in university housing. An example of this is if a student committed a violent rape against another student in a university residence hall. The student assailant could potentially face criminal charges, student disciplinary proceedings, *and* student housing disciplinary proceedings.

Liaison with campus and local police force and legal counsel. Incidents of sexual violence on campus are complex because the victim often seeks assistance from both the university administration and the local police or district attorney's office. Researchers and practitioners have noted that successful adjudication of most cases depends on the skills of judicial affairs administrators and the working relationship they have purposefully and proactively established with legal and law enforcement officials (Waryold, 1996). Concurrent criminal charges against the accused do not preclude on-campus disciplinary proceedings (Kaplin & Lee, 1995; Waryold, 1996), yet, attorneys representing the accused student often inquire whether disciplinary hearings can be delayed until after the criminal charges have been resolved.

It is important to note, however, that within a college community, the accused and the victim may have classes with one another, work together, live near each other, or see each other at campus events. Student affairs administrators have the professional responsibility to ensure that on-campus disciplinary actions proceed in a timely manner for the sake of the victim, the perpetrator, and overall campus safety and security. Having a positive and professional relationship with the district attorney's office, municipal law enforcement agencies, university police, the attorney(s) representing the university, the attorney(s) representing the accused, and the attorney(s) representing the victim is crucial to a positive resolution for all parties involved (Waryold, 1996).

Promote campus antiviolence policies and programs. Campus violence prevention programs should be prevention-focused, research-based, coordinated, and synergistic and supported by infrastructure (Langford, 2004). At one institution, sexual harassment policy and grievance procedures helped to decrease reported levels of faculty/staff sexual harassment of female undergraduate students (Williams et al., 1992).

In conclusion, campus administrators and student affairs professionals must stay current on the crime prevention programs, strategies, and best practices within academia. Research has shown that colleges and universities are paying increasingly more attention to safety and security issues on campus (Belknap, Fisher, & Cullen, 1999; Carr, 2005), and violence toward women on campus is of special concern for student affairs administrators and campus personnel alike (Belknap et al., 1999; Karjane et al., 2002; Malveaux, 2004; NACVAW, 2004). As crime rates on campus begin to equal those of their surrounding communities, and women are accounting for a greater percentage of the population of students, faculty, and staff, prevention of crimes against women, including sexual assault, rape, and dating/domestic violence, is rapidly becoming a sensitive issue on college campuses. While the postsecondary educational community continues to deal with violence against women, we might be well served to remember the massacre of January 1989. While such incidents are rare, the rising crime rates against women on campus, accompanied by women's vast underreporting of crimes, means that we have individual tragedies occurring on campuses every day. It is the collective responsibility of student affairs personnel, university administrators, students, faculty, and staff to work toward preventing violence against women on college and university campuses.

Additional Resources for Campus Administrators

Amnesty International
http://web.amnesty.org/actforwomen/index-eng

Domestic Violence Awareness Month Project
http://dvam.vawnet.org

National Center for Victims of Crime (NCVC)
http://www.ncvc.org

National Coalition Against Domestic Violence (NCADV)
http://www.ncadv.org

National Gay and Lesbian Taskforce (NGLT)
http://www.thetaskforce.org

National Organization for Women
http://www.now.org/issues/violence/

National Resource Center on Domestic Violence (NRCDV)
http://www.nrcdv.org

National Sexual Violence Resource Center (NSVRC)
http://www.nsvrc.org

National Violence Against Women Prevention Research Center
    (NVAWPRC)
http://www.vawprevention.org

Security On Campus, Inc.
http://www.securityoncampus.org

Silentwitness.net College Program
http://www.silentwitness.net/sub/colleges_program.htm

Stalkinghelp.org
http://www.stalking.org

U.S. Department of Education, Office of Postsecondary Education Campus
    Security Statistics
http://www.ope.ed.gov/security/search.asp

U.S. Department of Health and Human Services, Office on Women's
    Health
http://www.4woman.gov/violence/

U.S. Department of Justice, Office on Violence Against Women
http://www.usdoj.gov/ovw

University of Minnesota Center Against Violence & Abuse (MINCAVA)
http://www.mincava.umn.edu

University of New Hampshire Sexual Harassment and Rape Prevention
Program (SHARPP)
http://www.unh.edu/sharpp/

References

American Association of University Women (AAUW) Legal Advocacy Fund (2000). *A license for bias: Sex discrimination, schools and title IX.* Washington, DC: American Association of University Women.

American Council on Education Office of Women in Higher Education (1992). Eliminating sexual harassment on campus. *Educational Record, 73*(1), 50.

Baum, K., & Klaus, P. (2005). *Violent victimization of college students, 1995–2002.* Bureau of Justice Statistics Special Report, National Crime Victimization Survey (No. NCJ 206836). Washington, DC: U.S. Department of Justice, Office of Justice Programs.

Belknap, J., Fisher, B. S., & Cullen, F. T. (1999). The development of a comprehensive measure of the sexual victimization of college women. *Violence Against Women, 5,* 185–214.

Bohmer, C., & Parrot, A. (1993). *Sexual assault on campus: The problem and the solution.* New York: Lexington Books.

Boyer, E. L. (1990). *Campus life: In search of community.* Princeton, NJ: Carnegie Foundation for the Advancement of Teaching.

Brooks, L., & Perot, A. R. (1991). Reporting sexual harassment. *Psychology of Women Quarterly, 15,* 31–47.

Caputi, J., & Russell, E. H. (Eds.). (1992). *Femicide: The politics of woman-killing.* New York: Twayne Publishers.

Carr, J. L. (2005). *Campus violence white paper.* Baltimore, MD: American College Health Association.

Carroll, C. M., & Bristor, J. M. (1993). Sexual harassment on campus: Enhancing awareness and promoting change. *The Educational Record, 74*(1), 21–26.

Catalano, S. (2005). *Criminal victimization, 2004.* Bureau of Justice Statistics, National Crime Victimization Survey (No. NCJ 210674). Washington, DC: U.S. Department of Justice, Office of Justice Programs.

Cortina, L. M., Swan, S., Fitzgerald, L. F., & Waldo, C. (1998). Sexual harassment and assault: Chilling the climate for women in academia. *Psychology of Women Quarterly, 22,* 419–441.

Davie, S. L. (2001). *University and college women's centers: A journey toward equity.* Westport, CT: Greenwood.

DeKeseredy, W. S., & Schwartz, M. D. (1998). *Woman abuse on campus: Results from the Canadian National Survey.* Thousand Oaks, CA: Sage Publications.

Dey, E. L., Korn, J. S., & Sax, L. J. (1996). Betrayed by the academy: The sexual harassment of women college faculty. *The Journal of Higher Education, 67*(2), 149–173.

Dziech, B. W., & Weiner, L. (1984). *The lecherous professor: Sexual harassment on campus.* Boston: Beacon Press.

Domestic Violence Awareness Month. (n.d.). Retrieved April 8, 2006, from http://www.dvam.vawnet.org

Equal Employment Opportunity Commission. (1980). Sexual harassment guidelines, 29 C.F.R. § 1604.11(a). Washington, DC: Government Printing Office.

Feminist Majority Foundation, The. (2005). *Choices* campus campaign. Retrieved April 8, 2006, from http://www.feministcampus.org

Finn, P. (1995). *Preventing alcohol-related problems on campus: Acquaintance rape—A guide for program coordinators.* Newton, MA: Higher Education Center for Alcohol and Other Drug Prevention.

Fisher, B. S., & Cullen, F. T. (2000). *The extent and nature of the sexual victimization of college women: A national-level analysis.* Rockville, MD: National Criminal Justice Reference Service.

Fisher, B. S., Cullen, F. T., & Turner, M. G. (2000). *The sexual victimization of college women* (No. NCJ 182369). Washington, DC: U.S. Department of Justice.

Fisher, B. S., Sloan, J. L., & Cullen, F. T. (1995). *Final report: Understanding crime victimization among college students: Implications for crime prevention.* Washington, DC: U.S. Department of Justice.

Fisher, B. S., Sloan, J. J., Cullen, F. T., & Lu, C. (1998). Crime in the ivory tower: The level and sources of student victimization. *Criminology, 36*(3), 617–710.

Fitzgerald, L. F., Shullman, S. L., Bailey, N., Richards, M., Swecker, J., Gold, Y., Ormerod, M., & Weitzman, L. (1988). The incidence and dimensions of sexual harassment in academia and the workplace. *Journal of Vocational Behavior, 32*(2), 152–175.

Goodwin, M., Roscoe, B., Rose, M., & Repp, S. (1989). Sexual harassment: Experiences of university employees. *Initiatives, 52,* 25–33.

Green, J. (2005). Commemorating the Montreal massacre, for the 15th time. *Canadian Dimension, 39*(1), 2.

Gross, A. M., Winslett, A., Roberts, M., & Gohm, C. L. (2006). An examination of sexual violence against college women. *Violence Against Women, 12*(3), 288–300.

Hall, B. R., & Sandler, R. (1986). *The campus climate revisited: Chilly for women faculty, administrators, and graduate students.* Washington, DC: Project on the Status of Women, Association of American Colleges.

Hanson, K., & Gidycz, C. (1993). Sexual assault prevention program. *Journal of Counseling and Clinical Psychology, 61,* 1046–1052.

Hart, T. (2003). *Violent victimization of college students.* Bureau of Justice Statistics Special Report, National Crime Victimization Survey, 1995–2002 (No. NCJ 196143). Washington, DC: U.S. Department of Justice, Office of Justice Programs.

Hobson, C. J., & Guziewicz, J. (2002). Sexual harassment preventative/protective practices at U.S. colleges and universities. *College Student Affairs Journal, 21*(2), 17–29.

Hughes, J. O., & Sandler, B. R. (1986). *In case of sexual harassment: A guide for women students.* Washington, DC: Association of American Colleges.

Kansas Coalition Against Sexual and Domestic Violence. (2001, April). *April: Sexual assault awareness month.* Topeka: Author.

Kaplin, W., & Lee, B. (1995). *The law of higher education.* San Francisco, CA: Jossey-Bass.

Karjane, H. M., Fisher, B. S., & Cullen, F. T. (2002). *Campus sexual assault: How America's institutions of higher education respond.* Washington, DC: U.S. Department of Justice.

Kasper, B. (2004). Campus-based women's centers: A review of problems and practices. *Affilia, 19*(2), 185–198.

Keels, C. L. (2004). The best-kept secret: Crime on campus. *Black Issues in Higher Education, 21*(6), 20–27.

Kirkland, C. J. (2002). *Campus stalking.* Sacramento, CA: California Coalition Against Sexual Assault.

Knapp, L. G., Kelly-Reid, J. E., Whitmore, R. W., Huh, S., Zhao, L., Levine, B., Ginder, S., Wang, J., & Broyles, S. G. (2005). *Staff in postsecondary institutions, fall 2003, and salaries of full-time instructional faculty, 2003-2004* (NCES 2005-155). Washington, DC: U.S. Department of Education, National Center for Education Statistics.

Koss, M., & Cleveland, H. (1996). Athletic participation, fraternity membership and date rape: The question remains—Self-selection or different causal processes? *Violence Against Women, 2*(2), 180–190.

Koss, M., Gidycz, C., & Wisniewski, N. (1987). The scope of rape: Incidence and prevalence of sexual aggression and victimization in a national sample of higher education students. *Journal of Counseling and Clinical Psychology, 55*(2), 162–170.

Krug E., Dahlberg L. L., Mercy J. A., Zwi A. B., & Lozano R. (Eds.). (2002). *World report on violence and health.* Geneva: World Health Organization.

Langford, L. (2004). *Preventing violence and promoting safety in higher education settings: Overview of a comprehensive approach.* Washington, DC: U.S. Department of Education.

Lederer, L. (Ed.) (1980). *Take back the night: Women on pornography.* New York: W. Morrow.

Lott, B., Reilly, M. E., & Howard, D. (1982). Sexual assault and harassment: A campus community case. *Signs, 8,* 296–319.

Makepeace, J. M. (1981). Courtship violence among college students. *Family Relations, 30*(1), 97–102.

Malveaux, J. (2004). From Kobe Bryant to campus rape. *Black Issues in Higher Education, 21*(6), 30.

Martell, D., & Avitable, N. E. (1988). Feminist community organizing on a college campus. *Affilia, 13,* 393–411.

McKinney, K. (1990). Sexual harassment of university faculty by colleagues and students. *Sex Roles, 23*(7 8), 421 438.

Miller, B., & Marshall, J. C. (1987). Coercive sex on the university campus. *Journal of College Student Personnel, 28,* 38–47.

Montana Coalition Against Domestic and Sexual Violence (2000). *Stalking.* Retrieved April 8, 2006, from http://www.mcadsv.com/index.php?name = DV-Stalking

Moses, Y. T. (1989). *Black women in academe: Issues and struggles.* Washington, DC: Association of American Colleges, Project on the Status and Education of Women.

National Advisory Council on Violence Against Women (NACVAW) and the Violence Against Women Office (2004). Promoting safety and nonviolence on college and university campuses. In NACVAW and Violence Against Women Office, *Toolkit to end violence against women.* Washington, DC: Author.

National Center for Victims of Crime. (2004). Stalking fact sheet. Washington, DC: Stalking Resource Center.

Paludi, M. A. (1996). *Sexual harassment on college campuses: Abusing the ivory power.* Albany, NY: State University of New York Press.

Paludi, M. A., & Barickman, R. (Eds.) (1991). *In their own voices: Responses from individuals who have experienced sexual harassment and supportive techniques for dealing with victims of sexual harassment.* Albany: State University of New York Press.

Paludi, M. A., & DeFour, D. C. (1989). Research in sexual harassment in the academy: Definitions, constraints, responses. *Initiatives, 52,* 43–49.

Parker, J., & Freedman, J. (1999). Women's centers/women's studies programs: Collaborating for feminist activism. *Women's Studies Quarterly, 27,* 114–121.

Perry, R. (2002). *Raising voices: Eight University of Wisconsin-Madison students tell personal stories of dating violence.* Madison, WI: University Health Services and the Women's Studies Program, University of Wisconsin-Madison.

Pitts, V. L., & Schwartz, M. D. (1993). Promoting self-blame in hidden rape cases. *Humanity and Society, 17*(4), 383–398.

Rennison, C. M. (2002). *Rape and sexual assault: Reporting to police and medical attention, 1992–2000.* Bureau of Justice Statistics Selected Findings (No. NCJ 194530). Washington, DC: U.S. Department of Justice, Office of Justice Programs.

Rennison, C. M. (2003). *Intimate partner violence, 1993–2001.* Bureau of Justice Statistics, Crime Date Brief (No. NCJ 197838). Washington, DC: U.S. Department of Justice, Office of Justice Programs.

Rennison, C. M., & Welchans, S. (2000). *Intimate partner violence.* Bureau of Justice Statistics Special Report (No. NCJ 178247). Washington, DC: U.S. Department of Justice, Office of Justice Programs.

Riggs, R. O., Murrell, P. H., & Cutting, J. C. (1993). *Sexual harassment in higher education: From conflict to community.* ASHE-ERIC Higher Education Report No. 2. Washington, DC: The George Washington University School of Education and Human Development.

Roscoe, B., Goodwin, M. P., Repp, S. E., and Rose, M. (1987). Sexual harassment of university students and student-employees: Findings and implications. *College Student Journal, 21,* 254–273.

Sampson, R. (2002). *Acquaintance rape of college students.* Problem-Oriented Guides for Police Series, No. 17. Washington, DC: U.S. Department of Justice, Office of Community Oriented Policing Services.

Sandler, B. R. (1986). *The campus climate revisited: Chilly for women faculty, administrators, and graduate students.* Washington, DC: Association of American Colleges, Project on the Status and Education of Women.

Sandler, B. R., & Shoop, R. J. (1997). *Sexual harassment on campus: A guide for administrators, faculty, and students.* Boston, MA: Allyn and Bacon.

Schneider, K. T., Swan, S., & Fitzgerald, L. F. (1997). Job-related and psychological effects of sexual harassment in the workplace: Empirical evidence from two organizations. *Journal of Applied Psychology, 82,* 401–415.

Tangri, S. S., Burt, M. R., & Johnson, L. B. (1982). Sexual harassment at work: Three explanatory models. *Journal of Social Issues, 38,* 33–54.

Tenerowicz, L. (2001). Student misconduct at private colleges and universities: A roadmap for "fundamental fairness" in disciplinary proceedings. *Boston College Law Review, 42,* 653–694.

Terpstra, D. E., & Baker, D. D. (1986). A framework for the study of sexual harassment. *Basic and Applied Social Psychology, 7*(1), 17–34.

Tjaden, P., & Thoennes, N. (1998). *Stalking in America: Findings from the National Violence Against Women Survey.* Washington, DC: National Institute of Justice, U.S. Department of Justice, Centers for Disease Control and Prevention, and U.S. Department of Health and Human Services.

U.S. Department of Justice (USDOJ). (1999). *Cyberstalking: A new challenge for law enforcement and industry.* Report from Attorney General to Vice President. Washington, DC: U.S. Department of Justice.

U.S. Department of Justice (USDOJ). (2002). *Creating an effective stalking protocol.* Report submitted by the National Center for Victims of Crime. Washington, DC: U.S. Department of Justice.

U.S. Department of Justice (USDOJ). (2006). *Criminal victimization in the United States, 2004 statistical tables.* Washington, DC: U.S. Department of Justice and Bureau of Justice Statistics.

U.S. Department of Justice (USDOJ), Federal Bureau of Investigation (FBI). (2002). *Crime in the United States, 2002.* Retrieved April 8, 2006, from http://www.fbi.gov/ucr/cius_02/html/web/appendices/07-appendo2.html

Waryold, D. M. (1996). Handling sexual assault and relationships with law enforcement officials. *New Directions for Student Services, 73,* 79–88.

White, J. W., & Koss, M. P. (1991). Courtship violence. Incidence in a national sample of higher education students. *Violence and Victims, 6,* 247–256.

Williams, E. A., Lam, J. A., & Shively, M. (1992). The impact of a university policy on the sexual harassment of female students. *The Journal of Higher Education, 63*(1), 50–64.

Wilson, W., & Durrenberger, R. (1982). Comparison of rape and attempted rape victims. *Psychological Reports, 50,* 198.

Wirt, J., Choy, S., Rooney, P., Provasnik, S., Sen, A., & Tobin, R. (2004). *The condition of education 2004* (NCES 2004-077). Washington, DC: U.S. Department of Education, National Center for Education Statistics.

Yeater, E., & O'Donohue, W. (1999). Sexual assault prevention programs: Current issues, future directions and the potential efficacy of interventions with women. *Clinical Psychology Review, 19*(7), 739–771.

INSTITUTIONAL CONTEXT
AND RESPONSES

7

SAFETY IN THE COMMUNITY COLLEGE ENVIRONMENT

Charlene M. Dukes and Tracy Harris

C ommunity college students often find themselves in challenging situations and circumstances that extend far beyond the physical boundaries of the campus. This chapter examines issues of safety on an open campus[1], including situations that may blur physical and intellectual borders of community college campuses wherein the potential for violence arises. The chapter also addresses approaches for institutions to partner with the surrounding community to promote campus safety.

Development of the Community College Environment

Community colleges play a unique role in the higher education marketplace and represent a unique segment of American higher education (Milliron & de los Santos, 2004). One of the reasons for this uniqueness is the phenomenal student enrollment growth. Data compiled by the American Association of Community Colleges (AACC, 2000) identified 1,157 community colleges in the United States serving over 11.6 million students. Many community colleges, because of tremendous enrollment growth, have been challenged to reassess vision and mission statements, strategic and operational plans, and community needs. Meeting the social, educational, and personal needs of communities while working in partnership with local and state legislators on

---

[1] "Open campus" is synonymous with open access or open door higher education institutions. Cohen and Brawer (1987) described community colleges as "offering educational opportunities at the students' convenience, day and night, on campus and off."

funding and accessibility issues will be critical for institutions in the future (Smith & Vellani, 1999) This growth spurt by community colleges has created other institutional challenges as well. Burgeoning enrollments, demographic shifts, growth in services, needs of a growing non-English-speaking constituency, and remedial education all add to a complex web of various formats of institutional structures designed to serve the greater needs of the community (AACC, 2000). As a consequence, administrators from community colleges across the nation are struggling to identify staffing resources and increase the level of awareness necessary to create a safe campus environment among constituents (students, employees, and visitors) and the surrounding community. This chapter focuses on issues related to safety and the community college campus.

Brief History of the Community College

Joliet College is on record as the first public two-year college to provide a core general liberal arts education, in 1901 (Joliet Junior College, 2005). Community college growth in the 1960s was expansive and global, serving the baby boomers of the 1940s and the growing postwar U.S. economy. In 2000, AACC found that 44% of all American undergraduate students and more than half of students with freshman and sophomore status attend community and technical colleges (AACC, 2000). Thus, community colleges share a common commitment for open access to meet the educational and social development needs of a distinctive population of students. Increasingly, community colleges have redefined their institutional missions because of changing student demographics, competitive academic marketplaces, and the disparate academic needs of students. AACC describes the average community college student as female, enrolled part time, 29 years of age or older, and uses English as the second language (AACC, 2000).

Simultaneously, the growing demand for education and the escalating costs of private colleges and universities continue to force many students, and parents, to consider community colleges as their first choice in the college selection process. Other critical issues identified by Milliron and de los Santos (2004) as unique to community colleges include "educating first-generation college students, responding to increasingly diverse student participation, affording appropriate levels of academic support, providing adult basic education and senior programs, serving a growing segment of the population interested in workforce training and professional development, and overcoming the digital divide" (p. 107). Colleges and universities have become more integral components of the communities in which they are located. As growing numbers of younger and mature adults consider a college education, they, too, become concerned about the nonacademic environment and the college's ability to ensure a safe, healthy, and inviting collegiate experience.

Campus Crime: Why Is This an Issue?

Violence in American society has become a regular part of the college and university campus experience (Bennett-Johnson, 2004). According to the Federal Bureau of Investigation, Bureau of Justice, national statistics reveal that violent crime (defined as homicide, forcible rape, etc.), since 1993–2002, has declined steadily. At the same time, national statistics for burglary, property crime, and motor vehicle theft have not risen dramatically since 2000 (Federal Bureau of Investigation [FBI], U.S. Department of Justice [USDOJ], 2004). However, drug abuse and arrests among young adults are becoming a national epidemic and continue to rise far beyond the expectation of law enforcement officials and the common citizenry (FBI, USDOJ, 2004).

Community colleges have not been immune to this rise in drug and alcohol use and have developed programs and expanded staffing in key critical areas, such as health education services and counseling, to prevent the ramifications of such abuse. A study by Presley, Leichliter, and Meilman (1998) found that 9% of college students reported being victimized through some form of violent behavior or harassment as a result of someone being involved with drugs and alcohol in or around campus. Additionally, this study found that 67% of those surveyed who used drugs or alcohol were responsible for actual physical violence against a person or property. Another interesting finding on school violence and drug abuse from the Core Institute (retrieved April 22, 2006 from http://www.siu.edu/~coreinst/) is that 20.7% of college students reported drug use in the past 30 days. Last, Marcus, Reio, Kessler, Cutler, and Fleury (2001) presented results of a three-year study on violence between students at the University of Maryland. The study focused on fighting and analyzed the results by gender and severity of injury. General fighting and other violent offenses were common occurrences, with 9% of students needing medical attention, and alcohol was found to be the prevailing factor in more than 40% of the violent crimes on campus.

National and local crime statistics are critical in comprehending the importance of providing a safe community college campus environment. Understanding the need and the ramifications for a safe campus are steps community colleges must take in developing policies and practices that affect both short- and long-term institutional planning. As policies are formulated, many institutions may need to reexamine their institutional missions and visions to build congruency and alignment with the educational and service requirements of the community, coupled with the desire to provide a safe environment. Taylor and Maas (1995) identified the attributes that community colleges of the future will be expected to support: (a) delivering instruction at any time of the day, (b) providing alternative ways of learning according to students' individual learning styles, (c) networking electronically across district boundaries, (d) serving as primary centers for workforce retraining, (e) catering to the needs of part-time students, and (f) assuming a greater leadership role within the community.

Community colleges are part of the fabric of the environs served. Furthermore, such colleges are expected to respond to a wide array and diversity of needs, including providing full academic and student support programs for day and evening students, while remaining affordable and accessible to the community at large. Community colleges in urban areas often experience the "spillover" effect of community crime and work closely with local and state law enforcement agencies to inform and protect their students. Roueche, Roueche, and Ely (2001) found that urban community colleges often lack sufficient resources to address the needs of economically disadvantaged communities, but they are expected to respond rapidly to policy mandates and emerging community expectations (Dee, 2004). Rural community colleges are not immune, and, similar to urban areas, the activity tends to mirror crimes committed in the adjacent community. In other words, community colleges are a microcosm of the communities they serve (Kozeracki, 2000).

One area of concern for many community colleges is the ability to create a "safe" campus environment within an "open-access" campus community. A report by the Federal Bureau of Investigation, U.S. Department of Justice (2004), titled *Crime Factors—Crime in the United States 2004*, cited several factors that may contribute to the varied incidence of crime on college campuses, such as differences in the youth population; mobility of residents and commuting patterns; economic conditions, including poverty levels and job availability; effective strength of law enforcement agencies; citizens' attitudes toward crime; and crime reporting practices. Pezza (1995) examined the nature of crime on college campuses and found that incomplete reporting and lack of understanding impeded successful safety intervention on campuses. Community colleges are clearly expected to respond affirmatively by providing adequate levels of safety and awareness, which promote positive academic learning environments and productive social experiences for all college constituencies.

Another issue that must be addressed is how community colleges, compared to other colleges and universities, view campus crime. Pezza (1995) recognized that there has been a lack of clarity related to how colleges, universities, and law enforcement personnel define crime and violence, coupled with a continuous underreporting of crimes at the college level. The American College Health Association (ACHA) discussed the scope of campus violence on college campuses and found significant underreporting among victims, with only 25% of crimes reported (http://acha.org). There are two possible reasons for this underreporting. First, the general public is unfamiliar with how the Federal Bureau of Investigation Uniform Crime Reporting (FBI UCR) structure is indexed to differentiate and classify criminal behavior, and, second, underreporting among victims may be based on personal decisions. The FBI UCR criticizes itself for underreporting while acknowledging that students are reluctant to report crime. As a result, student injury data are not captured or indexed, thereby decreasing the number of reported incidents (FBI, 1998).

Legislative Impact

Crime on college campuses has become an important issue for students and parents alike in selecting which institution to attend (Security On Campus, 2006). College Parents of America, Inc., is a national organization serving the needs of college-going students and assisting parents in making rational decisions regarding college selection and safety (http://collegeparents.org). A great deal of this organization's time is spent on campus safety issues and informing parents and students about what they need to know in selecting a "secure" institution. This organization and others have gained in popularity due to significant legislation that changed the dynamics of campus safety for all postsecondary institutions of higher learning. The Student Right-to-Know and Campus Security Act of 1990 (Public Law 101-542, § 201) is pivotal in redirecting the energies of many community colleges to assess the definitions and levels of crime on and around their campuses. Concurrently, this legislation has heightened the level of awareness among students and family members regarding the seriousness of using institutional information in the college selection process and reporting campus crime. Furthermore, local supporters and visitors to community college campuses can access information that can enlighten and strengthen partnerships with institutions and assist in the identification and prevention of crime and violence on campuses.

One of the most critical amendments to this act was made as a result of a college student who died as a victim of campus violence. The parents of Jeanne Clery recognized a lack of awareness of the college's crime history when their daughter decided to enroll at Lehigh University, and they acknowledged that access to this information would have been a factor in their college selection. The act was later renamed the Jeanne Clery Disclosure of Campus Security Policy and Campus Crime Statistics Act (Public Law 105-244). Security On Campus, Inc., is a nonprofit organization whose primary goal is to educate prospective and current students, parents, and the community regarding the significance and importance of the act. Institutions that do not comply with the act's regulations are subject to fines by the U.S. Department of Education and the loss of participation in federally funded financial aid programs (Security On Campus, 2006). This includes reporting crime statistics on campus, in or on a noncampus building or property, or on public property within or immediately adjacent to and accessible from the campus (U.S. Department of Education [USDOE], 2005).

Several studies have been conducted to examine the effectiveness of the Clery Act with regard to college students, faculty, and staff and their knowledge of campus crime and reporting/awareness requirements. A study by Janosik and Gehring (2003) found that student knowledge of the Clery Act and its use of the information for college personnel was low. Gregory (2003) found in a study by the Association for Student Judicial Affairs (ASJA) that most were aware of the Clery Act and worked closely with campus police on enforcement issues. However, awareness by and participation of ASJA members at community colleges was "lower than that of their four-year counterparts" (p. 9). This is an important issue because of the very nature of community colleges as open-access institutions. Many community college students are enrolled in courses that run throughout the day and evening hours. Consequently, ASJA members at community colleges should work closely with law enforcement officers to identify, report, and prevent crime to assure all students that the institution is actively involved in protecting the safety of their students while keeping them informed regarding the process.

One disadvantage Gregory (2003) found was that many community colleges suffer from staffing shortages, which places an undue burden on ASJA members to keep up with the paperwork to comply with reporting requirements. Another possible explanation posited by Gregory was that "many community colleges have fewer sworn police officers than their four-year counterparts" (p. 9). Too few sworn police officers can potentially compromise the responsibility of institutions to meet the safety needs of the college and to document and prevent campus crime. Ironically, while one would posit that high rates of crime reporting could negatively affect a student's decision to enroll at an institution, Gregory found that there was "little evidence that the introduction of the Clery Act impacted students' decisions to enroll or not enroll at an institution" (p. 11).

Janosik and Gregory (2002) studied the effects of the Clery Act on law enforcement and whether the act had any impact on reducing crime. Approximately 944 high-ranking college law enforcement officials were surveyed and 371 responded to a series of independent questions. Of the respondents, 57% felt that the Clery Act has been effective or very effective in improving the quality of campus crime reporting, and another 57% felt that the quality of campus safety improved overall. Internet and campus mail were the most common ways campus crime statistics and other pertinent information were disseminated to students and employees.

Calloway, Gehring, and Douthett (2000) conducted a survey to determine if two-year college admissions officers were complying with the Student Right-to-Know and Campus Security Act of 1990. Issues identified by these researchers concluded that "the open nature of community colleges, the varying of campus communities and the differences in enrollment patterns may contribute to increased lack of knowledge and support of such legislation" (p. 190). The Calloway et al. study confirmed that only 6% of the two-year colleges surveyed met the notice requirement of the Campus Security

Act to provide a summary of the college's security report to prospective students. Possible reasons include "institutions' being unaware of the change in the notice requirement or institutions' unwillingness to comply because of the added expense of production and dissemination" (p. 189). A final point of contention exists between the Family Educational Rights and Privacy Act (FERPA) on student privacy and reporting campus crime statistics (Calloway et al., 2000; Van der Kaay, 2001). Research by Van der Kaay questioned the legal boundary involving the student's right to privacy under FERPA at the expense of "compromising" the release of student crime and campus safety information. Legalists have attempted to separate the two issues by "distinguishing between the academic educational record and those special circumstances where disclosure of personal information may be appropriate" (p. 4).

Prevention Measures

Community colleges have a challenging road ahead of them in meeting the safety needs of students. The events of September 11, 2001, and subsequent legislation (i.e., the Patriot Act) have forced many colleges to reexamine their level of commitment to campus security and safety (Rivard, 2002). Many higher education institutions are broadening their understanding of crime and violence on college campuses and developing those relationships that support a safer student learning environment. The Department of Education's National Center for Education Statistics (NCES) and its Safety in Numbers task force researched crime and violence in schools and prepared a report that recommends and encourages greater knowledge and understanding of data collection procedures and using information to develop clear definitions for crime, violence, and discipline (NCES, 2005). Several of the report's recommendations, which have a direct correlation to higher education, include "improving school safety, addressing safety issues, determining whether goals are met, establishing resources to improve school safety, enhancing prevention programs and modifying ineffective discipline practices" (p. 90).

The Safety in Numbers task force recommended two steps that higher education can pursue to improve the level of understanding and commitment among its constituents on campus safety issues. First, schools should develop training modules that highlight the importance for all constituents to recognize, report, categorize, and record incidents of crime in their schools. Second, schools should develop strategies that highlight the advantages and significant uses of reporting incident data (NCES, 2005). For instance, knowing when, where, and how certain crimes are committed can assist in designing preventive measures to reduce the occurrence of such incidents. Several recommendations to address campus violence include stronger development of the campus community, adequate warnings about criminal activity, better screening of potential students who pose a threat, and developing a comprehensive, campus-wide response to crime (ACHA, 2006).

Colleges must support the campus community with "greater levels of education and awareness regarding violence and its causes and should develop prevention programs" (Flannery, & Quinn-Leering, 2000, p. 840). The importance of focusing on parents when addressing campus safety issues is paramount to any prevention program, with two key elements being communication and prevention. Kennedy's (1999) recommendations for campus prevention include installation of a state-of-the-art campus ID system, improved lighting, more patrol officers, security cameras, and a campus escort system. Roark (1987) studied college crime prevention and recommends "a multi-faceted approach requiring broad interdisciplinary and interprofessional planning" (p. 368). In other words, prevention means understanding the issue of crime and violence and those situations or circumstances that may put individuals at risk. Roark recommends that colleges segment prevention into one of three categories: tertiary, secondary, and primary.

This segmentation allows college staff to prioritize response strategies to existing crime-related issues and develop new strategies that focus solely on crime avoidance and prevention. Schneider (2001) posited that the key to crime prevention in schools is assessing the physical environment of the institution. Schneider contends that the physical environment of the institution influences human behavior and, as a result, developed what is known as the Crime Prevention Through Environmental Design (CPTED) model. Schneider believes the "key is identifying problems or flaws (crime mapping) in the environment and making changes which can encourage positive student behavior" (p. 1). Whether it is increasing police officer visibility, improving campus lighting, limiting building access, developing campus awareness seminars, or increasing security cameras, crime prevention involves a greater understanding by the members of the community and the campus itself regarding the expectations for and consequences of antisocial behavior.

Community Partnerships

Service learning opportunities have opened the door for many community colleges to engage and strengthen partnerships with the community (Hatcher, 2002). Furthermore, Hatcher's commentary was supported years earlier by Boyer, who recommended that community college embrace "the social, civic, and ethical problems faced by members of its community, because in many cases, the community college is the only educational service provider for many students" (Boyer, 1996, p. 19). This civic engagement reaches far beyond the classroom. The entire college community as well as the external community must understand that campus safety is everyone's civic responsibility.

The Kellogg Commission (1999) addressed the criticality of college campuses and town/gown relationships in support of community engagement. Earlier, Upcraft and Gardner (1989) developed a standard for institutions to consider in creating an environment for student success, including: (a) personal characteristics, (b) demographics (race, gender, and age), (c) cultural characteristics (ethnic background and socioeconomic status), (d) institutional characteristics, and (e) institutional climate. Institutional climate can be closely associated with institutional culture, which, for most community colleges, remains difficult to transform, even 15 years after the Upcraft and Gardner report. The culture of the institution should reflect the level of civic engagement expected or desired at an institution. The challenge for community college leaders is changing the institutional culture so that campus safety and prevention is seen as a priority at the college. If institutions are successful in changing this mindset, the more likely it is that awareness of and interest in campus security will increase, and campus crime should decrease.

According to Smart (2003), two-year institutions have a more complex campus culture than many four-year institutions, and the impact of college culture can have a negative effect on campus-wide effectiveness in serving the needs of the students, maintaining college enrollments, improving student retention, and encouraging community service initiatives. Engaging in regular dialogue with community law enforcement agencies, political and community leaders, secondary school officials, students, and parents may assist with transforming the culture and creating greater opportunities for civic engagement and community collaboration in improving campus safety.

Conclusion

Providing a safe and secure environment on community college campuses is critical to student success and employee comfort. As violent behavior increases in the public school setting, it is finding its way onto college campuses. Students are reporting property thefts, physical altercations, and sexual assaults. One needs only to read any major higher education publication or local newspaper to learn of incidences of crime associated with intercollegiate athletics, sorority, fraternity, and co-curricular clubs/organization hazing, student-to-student conflict, and neighborhood brawls finding their way to the college campus. Institutional leaders are well positioned to assume the mantle of leadership and redirect staff energies to ensuring that a code of civic engagement and an atmosphere of civility exist within the walls of the academy. Several strategies can be used to support the need for students to be aware of criminal activity and their responsibility in decreasing actual campus crime.

Those strategies include: (a) publishing crime statistics in the campus newspapers, on college websites, and disseminating the information in key publications (i.e., schedule of classes, college catalog, and student handbook; (b) developing a safety component in the institutions' first-year experience, freshman seminar, and/or new student orientation courses/programming; (c) rewriting codes of conduct to speak directly to the commission of and accessory to crimes on and off the college campus and appropriate disciplinary sanctions; (d) surveying the physical environment and providing resources to ensure appropriate lighting, placement of call booths across the college, access to escort services, regular patrols of parking lots, and locating cameras in key positions inside and outside of buildings; (e) creating student/employee safety committees with membership from the community; (f) forming partnerships with local law enforcement agencies in support of decreasing crime and criminal activity; (g) providing nonconfrontational ways for students and employees to report crime and identify perpetrators; and (h) continuously training students and employees in how to identify and prevent crime, to their persons and their property.

As safety and security issues become more prevalent within the community college setting, institutional leaders will find themselves having to assure students, family members, employees, and the community at large that campuses are and can be protected environments, and that resources are in place to effectively manage unwarranted and intolerable behaviors. Administrators will need to pay close attention to the physical and emotional accoutrements of safety, including increasing a police or security presence, providing self-help sessions or seminars, and, potentially, requiring members of the college community to be photographically identifiable, similar to many government agencies. Susceptibility of campuses to persons who have no legitimate educational business to conduct on the campus opens the way for unwelcome elements to move through the institution in undetectable ways. Institutions of higher education must monitor new federal, state, and local legislation and current legislation that mandates particular responses to safety concerns. Implementation and communication to the entire college community will be critical to create and sustain feelings of safety and security among key constituents.

Personal safety is a concern for everyone, and community colleges are uniquely poised to partner with local and state law enforcement, profit and not-for-profit organizations, and community and civic agencies to ensure that learning environments are rich and replete with student and employee involvement in creating and sustaining learning environments focused on crime prevention.

References

American Association of Community Colleges (AACC). (2000). *National profile of community colleges: Trends and statistics* (3rd ed.). Washington, DC: American Association of Community Colleges, Community College Press.

Bennett-Johnson, E. (2004). The root of school violence: Causes and recommendations for a plan of action. *College Student Journal, 38*(2), 1–3.

Boyer, E. (1996). The scholarship of engagement. *Journal of Public Outreach, 1*(1), 11–20.

Calloway, R., Gehring, D., & Douthett, T. (2000). Two-year college compliance with the notice requirement of the Campus Security Act. *Community College Journal of Research & Practice, 24*(3), 181–191.

Cohen, A., & Brawer, F. (1987). *The collegiate function of community colleges.* San Francisco: Jossey Bass, pp. 4–7.

Dee, J. (2004). Turnover intent in an urban community college: Strategies for faculty retention. *Community College Journal of Research and Practice, 28,* 593–609.

Federal Bureau of Investigation. (1998). *Uniform crime report of the United States.* Washington, DC: U.S. Government Printing Office.

Federal Bureau of Investigation (FBI), U.S. Department of Justice (USDOJ). (2004). *Crime factors—Crime in the United States 2004.* Retrieved April 22, 2006, from http://www.fbi.gov/ucr/cius_04/summary/crime_factors/index.html

Flannery, D., & Quinn-Leering, K. (2000). Violence on college campuses: Understanding its impact on student well-being. *Community College Journal of Research & Practice, 24*(10), 839–855.

Gregory, D. (2003, Nov/Dec). Effect of the Clery Act on campus judicial practices. *Journal of College Student Development,* 1–12.

Hatcher, J. (2002). Campus-community partnerships: The term of engagement. *Journal of Social Issues, 58*(3), 503–517.

Janosik, S., & Gehring, D. (2003). Impact of the Clery Crime Disclosure Act on student behavior. *Journal of College Student Development, 44*(1), 81–91.

Janosik, S., & Gregory, D. (2002). *The Clery Act and the views of campus law enforcement officers.* Educational Policy Institution of Virginia Tech Policy Paper. (ERIC Document Reproduction Service No. ED482463). Blacksburg, VA: Educational Policy Institute.

Jeanne Clery Disclosure of Campus Security Policy and Campus Crime Statistics Act, 20 U.S.C. § A1092f (1990).

Joliet Junior College (n.d.[**Au: 2005 in text**]). *Historical overview of Joliet Junior College.* Retrieved April 28, 2005, from http://www.jjc.edu/campus_info/history/

Kellogg Commission on the Future of State and Land-Grant Institutions. (1999). *Returning to our roots: The engaged institution.* Washington, DC: National Association of State Universities and Land Grant Colleges.

Kennedy, M. (1999). Keeping campuses safe. *American School & University, 71*(10), 66–70.

Kozeracki, C. (2000). Service learning in the community college. *Community College Review, 27*(4), 54–71.

Marcus, R., Reio, T., Kessler, L., Cutler, K., & Fleury, J. (2001, August). *Interpersonal violence between college students: Proximal influences.* Paper presented at the annual convention of the American Psychological Association, Washington, DC.

Milliron, M., & de los Santos, G. (2004). Making the most of community colleges on the road ahead. *Community College Journal of Research and Practice, 28,* 105–122.

National Center for Education Statistics (NCES). (2005). *Indicators of school crime and safety: 2005.* Retrieved March 20, 2006, from http://nces.ed.gov/program/crimeindicators/index.asp

Pezza, P. (1995). College campus violence: The nature of the problem and its frequency. *Educational Psychology Review, 7*(1), 105–123.

Presley, C., Leichliter, J., & Meilman, P. (1998). *Alcohol and drugs on American college campuses: A report to college presidents.* Carbondale: CORE Institute, Southern Illinois University.

Rivard, N. (2002, April). On the campus: Rethinking security. *University Business,* 30–32.

Roark, M. (1987). Preventing violence on college campuses. *Journal of Counseling and Development, 65,* 367–371.

Roueche, J., Roueche, S., & Ely, E. (2001). Pursuing excellence: The Community College of Denver. *Community College Journal of Research and Practice, 25,* 517–537.

Schneider, T. (2001). *Safer schools through environmental design* (ERIC Digest No. 144). Washington, DC: Office of Educational Research and Improvement.

Security On Campus. (2006). *The Jeanne Clery Act.* Retrieved March 15, 2006, from http://www.securityoncampus.org/crimestats/cleryact.html

Smart, J. (2003). Organizational effectiveness of two-year colleges: The centrality of cultural and leadership complexity. *Research in Higher Education, 44*(6), 673–703.

The Student Right to Know and Campus Security Act, 20 § 201 (1990).

Taylor, L., & Maas, M. (1995). *The community college of the future. ERIC Digest, 120* (ERIC Document Reproduction Service No. ED381191).

Upcraft, L., & Gardner, J. (1989). *The freshman year experience: Helping students survive and succeed in college.* San Francisco: Jossey-Bass.

U.S. Department of Education. (2005). *The handbook for campus crime reporting.* Washington, DC: Office of Postsecondary Education.

Van der Kaay, C. (2001). *Student privacy versus campus security: Has recent legislation compromised privacy rights?* University of South Florida: Department of Leadership Development (ERIC Document Reproduction Service No. ED468176).

8

CALL FOR COMMUNITY-BASED EDUCATION

The State of Public Safety Issues at Minority-Serving Institutions

Marybeth Gasman and Noah D. Drezner

As demonstrated by the previous chapters in this book, college and university administrators are grappling with crime and safety issues. In some cases, these issues are a result of the unique environment (e.g., location or student population) produced by institutions of higher education (Wilkinson, 2002). In other situations, however, colleges and universities are feeling the pressure of external forces, such as violence and HIV/AIDS. This chapter explores public safety issues as they manifest at the nation's minority-serving institutions (MSIs), including historically Black colleges and universities (HBCUs), Hispanic-serving institutions (HSIs), and tribal colleges and universities (TCUs). Because these institutions have a commitment to racial uplift among specific populations, public safety issues can play out in unique ways on their campuses.

Before delving into the issues that MSIs face, we think it necessary to provide some historical and contextual information pertaining to these institutions to give the reader a sense of the unique nature of MSIs in the higher education landscape. Although all three types of institutions—historically Black colleges and universities, Hispanic-serving institutions, and tribal colleges and universities—fall into the category of minority-serving, they have varied histories.

Historically Black Colleges and Universities

A few Black colleges (e.g., Cheney, Lincoln, and Wilberforce) appeared in the North immediately before the Civil War, but the majority were established in the postbellum years (Butchart, 1980). These Black colleges were the result of efforts by religious missionary organizations who worked with the federal government's Freedmen's Bureau to educate former slaves. With the passage of the second Morrill Act in 1890, the federal government again took an interest in Black education, establishing public Black colleges. This act stipulated that those states practicing segregation in their public colleges and universities would forfeit federal funding unless they established agricultural and mechanical institutions for the Black population.

At the end of the 19th century, private Black colleges had exhausted funding from missionary sources. Simultaneously, a new form of support emerged—White northern industrial philanthropy. Among the leaders of industry who initiated this type of support were John D. Rockefeller, Andrew Carnegie, Julius Rosenwald, and John Slater. These industry captains were motivated by both Christian benevolence and a desire to control all forms of industry in the regions where their philanthropies operated (Anderson, 1988; Watkins, 2001).

Until the *Brown v. Board of Education* decision in 1954, both public and private Black colleges in the South remained segregated by law and were the only viable educational option for African Americans. The Supreme Court's landmark ruling meant that Black colleges, for the first time, would be placed in competition with White institutions in their efforts to recruit Black students (Gasman, 2007; Thompson, 1973).

During the 1960s, the federal government took a greater interest in Black colleges (Gasman, 2007; Thompson, 1973). In an attempt to provide clarity, the Higher Education Act of 1965 defined a Black college as "any . . . college or university that was established prior to 1964, whose principal mission was, and is, the education of black Americans" (Higher Education Act, 1965). Recognition of the unique aspect and purpose of Black colleges implied in this definition has led to increased federal funding for these institutions.

Currently, more than 300,000 students attend the nation's 105 historically Black colleges (40 public four-year, 11 public two-year, 49 private four-year, and 5 private two-year institutions). This number amounts to 16% of all African American college students. Overall, the parents of African American students at Black colleges have much lower incomes than do parents of Black students at predominantly White institutions (Wenglinsky, 1999). However, many researchers who study Black colleges have found that African Americans who attend HBCUs have higher levels of self-esteem and find their educational experience more nurturing (Brown & Freeman, 2004; Fleming, 1984; Ross, 1998, 2003). Moreover, graduates of Black colleges are more likely to continue their education and pursue graduate degrees than are their counterparts at predominantly White institutions (Wenglinsky, 1999). Despite the fact that only 24% of African American college students attend Black colleges, these institutions produce the majority of our nation's African American judges, lawyers, doctors, and teachers (American Association of University Professors [AAUP], 1995).

Hispanic-Serving Institutions (HSIs)

The term Hispanic-serving institution is really a misnomer; a better description would be Hispanic-enrolling. When the Higher Education Act of 1965 was reauthorized in 1992, the federal government inserted a legal definition of HSIs under Title III—"Institutional Aid"—of the act (Hispanic Association of Colleges and Universities [HACU], 2005). As a result, HSIs were defined as accredited degree-granting colleges and universities with Hispanic students accounting for 25% or more of the undergraduate enrollment. However, in 1998 the Higher Education Act was reauthorized once again, and HSIs were placed under Title V—"Developing Institutions" (largely as a concession to HBCU leaders who argued that HSIs were siphoning off their funding). Under Title V, the new definition was narrowed to include universities with 25% Hispanic full-time students in the undergraduate population. Moreover, to qualify for Title V federal grants, these HSIs had to provide evidence that a minimum of 50% of their Hispanic students fell below the U.S. Census's poverty-level restrictions (Laden, 2004).

With the exception of a few institutions, most HSIs emerged in the last 30 years as a result of shifts and growth in the Hispanic population in the U.S., including demographic shifts within large urban cities, the Civil Rights Movement of the 1960s opening campuses up to nontraditional populations, and the increased availability of need-based financial aid with the passing of the Higher Education Act of 1965 (Benitez, 1998; Laden, 2001, 2004). The only institutions expressly established to educate Latino students are Hostos Community College (New York), National Hispanic University (California), and Boricua College (New York)—all created, as a result of the Civil Rights Movement, in the 1960s and '70s. According to Berta Laden (2004),

> Dual factors of continued Latino immigration of the U.S. and internal de-mographic shifts in the past three decades brought many national and aca-demic border crossers to college for the first time. In search of jobs and improved economic conditions, Latinos continue to move into large urban cities and into less populated, rural or farming areas in the central U.S. where they have not resided before . . . As the Latino presence in some of these postsecondary institutions has risen to at least one-fourth or more of the student enrollment, these colleges and universities have increasingly been identified as HSIs. (p. 188)

However, there is mixed reaction to the term HSI. In fact, while some insti-tutions use the designation in marketing and promotional materials, others do not even acknowledge it. This paradox makes it difficult to talk about HSIs as a group.

Hispanic and Latino enrollment is increasing rapidly at HSIs, primarily due to the remarkable growth of this population (it is reported to have grown 55% between 1990 and 2000). As a result of such demographics, we are likely to see increases in the number of HSIs (U.S. Census Bureau, http://www.census.gov/). For example, since 1992, there has been an almost 100% in-crease in the number of institutions that have at least 25% Hispanic enroll-ment (HACU, 2005; Laden, 2001).

Tribal Colleges and Universities

Very little is known about tribal colleges and universities (TCUs), probably because these institutions are often remote, resource-poor, two-year colleges, with little infrastructure for systemic research (Ambler, 2003a; Vernon, 2002). The Navajo Nation created the first tribal college in 1968, now Dine College in Arizona. In response to the larger Civil Rights Movement of the 1960s, the college's purpose was to provide affordable and culturally specific education to American Indians to help prevent further assimilation by Na-tive Americans (Crum, 1989; Oppelt, 1990). Today, there are 28 tribally con-trolled colleges and three federally chartered tribal colleges, all members of the American Indian Higher Education Consortium (AIHEC). Founded in 1972, AIHEC supports the work of tribal colleges and the movement for national tribal college self-determination (http://www.aihec.org). Traditionally, these tribal colleges are located on reservations or other tribally controlled lands, most of which are isolated communities. As a result of being part of closer-knit neighborhoods, tribal colleges inherently have a more interactive town/gown relationship than do most American colleges and universities focusing on service to their communities (Cunningham & Parker, 1998; Pavel, Inglebret, & Banks, 2001).

Enrollment in TCUs has increased dramatically over the past 25 years. In 1982, enrollment at TCUs was 2,100; by fall 2001, enrollment had grown to 13,961, an increase of 565% (Ambler, 2003a, 2003b; AIHEC, n.d.; Snyder, Tan, & Hoffman, 2003). These institutions, primarily two-year schools, offer open admissions However, there are two tribal colleges that offer master's degree programs (Oglala Lakota College and Sinte Gleska College) as well as two schools that offer bachelor's degrees (Haskell Indian Nations University and Salish Kootenai College) (AIHEC, n.d.). Currently all AIHEC members are in the process of receiving regional accreditation, part of a move to encourage students to transfer to four-year institutions and continue their postsecondary education (Ambler, 2003a, 2003b; Vernon, 2002).

Public Safety Issues at Historically Black Colleges and Universities

In the case of HBCUs, some of the most prevalent public safety issues include alcohol and drug abuse, HIV/AIDS, homophobia, and hazing.

Alcohol and Drug Abuse

According to the National Institute on Alcohol Abuse and Alcoholism (2002), 40% of college students are binge drinkers. Of particular interest to HBCUs, the study found that those students least likely to drink attend two-year institutions, religious institutions, commuter schools, and HBCUs. For example, in a recent survey of HBCU students conducted by Reginald Fennell, only 15.7% identified themselves as binge drinkers (drinking five or more drinks in one sitting). Fennel also found that 18.2% of the students surveyed were regular users of marijuana. However, only 2.2% indicated they had used cocaine regularly, whereas 2.6% of those asked reported using crack or freebase forms of cocaine. In the case of both alcohol and drugs, men were more likely than women to abuse these substances.

When compared to African American students at predominantly White institutions (PWIs), these numbers are interesting. For example, according to a 1996 study of drug use among African Americans at PWIs, only 9% of students surveyed regularly used marijuana. Within the context of HBCUs, most students indicated they drank alcohol to relax, whereas within the PWI environment, the most frequent reason for drinking was to escape one's problems (Globetti, Globetti, Lo, & Brown, 1996). Perhaps the fact that HBCU students are far less likely to have to contend with racism on a daily basis plays a part in their physical and mental well-being and lack of stress (Allen, Epps, & Hanif, 1991; Fleming, 1984).

HIV/AIDS

One of the most pressing public safety issues facing HBCUs in the 21st century is the rapid spread of AIDS in the African American community. According to the Centers for Disease Control and Prevention, the HIV/AIDS epidemic is a health crisis for African Americans. In 2001, HIV/AIDS was among the top three causes of death for African American men ages 25–54 and among the top four causes of death for African American women ages 25–34 (http://www.census.gov). Moreover, according to the 2000 U.S. Census, African Americans accounted for approximately 12% of the nation's population; however, they represented 40% of the 929,985 AIDS cases in the United States (http://www.census.gov). Much of the spread of HIV/AIDS among African Americans has been linked to homophobia, religious objections to condom use, and lack of education about the disease (Hawkins, 2005). Homophobia refers to the fear that some individuals have of gays and lesbians, a fear that is prevalent in many African American communities (Hawkins, 2005). Much of this homophobia stems from Christian religious beliefs that also preclude use of condoms or other forms of birth control. Although many of these AIDS cases occur outside the college and university community, the disease is finding its way onto Black college campuses more and more often (Hawkins, 2005; Yates, 2004). Not only are student affairs and health staff members forced to contend with this crisis, but researchers within the Black community are taking it upon themselves to find solutions to the epidemic plaguing their race.

As a hands-on way of combating the toll of HIV/AIDS on Black students, many HBCUs have instituted AIDS education programs for their undergraduate populations. For example, the National Association for Equal Opportunity in Higher Education (NAFEO) and the American Red Cross have jointly sponsored training institutes aimed at teaching students how to talk about HIV/AIDS with their peers. These institutes have taken place at Bethune-Cookman College and Shaw, Hampton, and Tuskegee universities. Moreover, NAFEO has worked with several HBCUs to develop community outreach to educate those living in the areas directly surrounding Black colleges about prevention and the risks related to the disease (Roach, 1999).

In spring 2004, the 12 HBCUs in North Carolina came together to discuss HIV/AIDS among Black students. This event, entitled "Stomp out HIV/STDs" and co-sponsored by the North Carolina Division of Public Health, was held in response to what the Division of Public Health termed an outbreak of HIV infections among college students. The state found that out of the 84 new HIV cases, 73 were Black males at HBCUs (Yates, 2004). According to the Division of Public Health, the epidemic was a result of the developmental nature of college. Students, regardless of institutional type and race, experiment with drugs, alcohol, and sex, with little effort to educate them about the AIDS virus. According to David Jolly, an assistant professor of health education at North Carolina Central University: "[Students] convince themselves that nothing will happen. They think that HIV is not a disease that pertains to them. It happens to older White guys or drug users or down-and-out crack heads, some group they're not part of" (Yates, 2004, pp. 10–11).

Moreover, according to Jolly, the key population to be reached is young Black men who have sex with other men. This is most difficult, given the deeply rooted homophobia in the culture of many HBCUs (Peterson, 1995). In Jolly's words,

> We need to make campuses more supportive environments for gay and lesbian students. They need to feel more comfortable being who they are. If these guys feel threatened and harassed, they are going to lead secret lives and it will be harder to educate and protect them. (Yates, 2004, p. 11)

In an effort to further the research on HIV/AIDS in the African American community, several HBCUs are piloting studies. For example, at Morehouse College in Atlanta, Georgia, a group of physicians, researchers, and administrators formed the AIDS Group. According to one of the group's members, Eileen M. Yancey, "Morehouse is on the cutting edge, conducting studies and research that you don't see happening anywhere else" (Hawkins, 2005, p. 28). She is currently working on a study aimed at reducing HIV/AIDS among sexually active Black heterosexual men and women. In another example, Howard University graduate Chris Cathcart recently launched a magazine, *Ledge*, aimed at shaking up students about HIV/AIDS. *Ledge* is a student-driven publication that seeks to enhance risk awareness and mobilize students to fight against the epidemic (Hawkins, 2005). The magazine is distributed free of charge to more than 80 HBCU campuses. In addition to individual HBCUs, the United Negro College Fund, the fund-raising arm of most private HBCUs, recently established the HIV/AIDS Orientation and Professional Education (HOPE) program. As part of this initiative, the organization will survey 26 HBCUs in 14 southeastern states about general attitudes toward condom use and sexual activity (Hawkins, 2005).

Homophobia

Homosexuality has traditionally been a difficult subject in some parts of the larger African American community—a community with deep religious roots (Hawkins, 2005). These religious traditions usually placed an emphasis on the sinful nature of homosexuality and made little room for individuals to be open about their sexual orientation (Hawkins, 2005). Although several prominent African American ministers have recently spoken out against the persecution of gays and lesbians, there remains a deep stigma against homosexuals among the Black population (Braithwaite et al., 1998). In recent years, a few HBCUs have begun to address issues of homophobia—in response to incidents on their campuses, the AIDS epidemic, or pressure from factions of the student body. In a prominent 2002 case at Morehouse College, college junior Gregory Love was beaten with a baseball bat by one of his residence hall colleagues, Aaron Price. Price believed that Love was making sexual advances toward him. Just three weeks after this incident, the president of Morehouse, Walter Massey, established a task force to discuss issues of homophobia on the small-college campus ("Beating at Morehouse College," 2002).

Other campuses are also addressing this issue by allowing the establishment of gay and lesbian student groups. However, this has been a difficult fight on HBCU campuses, with some organizations receiving death threats.

In an effort to ease tensions, the Human Rights Campaign, an organization dedicated to the rights of gay, lesbian, bisexual, and transgender individuals, has sponsored forums at various HBCUs, including Morehouse College and Johnson C. Smith and Dillard universities. Many student affairs professionals and campus chaplains are trying to show links between gay rights and civil rights, noting the parallels between the two movements. Still, some students and their parents find this work on behalf of gays and lesbians to be objectionable (Petrosino, 2003).

Hazing

In more recent years, one of the most dire problems faced by Black colleges has been hazing within their marching bands, fraternities, and sororities (Jones, 2004; Kimbrough, 2003; Nuwer, 2002). Although hazing is not limited to Black colleges, it does happen quite frequently at these institutions due to the popularity of marching bands and the number of Black fraternities and sororities on Black college campuses (Jones, 2004; Kimbrough, 2003; Nuwer, 2002). Hazing is defined as the physical or verbal abuse used to initiate an individual into an organization (Nuwer, 2003). In addition, while all national fraternities and sororities have banned the practice of hazing, replacing it with intake processes, evidence suggests that it continues to take place and continues to be a significant problem on Black college campuses (Kimbrough, 2003).

As illustrated in the movie, *Drumline*, positions in Black college marching bands are highly sought after. Competition for membership is fierce, with many students being cut even though they came to a particular institution specifically because of the band. Part of the process of becoming members is the ordeal of the initiation rite, which often turns violent. For example, in 2002 at Florida A&M University (a public Black college in Tallahassee), new inductees into the institution's famed marching band were hit in the head for missing dance steps and ordered to "assume the position" at band parties (i.e., to be paddled). Often, the students were paddled until their buttocks swelled; one student suffered from kidney failure after the beatings. According to the former band director of the Florida A&M Marching 100, this type of behavior has been going on in marching bands since the 1950s. The membership rituals for marching bands mirrored those of fraternities, whose initiation rites they copied (Pudlow, 1998). As a result of the hazing, 12 members of the Florida A&M marching band were suspended from school. However, parents of the student victims wanted the institution to do more and called for an investigation and subsequent educational activities for students. Although parents acknowledged that hazing takes place in the Black Greek system, they saw membership in fraternities and sororities as optional—students could choose not to participate. For most music and music education majors at Black colleges, especially scholarship recipients, membership in the band is mandatory. Administrators at several Black colleges are encouraging students to "break the code of silence" around hazing by pointing to the dangerous ramifications of the activity (Kimbrough, 2003).

Most of the hazing on Black college campuses takes place within the fraternities and sororities (Kimbrough, 2003). Over the past 20 years, there have been countless hazing infractions in the Black Greek system (Kimbrough, 2003; Nuwer, 2002). Whereas much of the hazing within the White Greek system involves alcohol abuse, violence and physical abuse are most prevalent within the Black system (Nuwer, 2002). In recent years, incidents have taken place at many Black colleges, including the University of Maryland, Eastern Shore. At this public Black institution, members of Kappa Alpha Psi fraternity paddled one of their pledges until the blood vessels in his buttocks ruptured, causing the start of gangrene, and making it necessary for the student to have reconstructive surgery (Ruffins & Evelyn, 1998). Similarly, incidents have taken place at Fort Valley State University in Georgia, Alabama A&T University, Morehouse College, and Alabama State University, among many others. Another disturbing practice is branding, a standard rite of passage for most Black fraternities. This ordeal resembles the branding of cattle (or, during the antebellum period, African slaves). University deans of students as well as members of the national fraternity and sorority offices are discussing how this behavior can be stopped (Nuwer, 2002).

In 1990, the Black Greek organizations "officially" cracked down on hazing in response to the death of a Morehouse College student pledging Alpha Phi Alpha. The National Pan-Hellenic Council ended pledging and put in place a "New Member Intake Process." While some student affairs practitioners working closely with the intake processes believe that hazing has been minimized, others feel that pledging has become worse as it has moved underground (Richmond as cited in Ruffins & Roach, 1997). Some experts claim that the only hazing college officials hear about is when it results in severe injury or death, noting that if a new member avoids that fate and lives, he usually regards surviving the beating as a badge of courage (Richmond as cited in Ruffins & Roach, 1997). In spite of the fact that the majority of violent hazing takes place within fraternities, over the past 10 years, Black sororities have also put their new initiates through brutal rituals, often insulting and beating them. None of the national sororities condone this kind of behavior (Richmond as cited in Ruffins & Roach, 1997).

Researchers are often perplexed by the Black on Black violence that takes place within fraternities and sororities (Kimbrough, 2003; Nuwer, 2002). University of Pennsylvania sociologist Antonio McDaniel explains this by saying that, often, Black men internalize society's treatment of African Americans: "As a people, we have a long history of being beaten and branded and enslaved. So it is simply a sign of extreme nihilism and alienation when we willingly submit to beating and branding" (McDaniel as cited in Ruffins & Roach, 1997, p. 22).

Other officials at Black colleges think the problem of violent hazing stems from lack of supervision of fraternities and sororities (Nuwer, 2003). The majority of the most violent incidents—those that gain national media coverage—happen in off-campus housing, over which campus security and student affairs staff members have no influence or power (Kimbrough, 2003; Nuwer, 2003). When fraternities and sororities live in on-campus housing, the need for liability insurance gives colleges, universities, and the national Greek organizations more control over local chapters. Most White Greek organizations have their own houses on campuses or live in residence halls as a group and thus are under more pressure to cease beating their new members (Nuwer, 2002, 2003). However, most African American fraternities and sororities do not have the economic resources to build houses. Moreover, Black Greek organizations are more likely to donate to scholarships than to elaborate housing (Gasman & Anderson-Thompkins, 2003; Ruffins & Roach, 1997).

Public Safety Issues at Hispanic-Serving Institutions

As mentioned earlier, Hispanic-serving institutions are diverse in makeup and background (Laden, 2004). For purposes of this chapter, we consider an HSI a Hispanic-enrolling institution. Because the group of institutions included in this category is so varied, it is difficult to discuss them as a whole. Moreover, the media, policymakers, and even many scholars rarely use this government-devised designation. Despite this lack of clarity about who HSIs are, it is possible using this definition to provide descriptive statistics regarding the crime activity at HSIs and to explore the impact of HIV/AIDs on these campuses.

Crime

According to Security On Campus, Inc. (http://securityoncampus.org), an organization that maintains crime statistics on the majority of American colleges and universities, there were no murders on HSI campuses between 2000 and 2003. However, there has been considerable violent crime, especially at California State-Northridge, New Mexico State University, and the University of New Mexico. These institutions have also had more instances of rape than have the other HSIs (Security On Campus, Inc.).

Burglary has been a significant problem at all but a few HSIs, with the most instances at Florida International and the University of New Mexico. Auto theft is also of concern to administrators at HSIs, with California State-Fresno, California State-Long Beach, Florida International, and the University of New Mexico experiencing the most theft. The problem with discussing crime statistics at HSIs is that it is difficult to discern whether these statistics are indicative of HSIs or merely of the cities in which they are located (U.S. Department of Education [USDOE], 2006).

HIV/AIDS and Homophobia

Although Latinos represent only 9% of the overall population in the United States, they account for 17% of the AIDS cases (University of California, San Francisco [UCSF], 2005). A study completed in 1994 by the Centers for Disease Control and Prevention (CDC) found that 41% of all AIDS cases among Latino men were the result of unprotected sex with other men, and 36% were the result of injection drug use. The CDC also found that 46% of the cases among Latinas were the result of heterosexual sex, whereas 39% were due to injection drug use. Most troubling is the fact that among Latino gay/bisexual men, the rates of HIV/AIDS are increasing more quickly than those of White gay/bisexual men. According to researchers at the University of California, San Francisco, this staggering increase is most likely due to the fact that many Latino men who have sex with other men do not self-identify as gay/bisexual. They refuse to acknowledge the gay/bisexual label because of the stigma this lifestyle suffers in Latino communities, both on HSI campuses and within the larger Latino population. Moreover, researchers also found that most men did not use condoms regularly, if at all (UCSF, 2005). According to the research team, "Machismo dictates that intercourse is a way to prove masculinity," and wearing condoms, according to many Latino males, does not represent masculine behavior (UCSF, 2005).

To counteract the effects of these conditions, many HSIs are reaching out to the Latino population in ways that appeal to their community. For example, Latinos are more likely to respond to advice from those with whom they are familiar (UCSF, 2005). As such, HSIs are putting resources into counseling programs that continually and systematically reach out to the Latino population. They are encouraging the Latino student community to "break the silence about sexuality in their communities, address homophobia, and address specific cultural aspects that may be detrimental to healthy sexuality, such as not allowing power for women, and encouraging men to prove their masculinity through intercourse" (UCSF, 2005, p. 2). HSIs are also using peer educators to conduct peer-to-peer workshops on their campuses. During the workshops, student leaders hand out condom kits and instructions to participants. Moving beyond the issues of HIV/AIDS, these peer workshops incorporate broader issues, such as violence, drug use, and healthy relationships (Gurman & Borzekowski, 2004).

Public Safety Issues at Tribal Colleges and Universities

Tribal colleges and universities (TCUs) are located primarily within American Indian reservations and are connected to their communities more closely than are traditional American colleges (Rowell, 1997). For this reason, TCUs are often involved in local issues. They are looked upon as part of the community structure rather than as ivory towers disconnected from the masses (Ambler, 2003a, 2003b; Rowell, 1997; Sileo & Gooden, 2003). Tribes frequently turn to them for help solving community problems. If drugs, gangs, unemployment, poverty, alcoholism, and sexually transmitted diseases are a problem on reservations, then it makes sense that the reservations' students and their colleges are affected, at least indirectly.

Safety in the general American Indian community is a great concern, and the statistics are bleak. The poverty rate on tribally controlled land is 60.3%, three times the national average. Additionally, recent studies show that 40% of the tribal adult population abuses alcohol and drugs and is twice as likely to die from substance abuse as any other minority group (Ambler, 2003a). Further, American Indian youth are more likely than youth in other minority groups to commit suicide, with 28% of the population reporting they have considered ending their life (Ambler, 2003a). As if that were not enough, young Native American men are three times more likely to die from a car accident or other unintentional injuries than their non–American Indian peers (Ambler, 2003a).

Oppression, Prejudice, and Racism Toward American Indians

Many scholars conclude that past and current oppression, prejudice, and racism toward indigenous peoples feed into the public safety issues in and around TCUs (Ambler, 2003a, 2003b; Hunt, Gooden, & Barkdull, 2001; Sileo & Gooden, 2003). Hunt et al. (2001) believe that past experiences inflicted on Native American communities resulted in feelings of shame, depression, negative self-image, and powerlessness. After generations of oppression, indigence, and lack of opportunities, it is understandable that Native Americans are more susceptible to unsafe life situations than the majority of the population (Hunt et al., 2001; Sileo & Gooden, 2003). Other researchers have found that ongoing cycles of neglect, violence, and substance abuse on reservations leave American Indians susceptible to HIV/AIDS (Hunt et al., 2001; Sileo & Gooden, 2003; Vernon, 2002).

Tribal colleges realize they must tackle these issues. Many of the TCUs have begun to respond to these safety issues by setting up counseling sessions, discussion groups, and preventive workshops on physical and substance abuse (Hunt et al., 2001; Sileo & Gooden, 2003; Vernon, 2002). Additionally, tribal colleges are encouraging students to pursue careers in health-related fields, such as nursing, as a way to educate the general Native American population (Ambler, 2003b). Half of tribal colleges currently offer recreation centers and other facilities to encourage students to maintain their health and practice good nutrition habits.

HIV/AIDS and Homophobia

Besides substance abuse and nutritional matters, tribal colleges are concerned with HIV/AIDS prevention among indigenous communities and on campuses. New reports of HIV/AIDS infections and related deaths have increased steadily since 1998. Research shows that infection among Native

Americans typically happens while they are young adults through unsafe sex and use of shared drug needles (Sileo & Gooden, 2003).

As in many U.S. cultures, within American Indian culture, discussions about sex are considered taboo. Barriers to talking about sex create misinformation and ignorance and make sexually transmitted disease prevention nearly impossible. For example, there is a false belief that a Nation's isolation on the reservation prevents the spread of AIDS. Researchers find that American Indian communities are further behind the general population in knowledge about HIV transmission, prevention, and the importance of those sexually active being tested (Ambler, 2003b; Boyer, 2003).

To increase awareness and educate fellow American Indians on HIV/ AIDS topics, Salish Kootenai College in Pablo, Montana, created the Building Effective AIDS Responses (BEAR) project. Part of BEAR's message, beyond prevention, is to inform tribal communities and students at tribal colleges that although AIDS does not have a cure, long-term management of the disease has improved. This message is important; when HIV/AIDS is not discussed or treated, the risk for infection within the community rises (Boyer, 2003).

Further exacerbating the HIV/AIDS epidemic within the Native American population is the recent increase in homophobia within reservations, tribal colleges, and communities in general. Traditionally, sexual minorities such as gay, lesbian, bisexual, and transgender people were revered by American Indians. In the Algonquin language, they were referred to as *nizh manitoag*, or two-spirited (Brown, 1997). However, Christian antihomosexual influences have infiltrated Native American culture (Sileo & Gooden, 2003). What was once accepted is now seen as "deviant and immoral" (Vernon, 2002, p. 125). As a result, there is a large closeted gay community—akin to the African American "down-low" community (King, 2004)—in which men discreetly have sex with other men while maintaining a front of sexual conformity through marriage to a woman. Scholars believe that these dual relationships increase HIV transmission because they often include unprotected sex (Rowell, 1997).

Tribal colleges have taken on the difficult role of HIV/AIDS education both on campus and within the greater reservation. Understanding that they need help disseminating the message, many Native American health educators have contacted tribal elders for their support and have received the needed assistance (Ambler, 2003b; Boyer, 2003). Additionally, AIHEC, along with the federal Office of Minority Health, created the HIV/AIDS Prevention Education Project in which students team with health experts to teach their peers about the disease. This project has also funded free, anonymous HIV testing at tribal colleges.

When HIV/AIDS hits a college, it creates an opportunity for a "teachable moment." Si Tanka University in South Dakota responded in just such a positive way when a student was diagnosed with HIV. In 2002, a student at the Huron campus found out that he contracted HIV after trying to donate blood. One tribally owned newspaper then reported a "full-blown AIDS scare," resulting in the arrest of the student on charges that he was intentionally exposing others to HIV infection. Si Tanka took the opportunity presented to it to develop a public health campaign, including bringing in speakers and holding public forums. The campaign later grew into The Spirit of Courage mentoring program in which every student was paired with a faculty or staff member to provide the student with the opportunity to ask questions and confide in one person about traditionally taboo topics (Boyer, 2003).

Alcoholism and Related Issues

According to a 1993 report issued by the U.S. Department of Health and Human Services, 95% of American Indians are affected, directly or indirectly, by alcohol abuse (Krause, 1998). Native Americans are more than twice as likely to die from preventable accidents than the rest of the U.S. population, and some research suggests that nearly three-quarters of all accidental deaths in the American Indian population are related to alcohol use (Hunt et al., 2001; Silco & Gooden, 2003; Vernon, 2002). In fact, the magnitude of alcoholism might be even greater than reported. Mortality statistics do not attribute deaths from liver cirrhosis, suicide, homicide, kidney dysfunctions, and diabetes mellitus to alcoholism, even though there is an established connection (Krause, 1998; Mitchell & Patch, 1981). The National Institute on Alcohol Abuse and Alcoholism, for example, reports that American Indians are three times more likely as other Americans to die from various forms of liver disease (Krause, 1998: Mitchell & Patch, 1981). This has made it imperative that tribal colleges be part of the intervention and education process.

Alcoholism within the indigenous populations affects the next generation at a higher rate than it does in other American ethnic groups. According to the U.S. Department of Health and Human Services, newborns in these communities are diagnosed with fetal alcohol syndrome (FAS) at twice the national average (Substance Abuse and Mental Health Services Administration [SAMHSA], 2002). To combat the pervasive and deleterious results of alcoholism, education at all levels is needed (Krause, 1998; Mitchell & Patch, 1981). Mitchell and Patch (1981) suggest that alcohol education be integrated directly into school and college curricula. In addition to classroom discussions, they encourage educators to develop both preventive and rehabilitative services for students and the general population. Tribal colleges are hoping that the extensive resources and energy they are spending to combat alcohol use among their students will aid not only students but also their families and younger siblings as well, slowing down the rapid cycle of alcohol abuse (Krause, 1998; Mitchell & Patch, 1981).

For tribal populations, education from within the community is very important (Mitchell & Patch, 1981). The federal government's Substance Abuse and Mental Health Services Administration (2002) asserts that the most effective way to reach American Indians on topics such as alcoholism is to use members of the community who can incorporate cultural concepts and "bicultural realities" more easily. As in other minority communities, there is an added level of trust when someone from the community is part of the information process (Gasman & Anderson-Thompkins, 2003; Krause, 1998; Mitchell & Patch, 1981).

Suicide

American Indian youth (ages 15–24) are 3.3 times more likely to commit suicide than the national average (*Suicide prevention among Native American youth*, 2005). This behavior is pervasive in both small and large tribal communities. Of more disturbing concern is the fact that the suicide trends run counter to what is occurring in the rest of the U.S. population. While suicide rates in other racial and ethnic groups in the United States declined in the 1990s, they increased in Native American communities (*Teen suicide among American Indian youth*, 2005).

Only a small portion of the suicide literature is devoted to indigenous populations (*Suicide prevention among Native American youth*, 2005). However, it is clear that the phenomenon of suicide within the American Indian community is different from within the general population (*Suicide prevention among Native American youth*, 2005). According to U.S. Surgeon General, Vice Admiral Richard Carmona, "In many . . . tribal communities, suicide is not just an individual clinical condition, but also a community condition" (*Suicide prevention among Native American youth*, 2005). Therefore, it requires different approaches to prevention.

The U.S. Department of Health and Human Services reports numerous models of reservation-based preventive care being developed or currently in use at tribal colleges. For example, over the past decade, the Jicarilla Apache of northern New Mexico reduced one of the highest suicide rates in the United States by approximately 60%. They accomplished this by creating a community-based intervention program strategy developed by tribal college and tribal leaders, community members, youth, clinicians, researchers, and Indian Health Services. The curriculum engages the entire community, including the tribal government, schools, colleges, and law enforcement agencies (*Suicide prevention among Native American youth*, 2005).

To address the risk for suicide in the American Indian population, the federal government established the Garrett Lee Smith Memorial Act in October 2004 (Garrett Lee Smith Memorial Act, 2004). The act, which makes available $11 million in grants, enables states, Indian Nations, and tribal colleges and universities to develop suicide prevention and intervention programs.

For many years, formal and informal programs have been in place at tribal colleges and universities (Ambler, 2003a). Faculty and staff regularly help students to thrive when it seems that the odds are against them. Scholars have identified these informal support systems within the tribal colleges as a form of "cultural resilience" (Ambler, 2003a). TCUs are strengthening these informal support networks—making them into formal programs—to help prevent students from falling into depression and engaging in self-destructive behavior. Fort Peck Community College has even taken the idea of "cultural resilience" into its reservation's middle schools, helping to counter violence and depression at an early age.

The Need for More Educational Funding

While AIHEC received federal funding for health education, and Congress established the Garrett Lee Smith Act, Marjane Ambler (2003b) cautions that grants are not typically available to address health disparities in the American Indian community. This type of financial support is available for

Hispanic and Black community projects, but the government often omits American Indians. Further, the federal grant process is skewed toward those with grant-writing experience and expertise, which is lacking among tribal college personnel. It is clear that greater access to federal funds would benefit tribal colleges in their mission to make not only their campuses, but also their communities, safer.

Conclusion

Public safety at minority-serving institutions surpasses mere monitoring of and responding to crime. While each of the MSI types investigated in this chapter operates from a unique perspective and has a distinct history, the campus safety issues each faces are augmented in similar ways by a history of oppression, lack of educational opportunity, and exclusion from public campaigns and funding streams. In each case, the solution is tied to these institutions' overall mission: uplifting the community. We see this as the largest difference between the public safety situation and response at traditionally White institutions and their minority-serving counterparts. For instance, all three MSI types are responding to the HIV/AIDS epidemic within their communities by acknowledging their respective cultures' homophobia and general disassociation with the issue.

It is through the mission of racial uplift that college administrators on these campuses are most successful at engaging their student bodies around violence, substance abuses, and unsafe sexual practices. We believe that administrators, student affairs professionals, and faculty members at minority-serving institutions must be aware of the needs of the specific minority community their institution serves. They need to be aware of the problems their students face and work to counteract them. By acknowledging these safety concerns and the specific needs of their students, colleges and universities can serve the greater community by educating a generation that can help combat the cycles of violence and self-destructive behavior explored in this chapter.

These institutions should share with one another their successes and failures in addressing these public safety issues. By identifying best practices and rooting out unsuccessful strategies, they might provide help to other campuses that are dealing with similar issues. With this information, MSIs can act quickly to mitigate the effects of a problem, whether it is hazing, homophobia, substance abuse, or suicide. These best practices can be shared through the consortiums of each group of institutions: the National Association for Equal Opportunity in Higher Education for historically Black colleges and universities; the Hispanic Association of Colleges and Universities for HSIs; and the American Indian Higher Education Consortium for Tribal Colleges.

References

Allen, W., Epps, E., & Haniff, N. (1991). *College in black and white: African American students in predominantly White and historically Black public universities.* Albany, NY: SUNY Press.

Ambler, M. (2003a). Cultural resistance. *Tribal College, 14*(4), 8–10.

Ambler, M. (2003b). Reclaiming native health. *Tribal College, 15*(2), 8–9.

American Association of University Professors (AAUP). (1995). Report on the status of Black colleges. *Academe, 23,* 17–23.

Anderson, J. (1988). *The education of Blacks in the South.* Chapel Hill: University of North Carolina Press.

Beating at Morehouse College raises debate over perceived homophobia. (2002, November 29). *Chronicle of Higher Education,* 30.

Benitez, M. (1998). Hispanic-serving institutions: Challenges and opportunities. *New Directions in Higher Education, 102,* 57–68.

Boyer, P. (2003). Small, rural, close, but not safe: Community-based educational programs are breaking rules to fight AIDS. *Tribal College, 15*(2), 10–14.

Braithwaite, R., Stephens, T., Sumpter-Gaddist, B., Murdaugh, H., Tayor, S., & Braithwaite, K. (1998). Sex-related HIV/AIDS prevention among African American college students: Issues of preventive counseling. *Journal of Multicultural Counseling and Development, 26*(3), 177–196.

Brown, L. B. (1997). Men and women, not-men and not-women, lesbians and gays: American Indian gender style alternatives. In L. B. Brown (Ed.), *Two spirit people: American Indian lesbian women and gay men,* pp. 5–20. New York: The Haworth Press, Inc.

Brown, M. C., & Freeman, K. (2004). *Black colleges: New perspectives on policy and practice.* Westport, CT: Greenwood Press.

Butchart, R. (1980). *Northern schools, southern Blacks, and reconstruction.* Westport, CT: Greenwood Press.

Crum, S. (1991). Colleges before Columbus. *Tribal College, 3*(2), 14–17.

Cunningham, A. F., & Parker, C. (1998). Tribal colleges as community institutions and resources. *New Directions for Higher Education, 102,* 45–56.

Fleming, J. (1984). *Blacks in colleges.* San Francisco: Jossey-Bass.

Garrett Lee Smith Memorial Act of 2004, S. 2634 (2004). 118 U.S. Stat. 1404, Public Law, 108–355.

Gasman, M. (2007). *Envisioning Black colleges: A history of the United Negro College Fund.* Baltimore: The Johns Hopkins University Press.

Gasman, M., & Anderson-Thompkins, S. (2003). *Fund raising from Black college alumni: Successful strategies for supporting alma mater.* Washington, DC: CASE books.

Globetti, G., Globetti, E., Lo, C., & Brown, C. (1996). Alcohol and other drug use among African-American students in a southern university. *Journal of Multicultural Counseling & Development, 24*(2), 118–129.

Gurman, T., & Borzekowski, D. (2004). Condom use among Latino college students. *Journal of American College Health, 42*(4), 169–178.

Hawkins, D. (2005, March 24). On the case of HIV/AIDS. *Black Issues in Higher Education,* 25–29.

Higher Education Act, 79 U.S. § 1219 (1965).

Hispanic Association of Colleges and Universities (HACU). (2005). HACU's legislative agenda for the Higher Education Act reauthorization. Retrieved April 10, 2006, from http://www.hacu.net

Hunt, D, E., Gooden, M., & Barkdull, C. (2001). Walking in moccasins: Indian child welfare in the 21st century. In A. L. Salle, H. A. Lawson, and K. Briar-Lawson (Eds.), *Innovative practices with vulnerable children and families* (pp. 165–187). Peosta, IA: Eddie Bowers Publishing.

Jones, R. (2004). *Black haze: Violence, sacrifice, and manhood in Black Greek letter fraternities.* Albany: State University of New York.

Kimbrough, W. (2003). *Black Greek 101: The culture, customs, and challenges of Black fraternities and sororities.* Madison, NJ: Fairleigh Dickinson University Press.

King, J. L. (2004). *On the down low: A journey into the lives of "straight" Black men who sleep with men.* New York: Broadway Books.

Krause, T. M. (1998, Fall). A potential model of factors influencing alcoholism in American Indians. *Journal of Multicultural Nursing & Health.* Retrieved April 10, 2005, from http://www.findarticles.com/p/articles/mi_qa3919/is_199810/ai_n8810819

Laden, B. (2001). Hispanic-serving institutions: Myths and realities. *Peabody Journal of Education, 76*(1), 73–92.

Laden, B. (2004). Hispanic-serving institutions: What are they? Where are they? *Community College Journal of Research and Practice, 28,* 181–198.

Mitchell, W., & Patch, K. (1981). Indian alcoholism and education. *Journal of American Indian Education, 21*(1). Retrieved April 10, 2005, from http://jaie.asu.edu/v21/V21S1alc.html

National Institute on Alcohol Abuse and Alcoholism (2002). *A call to action: Changing the culture of drinking at US colleges. Final report of the Task Force on College Drinking.* (NIH Publication No: 02-5010). Retrieved April 10, 2005, from http://media.shs.net/collegedrinking/TaskForceReport.pdf

Nuwer, H. (2002). *Wrongs of passage. Fraternities, sororities, binge drinking and hazing.* Bloomington, IN: Indiana University Press.

Nuwer, H. (Ed.). (2003). *The Hazing Reader.* Bloomington, IN: Indiana University Press.

Oppelt, N. T. (1990). *The tribally controlled Indian college: The beginning of self-determination in American Indian education.* Tsaile, AZ: Dine Community College Press.

Pavel, D. M., Inglebret, E., & Banks, S. R. (2001). Tribal colleges and universities in an era of dynamic development. *Peabody Journal of Education, 76*(1), 50–72.

Peterson, J. (1995). AIDS-related risks and same-sex behaviors among African American men. In G. M. Herek, & B. Greene (Eds.), *AIDS, identity and community: The HIV epidemic and lesbians and gay men.* Thousand Oaks, CA: Sage Publications.

Petrosino, F. (2003, July/August). HBCUs tackle homophobia with diversity initiatives. *Crisis,* 10–11.

Pudlow, J. (1998). Sour note for the Marching 100. *Black Issues in Higher Education, 15*(21), 18–20.

Roach, R. (1999, December 9). The race to save lives. *Black Issues in Higher Education, 16*(21), 22–27.

Ross, M. J. (1998). *Success factors of young African American men at a historically Black college.* Westport, CT: Praeger.

Ross, M. J. (2003). *Success factors of young African American women at a historically Black college.* Westport, CT: Praeger.

Rowell, R. (1997). Developing AIDS services for Native Americans: Rural and urban contrasts. In L. B. Brown (Ed.) *Two spirit people: American Indian lesbian women and gay men* (pp. 85–95). New York: The Haworth Press, Inc.

Ruffins, P., & Evelyn, J. (1998). The persistent madness of Greek hazing. *Black Issues in Higher Education, 15*(9), 14–19.

Ruffins, P., & Roach, R. (1997). Frat-ricide: Are African American fraternities beating themselves to death? *Black Issues in Higher Education, 14*(8). Retrieved September 10, 2005, from http://www.diverseeducation.com

Sileo, T. W., & Gooden, M. A. (2003). HIV/AIDS prevention in American Indian and Alaska Native communities. *Tribal College, 14*(4), 44–49.

Snyder, T. D., Tan, A. G., & Hoffman, C. M. (2003). *Digest of education statistics 2003.* Washington DC: National Center for Education Statistics, U.S. Department of Education.

Substance Abuse and Mental Health Services Administration (SAMHSA). (2002). American Indian/Alaska Natives and substance abuse. *Prevention,* 5(16). Retrieved September 13, 2005, from http://www.ncadi.samhsa.gov

Suicide prevention among Native American youth: Hearing before the Committee on Indian Affairs, of the United States Senate, 109th Cong. (15 June 2005) (testimony of Surgeon General, Vice Admiral Richard H. Carmona).

Teen suicide among American Indian youth: Hearing before the Committee on Indian Affairs, of the United States Senate, 109th Cong. (2 May 2005) (testimony of Charles W. Grim, director of the Indian Health Service).

Thompson, D. (1973). *Private Black colleges at the crossroads.* Westport, CT: Greenwood Press.

University of California, San Francisco (UCSF). (2005). *What are Latinos' HIV prevention needs?* San Francisco: Center for AIDS Prevention Studies.

U.S. Department of Education (USDOE). (2006). *Campus crime and security statistics.* Retrieved April 10, 2006, from http://ope.ed.gov/security/

Vernon, I. S. (2002). Violence, HIV/AIDS, and Native American women in the twenty-first century. *The American Indian Culture and Research Journal, 26*(2), 115–133.

Watkins, W. (2001). *White architects of Black education.* New York: Teachers College Press.

Wenglinsky, H. (1999). *Students at historically Black colleges and universities: Their aspirations and accomplishments.* Princeton: Educational Testing Service.

Wilkinson, C. (2002). Addressing contemporary campus safety issues. *New Directions for Student Services.* San Francisco: John Wiley & Sons.

Yates, E. (2004, April 22). N.C. students, faculty address HIV outbreak. *Black Issues in Higher Education,* 10–11.

9

THE ROLE OF THE CAMPUS POLICE AND SECURITY DEPARTMENT IN THE 21ST CENTURY

An Essay Based on 30 Years of Experience

James A. Perrotti

I have spent over 30 years in university policing, the better part of my adult life. During that time, I have witnessed and been part of a transformation driven by actual crime and the fear of crime. University police and security at some institutions have become model agencies, nationally recognized for excellence as leaders in the field of protective services—for example, the Yale University Police Department and the University of Connecticut Police at Storrs. Others have not fully embraced the importance of security in university life. I have often heard university administrators say that before any learning can take place, there must be a safe and secure environment. A safe campus is a basic expectation of students, faculty, and staff as well as parents and families. When a member of the campus community is a victim of crime, the entire institution is affected in a variety of ways. For example, a series of crimes against persons might put the community on edge and spread fear. The perception and fear of crime causes the campus community great concern and affects the quality of life and learning.

Life on campus is an open environment where free expression and the exchange of ideas are core principles. There is often conflict between the need for security and maintaining an open environment. Freedom of

thought and expression are cherished, and many institutions of higher education have minimal controls over campus access due to their commitment to
an open environment. College and university students tend to be less aware
of the need for security and feel protected within the confines of their academic surroundings. These issues can be magnified by factors such as
whether the campus is in a rural or urban location and the level of security
present. With these limitations and realities, it is often a struggle to remain
an inviting neighbor *and* a secure institution. Campus security in today's
world requires unobtrusive methods with the least amount of interference.
This can be a tremendous challenge for campus administrators and those
responsible for security and safety.

The first step in creating a safe and secure environment is a commitment
by the administration to support a police or security program. This support
must be financial and philosophical. The campus community has the right
to demand the best from police and security personnel. To ensure the highest-
quality service, the college must commit to fund programs and offer a salary
structure that will attract highly trained personnel. Salary and benefits competitive with local police agencies and the security market are necessary to
recruit and retain talent. Attrition among police and security personnel creates an unstable environment and reduces the department's effectiveness. I
often hear my colleagues in the industry complain about the lack of funding
for important programs and attractive salaries. Parity with municipal agencies and market competitiveness seems to be the hardest for many organizations. The results of fully funding police and security can be seen in healthy
organizations that have a significant impact in reducing crime. A dysfunc-
tional department, with high turnover, recruiting difficulty, and weak leadership, will have a ripple effect on the campus community. Many campus
administrations have waited for a crisis to begin before making this commitment and, as a result, have experienced significant problems that lingered for
years and tarnished the school's reputation.

I have learned that a mission and value statement for the campus police
and security agency is critical to its success. Clarification of the department's
role on campus is the cornerstone of effectiveness. The mission and values
statement should be developed as a project for the entire department to have
true meaning and universal commitment. The statement should parallel the
mission of the university and be easily understood and committed to memory. A well-developed mission and values statement gives the department a

direction, a sense of worth and unity. Every task in which the department engages should be consistent with and support the mission. The clarity a mission creates is one of the most helpful tools any administrator can have.

I am a proponent of partnerships and collaborations in police and security. The days of working in isolation are gone forever, as they have proven to be limited in effectiveness. Community policing has been in place for many years in our country and has proven to be an effective style and philosophy. Developing partners is a basic element of community policing, and on a campus, one quickly learns the value of partnerships. The partnerships and opportunities for collaborations on campus are virtually endless. It is inherent within the institution that students, faculty, and staff will contribute time and energy to improve the quality of the environment. A police or security department that does not have partnership as a guiding principle will lose the advantage of community support and collaboration. Administrators should expect police and security to be partners in creating a safe and secure campus. This partnership improves the quality of life for the entire campus.

Campus police and security leaders must be included in the group of key decision makers on campus through regular meetings and communication. Although I often use *police* and *security* interchangeably, and the general responsibilities for safety of the campus community are similar, police and security have different roles and accountability. Police provide the scope of services similar to those of a municipal police department, which includes fully sworn personnel with police authority in their designated jurisdiction. Security services are typically defined as those that nonsworn personnel provide, services such as physical security.

Partnerships external to the institution are equally critical to police and security success. I have found a relationship with local police and community leaders is essential to effective operations. This type of relationship extends beyond an awareness of what is occurring outside campus borders. This should be a true partnership that includes exchange of information, training and education opportunities, and shared technology. A safe and secure environment does not end at the property line. There must be proactive measures by college administrators to form and maintain bonds with the community. These partnerships should include community leaders, politicians, clergy, and interested groups. Both campus and municipal police and security departments must align with these partnerships to be effective. Local, state, and federal law enforcement agencies also must be oriented to the campus and aware of any vulnerability that may exist. One important feature of this partnership is for each campus police and security department to enter into a mutual aid agreement and memorandum of understanding with surrounding local government. These agreements should be reviewed and updated regularly, with all police and security personnel required to be aware of the terms and conditions of the mutual aid agreements.

Since the U.S. Department of Education began to publish campus crime statistics, colleges and universities have taken a greater interest in campus security (Jeanne Clery Disclosure of Campus Security Policy and Campus Crime Statistics Act, 1990). These statistics have a direct impact on the perception of the safety on campus. The reporting requirements by the U.S. Department of Education have been the single most effective way of encouraging campus administrators to address security issues directly. Many institutions fear that reporting crime may have a negative impact on the institution's image, thus negatively affecting enrollment and academic standing. This concern has created resistance to acknowledging security issues and the risks they create. Campus police and security departments must collaborate with campus administrators to encourage open reporting.

Safety and security are major concerns for everyone despite the consequences of open reporting on image and enrollment. The campus image is improved when students, faculty, and staff are aware of security issues and are part of the solution. For example, if a series of street crimes should occur, it is important to alert the citizens of the community so they can take measures to improve their own safety, such as not walking alone or using an escort service. When a campus uses open reporting, everyone has an opportunity to decrease the risk of becoming a victim. Awareness is an important tool in developing community involvement to help reduce crime.

Keeping the campus police and security department up to date and aware of current issues requires dedicated and continuous training and education. While much of the training will relate to police and security topics, it is important to include high-level leadership programs. Training and education are by far the most effective tools in keeping the agency current with state-of-the-art policing practices and developing new skills. The development of future leaders who are prepared for advancement and the challenges of the next generation is the responsibility of all police agencies. We should do all we can to raise the professionalism of campus police and security.

Post-September 11, 2001

The post-September 11th world forced us to reexamine the complex systems that provide security to our nation. We all remember the days following the terrorists' attacks, the stunning magnitude of the events, and the realization of how vulnerable we really were. The nation's defense structure was scrutinized and challenged. Complex questions were raised. How would we organize our country to protect itself from another attack? Could a problem of this size be solved with any confidence in the lasting effectiveness of any program? Much progress has been made since the attacks at every level of government and in the private sector, and many colleges and universities have developed extensive plans for protecting their campus, such as creating specialized response teams and offering emergency disaster training. However, some schools have yet to recognize the immediacy of the threat.

Failure to acknowledge and prepare for the possibility of further acts of terrorism can have disastrous consequences. Planning and preparation for such an event can be a challenge for the campus community's students and staff. The need to remain open and accessible while reducing vulnerability can be daunting when freedom of movement on campus is the norm. Any attempt to hinder that freedom is perceived as a violation of academic privilege. Campus communities should make every effort to collaborate on security issues created in the post-9/11 world. The vulnerabilities of each campus should be identified and solutions developed. These vulnerabilities may include access to research facilities, computer systems, and individuals. These issues can be addressed and their impact minimized if community members are engaged in the problem-solving process. International terrorism on American soil is new to this country and to the campus community.

Terrorist threats to colleges and universities have been overlooked. The safety of college campuses has historically been the responsibility of internal security. Local law enforcement has not been expected to develop a strategy and contingency plans for a private institution that are sensitive to the student population and respond to the intricacies of an academic environment. The campus community, including senior-level leadership as well as local law enforcement, must be engaged and collaborative for the plan to be effective.

The threat of domestic terrorism on university and college campuses is very real. Many research projects on college campuses are targets of domestic terrorism, and for those campuses affiliated with hospitals and medical centers, the potential is escalated and more complex. There have been many cases of university and college campuses victimized by domestic terrorist organizations and individuals such as the Animal Liberation Front and the Earth Liberation Front. While some domestic terror suspects have been apprehended, such as Unabomber Theodore Kaczynski, responsible for several campus bombings, the risk to the campus community remains a strong concern. Security measures for areas where research is being done should be examined thoroughly and protective systems must be developed, such as stricter access control and video monitoring. A heightened level of security is accepted more easily by students, faculty, and staff when the need is clear and acknowledged. Previous attacks on university and college campuses have resulted in the loss of millions of dollars in property and research and have resulted in injuries to university personnel. Collaboration with faculty and students for security planning cannot be overlooked or overemphasized. Each member of the academic community must understand his or her individual responsibility to cooperate and be part of finding solutions.

The presence of chemical, biological, and radiological materials, commonly found in many research facilities, creates a security concern and an increased security risk. A security survey must be conducted and environmental risks assessed. For the areas of high or medium risk, an action plan must be developed, recognizing the need for researchers to have 24-hour access to the materials and facilities.

In planning for a terrorist event, detailed evacuation plans are essential. It is critical for colleges and universities to be part of the greater local government plan as well. Local government plans may include contingencies for housing, food, and medical care beyond the university populace. The campus environment creates a number of unusual conditions that also must be addressed, including the residential population. While many see the campus as a place to house and feed persons displaced by a terrorist event or natural disaster, it can also be subject to evacuation. The planning process should include representation by the campus community as well as local, state, and federal personnel. A thoughtful disaster plan in theory is useless during a real incident if it has been developed in isolation and resources external to the campus are deployed elsewhere.

When developing a blueprint to respond to a terrorist event, planners must recognize the possibility of a "compound hazard," such as a weather event or other incident not directly related to the terrorist act. These compound hazards may include demonstrations and riots as well as such environmental factors as the loss of power and water. These events can occur without warning, so the plan must encompass the campus and the surrounding area.

Special events and high-profile visitors to the college campus create another unusual challenge in the post-9/11 era. Managing special events and dignitary visits now requires a thorough understanding of the threat assessment process and a complete analysis of the event. Development of a comprehensive plan for these events forces the reallocation of precious resources already in short supply in many campus communities.

In speaking with colleagues in campus policing, I have discovered what appears to be a consistent lack of funding for homeland security projects post-9/11. Many basic protections are not implemented because of insufficient resources and budget, creating a continued risk. Campuses must commit to a plan to fund homeland security projects regularly until all risks and vulnerabilities are addressed. Colleges and universities will be better served by budgeting resources to identify and eliminate risks, rather than dealing with a crisis situation. Crisis management can be far more costly to an organization than risk management.

The 21st Century

When I began my career in university policing more than 30 years ago, the responsibilities and challenges were quite different from what they are today. Explaining what it was like then will help the reader understand campus security today and the direction of the future. My career in university policing began as a member of a department of approximately 30 sworn officers with full police powers, training, and certification, but totally in "plain clothes." The concept behind a plain-clothes department was to provide security but remain as unobtrusive as possible. Consider the idea of an invisible police department! We were necessary to the campus community, but we had little standing or real authority. University police were regarded as outsiders by the students, faculty, and staff. There was crime on campus, but it was not significant and was considered more a city problem. Morale was poor in the department and police services ineffective and costly. It was a dismal situation.

By the late 1970s, crime was on the increase. Enlightened students began to question college administrators out of concern for personal safety. Following pressure by the students for a more visible police force, officers were placed in uniform; however, the university did not want any similarities in uniform with the local police. The uniforms were royal blue and looked neon under bright lighting. Although well intentioned, the nontraditional color of the uniforms led to an even greater decline in morale, and the officers sank deeper out of sight. Crime continued to escalate, and the department struggled to remain responsive. While the royal blue uniforms improved the appearance of the police, the new image failed to encourage heightened visibility. A group of officers, of which I was part, sought to raise these concerns with the police chief in the hope that reforms would be considered. In the early 1970s, we were successful in our efforts, and the department changed to the traditional dark blue uniforms worn by city police. The discussion with the chief also opened the door to increased training and a movement toward a change in philosophy began. Despite these positive measures, city and campus crime continued to escalate, and a series of high profile incidents resulted in a critical review of university police operations.

The department began to evolve in response to the needs of the campus community. New leadership at the senior administrative level of the university also recognized and supported a change in philosophy. Policing would shift from a proprietary security function to a more professional police agency with an established mission and values. Standard police policy and procedure were adopted, and training and education included ethics and leadership. The campus community began to understand and appreciate the department's capabilities, and respect for and recognition of the department grew. Today the department stands at 83 sworn officers and has become a tremendous asset to the university and surrounding community.

Today, officers of the department take great pride in their profession and have confidence in the work they do. The department's administrative support has been outstanding and continues to recognize the value of an efficient and effective police service. The evolution of the police department was a true success story. While crime may never be eradicated, the instances are lower and staff work continually to solve problems that give rise to crime. The men and women of the university police stand shoulder to shoulder with local, state, and federal law enforcement as equals in training, experience, and resources. Committed to the principle of collaboration and community policing, the university has developed sound relationships with its community partners.

Many college and university police and security organizations have not enjoyed the success this university has experienced. Campus leaders do not always see the value of the department until a major incident occurs. This shortsightedness can have tragic consequences. When a university police or security agency is devalued, problems manifest themselves inside and outside the department. Campus security cannot tolerate neglect, and continued neglect will eventually create new issues for the entire campus community in the form of poor service and civilian complaints. Campus leaders must recognize the importance of a high-quality security function, whether it is sworn or proprietary, and provide adequate administrative support for it. Before any learning can take place, students must have a safe and secure environment.

The importance of diversity, in both the composition of departmental personnel and cultural competency, cannot be too underscored and valued. Gender, race, and ethnic diversity strengthen the agency and should be a guiding principle in the recruiting process. Affirmative measures should be taken to seek out diverse candidates for the applicant pool. The agency's reputation should be one that welcomes and supports diversity and should mirror the community it serves. In many police agencies, women and minorities are the last hired, and as a consequence, have the least seniority. In a strict seniority-based promotional system, they are outbid for leadership positions by nonminorities. Special attention must be paid to succession planning for department leadership to include women and minorities.

Reinforcement of strong ethical standards in campus police and security departments must be included in each day's plan. To gain the respect of the community, security personnel must perpetually demonstrate high ethical standards such as trust and commitment. Personnel must treat all individuals with equal respect and dignity. When the department is supported by the leadership of the institution, ethical policing comes naturally. The leadership of the department must also lead by example and not succumb to poor judgment with regard to ethical behavior. Department leaders must set the standard for ethical behavior and adhere to a personal and professional code of conduct.

Challenges

Campus police and security agencies today face new and more complex challenges than they did in the past. To keep the campus secure in the post-9/11 era, there is still much work to be done. Technology and the flow of information in the modern world can be a blessing and a curse. Police and security departments receive tremendous amounts of information every day and are expected to be current and informed. An agency must have an infrastructure that includes information technology and expertise to manage the flow of data. Responding to these demands requires state-of-the-art equipment and highly trained personnel. Advances in technology will continue at rapid pace, requiring campus security and police to keep up with both qualified personnel and necessary technology upgrades to respond to operational and strategic challenges. The computerization of crime statistics and information has provided a timely assessment of criminal activity and assisted departments in developing long-term strategies through crime mapping. Crime analysis programs have the added benefit of allowing department leadership to emphasize accountability through the presentation of crime data. Technology will continue to be a significant weapon in preventing and reducing crime.

Another significant challenge we face in the 21st century is a shift in our prison population and its direct effect on universities and colleges. In the 1990s, the American legal system supported incarceration with long sentences for criminal convictions, and the prison population grew to the largest numbers in history. New state-of-the-art prisons were built to manage the growing prisoner population, and the cost of maintaining the prison population grew at a staggering rate. Efforts to reduce crime resulted in "warehousing" offenders for long periods and at significant expense. The American taxpayer has borne the expense of this growing population, and, although we have benefited from a significant reduction in crime in the last decade, the growing prison population has become a greater concern. Political leaders are challenged to reduce rising prison costs, not only in supporting the system, but also in the value of human life. The concept of rehabilitation in our prison system is something many believe has failed. Recidivism is high, and a revolving door exists for many criminals.

Today, the prisoner release program has created new dilemmas. The number of convicts returning to our communities following short sentences and minimal rehabilitation efforts is growing. This phenomenon has caused an influx of people in need of monitoring and social services. State and local agencies are understaffed and underfunded, leaving released persons without formal monitoring and little support to reintegrate into society. These individuals often return to criminal activity in cities around university and college campuses. In addition, many released persons are employed by firms associated with the campus or even by the college or university. We should not be fearful of the released population; most are nonviolent and will not become repeat offenders. However, programs should be developed to support these individuals. Some may become students at your institution in an effort to improve their lives. Society and employers must work together to assist those who have paid their debt.

Violent offenders should be considered differently in terms of access to university property and personnel. A reasonable process of background checks, including criminal and sex offender history, should be incorporated into a comprehensive security plan.

Keeping the student body safe will always be of primary concern. The education of students and faculty, which includes risk recognition and programs to reduce those risks, is a priority for campus administrators and security personnel. Students also have a significant role in this process. We should be as supportive as possible in educating students in personal safety. Students on today's campus come from diverse backgrounds. Some have lived a life totally without the fear of crime, while others are more familiar with crime. Many international students distrust police and security because of their experience in their country of origin. Unfortunately, they can be victimized easily because of their fear of reporting crime to the authorities. Police and security should collaborate with international student organizations to provide security education and develop trust. In addition, campus police and security should collaborate with student groups to develop consistent lines of communication and trust. In doing so, security programs can be developed that accommodate all students while encouraging each to practice crime prevention and make informed decisions on personal security.

The university or college campus of today can be among the most diverse and liberal environments in our country. An academic center where individuality and expanded thinking are encouraged is one of the fundamental principles of higher education. Ideas are shared, positions debated, and social activism encouraged. The atmosphere created is a learning environment like no other. America is a nation of great achievement, in part due to our higher education institutions. To be part of this learning experience and enjoy the benefits on campus, one must be tolerant of the differences in people and philosophies. There are times when conflicts arise that can lead to large divisions on campus to the detriment of the institution. These can be politically and culturally charged with extreme positions and passions. To avert conflict, administrators and public safety should take a proactive approach and develop partnerships through collaboration. Police and security should not experience working with diverse groups on campus for the first time when a crisis develops. Programs that bring campus public safety together with student groups should be an ongoing priority. Hate crimes must be investigated aggressively, and the policy regarding such crime should reflect a zero tolerance approach. Police and security personnel require specialized training to recognize and investigate hate crimes.

No discussion of future challenges would be complete without commenting on drugs and alcohol. It is an unfortunate fact that college students use drugs and alcohol all too frequently. Most campus security administrators can recount numerous stories of students under the influence of drugs and alcohol with tragic consequences. The results of excessive consumption are documented in incidents such as those involving assault, sexual assault, theft, burglary, and property damage. It is unfortunate to see young adults realize, after being involved in an incident, that substance abuse has affected their behavior to the point of losing control. Good people have been marked for life when excessive consumption has resulted in uncharacteristic behaviors that contributed to an incident of crime. It is indeed difficult to understand what motivates young adults to consume alcohol to a point where their behavior causes personal harm. Binge drinking creates a great medical risk and can cause death from alcohol poisoning or a lethal alcohol/drug combination. Fortunately, the abuse of alcohol and drugs on college campuses is widely recognized. Campus administrators should familiarize themselves with the results of studies done on student substance abuse and programs developed to address the problem. Campus administrators have placed restrictions on alcohol use on campus and encouraged alcohol-free events.

Major events such as sports contests have received media attention after an alcohol-fueled crowd became unruly and rioted. People have been killed or injured, millions of dollars of property destroyed, and lives affected forever. Yet there seems to be no effective or lasting means to control consumption. Absolute prohibition merely drives the behavior underground. It has been my experience that young people on a college campus will find ways to circumvent any controls on the use of alcohol. Many believe drinking in college is a rite of passage and a tradition passed down from one generation to another. Parents seem to believe drinking in college is an acceptable pastime and something all students do to relieve the stress of academic life. Nothing could be further from the truth.

To address the problem, college administrators must first acknowledge the issues involving substance abuse, especially alcohol, openly and honestly. Encouraging students and parents to become involved in problem solving are also positive measures. Any controls put in place must be realistic and reviewed periodically for effectiveness. The solution to alcohol and drug abuse on college campuses rests not only with police and with security, but with the entire student body, administration, families, and faculty. Ignoring the problem will only compound it.

Recently, sexual assault on college campuses has received considerable attention. Unfortunately, sex crimes often go unreported. Police and sexual assault victim services groups have made significant strides in developing techniques that further the investigation and support the victim. More work must be done to raise victims' confidence in the system and increase reporting of such crime. Some colleges and universities have developed programs to facilitate reporting and adjudication of sexual assaults internally. These programs have come under intense criticism by organizations demanding better security and support for victims of sexual assault. It is apparent that academic institutions have great difficulty handling these cases internally. Many campuses have created committees, usually attached in some way to the office of student affairs, that are charged with hearing student disciplinary cases. Most cases reviewed by the committee can be handled in a satisfactory manner, but many can be overwhelming to the committees, which usually comprise faculty, students, and administrators. The complex nature of some cases is far too challenging for this type of review.

Sexual assault is a crime, and such cases are better served through criminal proceedings. The campus community should collaborate with police and security officials long before a case is reported. A strict zero tolerance policy on sexual assault sends a clear statement to everyone. Also relevant is the use of alcohol as a contributing factor in sexual assault. Unfortunately, when alcohol is present in a case, particularly overconsumption, successful prosecution can be a problem. Many prosecutors are reluctant to prosecute cases where individuals involved are intoxicated for fear of traumatizing the victims further. An effective security education program includes and addresses the use of alcohol and date rape drugs in sexual assaults. Security education programs help make students aware of the realities of sexual assault. The college campus can be an environment where discussions of sexual assault are open, policy is developed in a collaborative way, and reporting is encouraged.

As though the threat of international terrorism, sexual assaults, and drug and alcohol abuse were not enough to challenge campus security, youth gangs have now permeated our communities. A current challenge facing America is youth violence, which has risen quite dramatically over the last two years. Cities across our country are experiencing a wave of violent crime perpetrated by youthful offenders. Gun violence is particularly troubling among youth in our communities. Parents have growing concern that their children will be victims of violence. Will their child be the next one shot and killed? The issue of youth violence has begun to affect university and college campuses as well. Students, faculty, and staff have been the victims of crimes committed by neighboring youth. We know that "building a wall" around the campus and isolating it has a negative impact on the community. Turning away from the problem will prolong it. Many of these young people may eventually attend institutions of higher education, bringing with them their life experiences. Youth violence can and does lead to tomorrow's criminals. I strongly recommend that campus communities actively engage in collaborative efforts with their host communities.

While a variety of programs can be developed to address youth issues and begin the process of change, opportunities have been missed because of a lack of funding. Universities and colleges can still have a positive impact on youthful offenders with minimal resources, such as mentoring youth in the area through positive role models. Another is a program to give help with homework assignments. The list of potential programs is endless; however, it should include those that are simple, but have major impact. Success stories keep people interested and engaged. Partnering with the community in youth programs is essential today and for the future. There are sure to be many challenges to academic institutions in the days and years ahead; keeping the campus safe and secure is one of them. Supporting those responsible for safety and security should be a high priority for all colleges and universities. It is important to remember that before any learning can take place there must be a safe and secure environment in which to learn.

Conclusion

The emphasis on partnerships described in this chapter is not cliché, nor should it be considered a criticism of earlier methods of campus policing.

Relationship development is the responsibility of police and security leadership as well as campus administration and local, state, and federal police agencies. It is both a practical and operational necessity to build common goals with our allies and to share a vision and plan for the future.

A traditional safety philosophy no longer fulfills the needs and challenges of the modern college campus. Today's challenges require technical and financial support as well as carefully nurtured community partnerships. Understanding the concerns of both the internal and external communities and addressing problems collaboratively are key to effective policing. The recommendations in this chapter are the foundation of a program to address the rapidly changing campus environment. As stated earlier, before any learning can take place, there must be a safe and secure environment. The leaders of tomorrow rely on our services to ensure this environment.

Reference

Jeanne Clery Disclosure of Campus Security Policy and Campus Crime Statistics Act [originally passed as part of Student Right-to-Know and Campus Security Act of 1990], 20 U.S.C. § 1092 (1990).

10

THE INCOMPATIBILITY OF WEAPONS AND COLLEGE CAMPUSES

Charles Cychosz

Weapons are philosophically incompatible with the culture that most campus communities are trying to develop and maintain. Campuses generally value reasoned discussion and intellectual debate, deliberative problem solving, equity, and a sense of safety and security. These qualities are explicitly or implicitly valued on most campuses because they free students and faculty to invest in the learning enterprise. Weapons, however, have intruded into campus much as they have created a new presence in the nation's secondary schools and the corporate workplace. The presence of weapons affects the learning environment in a number of ways—from the serious effects of fear and intimidation to the less serious but disruptive impact of mischief and vandalism (Hemenway, Azrael, & Miller, 2001).

While many factors contribute to this phenomenon, the administrators of today's college campus must respond to the presence of weapons. This response increasingly involves the challenge of reconciling the philosophical foundations of the institution with contemporary realities of students, staff, and the communities in which they live.

Weapons Defined

Defining weapons initially may seem to be an unnecessary discussion of the obvious. To overlook this task, however, is to underestimate the ingenuity of young people and the rapid evolution of technology. Effective regulation of weapons begins with a clear definition of the devices covered by campus policies and practices. Any discussion of weapons, or any weapons policy, must acknowledge the array of devices that fall into this classification. Furthermore, campus administrators can consciously determine the scope of devices and activities they choose to regulate through campus policy. Engaging the campus community in this process is, of course, a path toward an effective policy.

Firearms are the focus of much of the concern about weapons. In the United States, firearms are widely available. For example, 2003 manufacturing data show 2.18 million firearms manufactured in the United States (Bureau of Alcohol, Tobacco, Firearms, and Explosives, 2003). Even allowing for substantial exports, this production supplements a large supply of existing weapons in most communities. Access to new weapons is subject to commercial regulations at one or more levels of government, with federal law providing the foundation for regulatory activity.

Federal regulations controlling purchase and possession of firearms are based on the Gun Control Act of 1968. This law provides the federal definition of firearms, defines the scope of transactions allowed, and places special restrictions on certain classes of weapons and ammunition. On a practical level, dealers are prohibited from selling weapons to any person who

- has been convicted of or indicted for a felony;
- is a fugitive who has been adjudicated as a mental defective;
- has been committed to any mental institution;
- is addicted to or an unlawful user of marijuana or a stimulant, depressant, or narcotic drug;
- is less than 18 years of age for the purchase of a shotgun or rifle or is less than 21 years of age for the purchase of a firearm other than a shotgun or rifle;
- is a nonresident of the state in which the licensee's place of business is located;
- is an alien illegally or unlawfully in the United States;
- has been dishonorably discharged from the armed forces;
- is subject to a court order that restrains such person from harassing, stalking, or threatening an intimate partner; or

- has been convicted in any court of a misdemeanor crime of domestic violence.

It is important to note that these restrictions apply to federally licensed firearms dealers. Nothing in this law applies these restrictions to individual transactions between unlicensed private firearms owners, although some state and local entities have extended these principles (Lockyer, 2005). In addition, recent revisions in these laws have expanded sales to out-of-state customers while restricting weapons from elementary and secondary schools. Campuses with federal facilities or federal parklands should take special note of the sections that define the scope of acceptable firearms possession on these types of properties. In 1993, the Brady Handgun Violence Prevent Act (Brady Act) required a National Instant Criminal Background Check System. This was intended to create a system to allow federal firearms license holders to verify that a customer was eligible to purchase a firearm under federal law. Again, this law applies only to transactions involving a federal firearms license holder.

Thus, federal firearms regulations restrict sales to those with felony convictions or certain other conditions or offenses, while adding some additional restrictions on handgun purchases. State and, occasionally, local regulations can be more restrictive, often requiring a purchase permit from a state or local authority. Because of the tradition of state control over these transactions, college administrators must determine the local and state regulations being enforced in their community. Sources of this information include the state attorney general and the local law enforcement agency. Finally, some states, like North Carolina or California, have promulgated state regulations limiting possession of weapons on all campuses under state jurisdiction. The Bureau of Alcohol, Tobacco, Firearms and Explosives has traditionally published an annual compendium of State Laws and Published Ordinances (Bureau of Alcohol, Tobacco, Firearms and Explosives, 2005). California, for example, produces a similar document with an overview of state and local ordinances for California communities (Lockyer, 2005).

Firearms are the focus of much of the weapons legislation and concern, in part due to their lethality. Of 14,408 murders reported to the Federal Bureau of Investigation (FBI) in 2003, 66% (9,638) were committed with a firearm (FBI, 2003b). In fact, slightly over half (7,701) of all murders were committed using a handgun. In contrast, 13% (1,816) were committed with knives, and 6% (946) were committed with hands, feet, and fists, while only four were reported for explosives. Because murders are generally reported to authorities and well investigated, they serve as a useful index of the scope of weapons used in serious violence. In a detailed review of elementary and secondary school-associated fatalities, 77.1% resulted from a firearm (Kachur et al., 1996). It is interesting to note that there is limited regional variation in the proportion of murders attributed to firearms (FBI, 2003a), ranging from a high of 68.1% in the Midwest to a low of 61.9% in the Northeast.

Because of the initiative necessary to obtain a firearm, possession of this type of weapon is not a casual undertaking for most people. While motivation for weapons possession is explored later in this chapter, firearms purchases involve more money and documentation than do purchases of other types of weapons. As such, obtaining a firearm legally involves a higher level of intentionality and forward planning than something like a knife does. The exception is person-to-person private firearms sales, which are largely unregulated transactions between private citizens.

Weapons as a concern on campus go well beyond firearms. Perhaps more ubiquitous are knives and similar edged weapons. Federal regulations (U.S.C. Title 15, Chapter 29) do not allow switchblade knives to be manufactured or distributed in interstate commerce. Most states have similar regulations restricting possession of them. Again, state laws vary, but many communities allow blades up to 2.5, 3, or 3.5 inches to be carried as a pocketknife. In addition, knives are easily purchased in a variety of locations and are relatively inexpensive, easily stored, transported, and concealed. Based on the limited epidemiological research on this topic, knives may be the weapon of choice for those seeking some defensive capability (Kieck, 2005). Knives may also be obtained on impulse under circumstances requiring less money and less planning. Longer edged weapons (e.g., machetes and swords) are easily overlooked when considering weapons. They are often decorative or ceremonial in purpose and certainly difficult to conceal. As such, they are not often referred to in campus weapons policies. Nonetheless, decorative swords are increasingly common, and impulsive use of these weapons can change their function rapidly from decorative to threatening or injurious. At the very least, ownership and display of these weapons on campus can lead the public to question the scope of weapons regulation there.

Firearms and knives have obvious offensive potential and are well recognized for their role in robberies, assaults, and similar crimes (FBI, 2003c).

Other weapons are predominantly defensive in orientation. Perhaps the most common of these is the small canister of pepper spray. These devices are widely available for purchase, easily concealed, and carried by many people on a key ring or in a pocket. Given the general perception of these devices as a defensive tool, many campus policies exclude these devices from policy and regulation. Policies that list them as weapons often allow possession of these devices explicitly for personal protection. Electric discharge stun devices are less easily obtained and, as a consequence, have received relatively little attention on most campuses. Because of the potential for offensive use as well as the potential for hazing-related use, these devices are good candidates for regulation by campus policy.

Finally, it is easy to overlook the potential for "explosives" as weapons. Nonetheless, recent campus experiences suggest that fireworks, firecrackers, and homemade versions of bottle and pipe bombs are in the possession of college-age students. While most of these are more likely to be created out of somewhat mischievous curiosity, they can be dangerous devices when they are stored or deployed in a crowded campus environment of residence halls and classrooms. Of course, on the other end of this continuum are potentially deadly explosive devices that are clearly intended to harm others. Policy strategies can prohibit the manufacture, modification, possession, or placement of potentially explosive devices. Possession of explosives, including homemade or modified fireworks, occurs often enough to generate discussion in the community. As noted later in this chapter, the campus community often notifies campus authorities of these activities, particularly through informal channels.

Another venue that occasionally involves explosives is campus chemistry laboratories. The actual malicious manufacture of explosives is relatively uncommon, but campuses have seen experiments gone awry and the mischief that has resulted in expensive hazardous materials disposal charges. Although not generally concerned about chemical compounds as weapons, campuses are increasingly sensitive to the toxicity or hazard potential of chemicals stored in their laboratories and are taking steps to ensure control over access to and limitations on the quantity in secure storage. Before taking these steps, campuses have seen these lab chemicals emerge as various types of environmental contamination—and certainly as safety concerns to the campus population.

Who Carries a Weapon?

Weapons are present on many college campuses every day. For instance, students carry weapons with a frequency that surprises even some seasoned campus staff. National statistics derived from the Core Alcohol and Drug Survey on 61 campuses during the mid-1990s suggests that 11% of men and 4% of women had carried a weapon in the last 30 days (Presley, Meilman, & Cashin, 1997). A survey of Pennsylvania State University students in 2000 found that 4% reported carrying a weapon or dangerous object while at school (Pennsylvania State University, 2000). In this same survey, students attributed weapons carrying to past violent experiences, worries of attacks by strangers, and feeling more in control of situations. More recently, in a sample of more than 10,000 students at 119 colleges, 4.3% had a working firearm while at college (Miller, Hemenway, & Wechsler, 2002).

While there are many reasons for possession of weapons by students, the most pervasive motivation is often self-protection. This same study revealed that weapon-carrying students had experienced harassment, violence, and threats of violence at a greater frequency than had the unarmed group. It is also interesting to note that the weapon-carrying group reported higher rates of binge drinking, other drug use, and substance abuse consequences (Miller, Hemenway, & Wechsler, 1999; Presley et al., 1997). Broader studies of weapons ownership (e.g., Coyne-Beasley, Baccaglini, Johnson, Webster, & Wiebe, 2005) have further supported the trend for firearms ownership to be more common among males and in regions of the country where gun ownership is higher.

Some of the research seeking ways to reduce firearms-related injuries has highlighted the lethal nature of weapons in otherwise impulsive actions. Specifically, the concept is that a simple altercation can too easily escalate to a fatal confrontation if one or both parties has a weapon. One of the most closely studied examples of this comes from the FBI analysis of law enforcement officer assaults (FBI, 2005). For the 2004 calendar year, there were 59,373 reported assaults on police officers. While firearms accounted for only 3.6% of the weapons involved in these assaults, they were used in 54 of the 57 officer fatalities. If a disagreement escalates to the point of an assault, the likelihood of a fatal outcome increases in the presence of a weapon. It is likely, proponents argue, that many more victims would survive if weapons were not in close proximity to participants in a dispute. FBI summary statistics for 2003 (FBI, 2003c) attribute more than 4,000 murders to arguments.

This same line of thinking has been the basis for special federal regulation of weapons possession among domestic violence offenders.

U.S. Department of Education statistics for 2003 (U.S. Department of Education, 2003) show 2,297 arrests and 1,877 disciplinary actions for illegal weapons possession in campus-related venues. Of these, 1,181 illegal weapons possession arrests and 1,670 disciplinary actions were reported as "on campus." Nationally, residence halls reported 311 arrests and 3 disciplinary actions. Public property was by far the most common location classification, accounting for 1,004 arrests and 127 disciplinary actions. Implied in these data is the relatively greater likelihood of encountering a weapon in public spaces, which are frequented by a broader cross-section of campus residents and visitors. The high number of arrests also implies a relatively strong law enforcement response to these incidents.

Another troubling element of weapons possession is the apparent co-occurrence of weapons possession with binge drinking and drug use. The disinhibiting effect of the substances results in less influence by normal social controls. When combined with the lethal nature of firearms, this behavior would seem to be an important target for risk reduction activities.

Along with the impulsive character and those using alcohol and other drugs are those young adults who develop feelings of suicide. The availability of firearms, particularly when associated with alcohol, also seems to enhance the lethality of suicidal behavior (Miller et al., 1999; Presley et al., 1997). Colleges across the country have struggled to support students and diminish suicide-related deaths. Limitations on the availability of weapons seem to be a logical intervention—another consideration for campuses creating weapons policies.

Similarly, faculty and staff on some campuses carry firearms under local concealed weapons permits. While states vary in the extent to which this is allowed, many Midwestern and Western states allow citizens to apply for concealed weapons permits. Acceptable reasons for requesting permits often include personal protection or such activities as handling or transporting bank deposits. There is rarely any formal notification of employers when these permits are issued. In fact, a number of campuses have had to notify the campus community of how state "right to carry" laws are interpreted on campus—for example, "Concealed weapons are not to be carried on University property. Concealed permit holders will notify University Police for instructions on temporary weapons storage" (Eastern Washington University,

2005, p. 1), or simply, "No concealed carry permit exempts a person from this policy" (University of Arizona Police Department, 2005, pp. 1–2). Of the 33 states that allow residents some form of concealed weapons authority, approximately 19 make exceptions for universities (Bureau of Alcohol, Tobacco, Firearms and Explosives, 2005). Little research has been published exploring the extent to which faculty and staff actually carry firearms. Anecdotal references to this question suggest that faculty and staff are likely to carry weapons for many of the same reasons as students do.

As campuses have strengthened their connection with local communities by becoming more open and accessible, visitors have found it easier to bring weapons to campus as part of their specific intent to prey on students and their property. In a similar vein, today's students are more mobile, often living, working, and socializing off campus. This blurring of boundaries has led to an evolution in crime reporting on campus. The U.S. Department of Education crime reporting requirements acknowledge this reality with off-campus crime reporting now a required component of how campuses are expected to report to parents and students. Thus, campuses become the target of crime perpetrated by people who have no affiliation with campus while students increasingly move beyond the traditional boundaries of campus.

How Can Campuses Respond?

Finally, the campus and community have come to expect, or at least accommodate, the notion that weapons are carried by law enforcement. This intrusion of weapons onto campuses is another reality that must be accommodated by contemporary college administrators. Campuses that employ sworn law enforcement officers generally screen employees according to state procedures for police officers. This generally takes advantage of contemporary strategies developed by states to ensure that police officers meet well-accepted levels of psychological stability and training before they carry weapons. Policies (or laws) that ban weapons from a campus generally make appropriate provisions for local law enforcement officers as well as state or federal officials who may carry weapons on campus as a part of their work. Professional courtesy generally leads to contact with local law enforcement officials when state or federal agents must come to a college campus. It is not uncommon, for instance, to have presidential visits or major public events that involve armed federal protective services or police officers from a variety of jurisdictions. Policies that acknowledge the role of weapons in law enforcement activity can accommodate these situations while encouraging communication with campus officials.

Another dimension of this question emerges for campuses that have a security force rather than a state-certified law enforcement presence. Security services often operate without firearms but may carry other devices, including tasers, impact weapons, or irritant sprays. Background investigations, thorough training, and clear use of force policies help the campus community trust that these weapons will only be used in ways that are consistent with local expectations and definitions of necessity.

In a case that may be of special interest to those institutions employing contract security services, the U.S. attorney for the Southern District of Texas announced convictions of Spartan Security Services (Financial Holdings, Inc.) for conspiracy to arm illegal aliens. This followed prosecution of several Spartan Security employees on weapons charges. Although Spartan primarily provides security to automobile dealerships, apartment houses, and nightclubs, this case highlighted the vulnerability of an institution that contracts for security services. Campuses with contract security may want to include explicit references to campus weapons policy when contracting for security services. Given the scope of the Spartan Security incident, it may also be prudent for campus administrators to conduct background reviews of any contract security employee who may be expected to carry a weapon in the course of his or her employment.

Finally, some campuses operate with a law enforcement authority that does not generally carry a firearm. While this is increasingly rare among large public institutions, it still occurs. This practice extends mostly from tradition and an interest in avoiding the liability associated with an armed law enforcement agency. Campus authorities that operate unarmed forces are reluctant to change to an armed force due to public perceptions, cost, and perceived risk. In these cases, departments may rely on a process of arming officers in response to a threat or a working agreement with an armed community police force. While an objective analysis of the circumstances requiring firearms typically leads law enforcement practitioners to conclude that these delayed arming strategies are ineffective, some campuses continue to operate successfully under this arrangement. Campus law enforcement and security agencies are at the forefront of responding to weapons as part of a growing commitment to safety on campus (Community Oriented Policing Services, 2005).

Weapons, like alcohol, are on our campus and must be managed with education, development and administration of appropriate policies, and consistent enforcement.

Policy Components

Contemporary circumstances have led most colleges to establish some kind of weapons policy. As noted earlier, it is very important for a campus community to articulate a policy regarding weapons possession. Some key components of such a policy are reviewed in the following section.

Comprehensive Policies Include Clear Definitions of Weapons, Including Ammunition

For example, the policy at the University of Texas at Austin includes the following language: "The following weapons are prohibited: firearms, an explosive weapon, a machine gun, a short barreled firearm, a firearm silencer, switchblade knife, knuckles, armor-piercing ammunition, a chemical dispensing device, a zip gun, a club, or night stick, and an illegal knife" (University of Texas at Austin, 2003).

The University of North Carolina-Charlotte addresses this question using the following language: "The definition of the term 'weapon' as used in this policy statement shall be identical to that in the corresponding State law. The term includes not only all firearms, but also powerful explosives and such devices as knives or clubs intended for use in personal combat" (University of North Carolina-Charlotte, 2001, p. III-11-1).

Paintball guns are not generally considered firearms under state or federal laws. Because they may be hazardous to someone who is not wearing appropriate protective equipment, some campuses have specifically regulated possession of these devices. Somewhat more challenging are firearm replicas such as Airsoft guns. This manufacturer produces spring-powered devices that shoot a plastic projectile. While the projectile is so light it is unlikely to do harm, the guns themselves are so realistic that police agencies have frequently been forced to respond to possession of these devices under the assumption that they are real firearms. Finally, campuses may occasionally see "potato guns," devices typically composed of PVC pipe and using lighter fluid for the explosive launch of the projectile. While these devices can be dangerous, they are not federally regulated as firearms. On campus, they are most likely to show up as a source of creative vandalism. Most campuses respond to these items as an educational challenge, but policy controls may be appropriate in some settings.

Thoughtful Consideration of the Various Constituencies Covered by Policy

There is a temptation to summarily ban weapons from campus. As with any other policy action, however, it is often more productive to discuss the impact of a proposed policy with the affected constituency. For example, banning weapons may overlook a campus Reserve Officers' Training Corps (ROTC) armory, or the fact that a campus trap and skeet club shoots at a local facility. If constituency groups will be affected by a weapons policy, one can often achieve greater compliance by inviting assistance from these groups in developing and implementing the policy.

Identification of Enforcement Authority

In many cases, the first line for enforcement of weapons policies is campus police departments. The following example from the College of Charleston illustrates this authority:

> Please notify our Campus Police . . . immediately if you witness or suspect possession of a weapon of any kind. Your help is invaluable in insuring the safety of all members of our community. Keeping our campus free from the tragedy of violence is a community effort. (College of Charleston, 2005, p. 1)

Similarly, from Stony Brook University:

> Intentional possession, or sale, of firearms or other weapons by anyone is strictly forbidden and is a violation of state and federal law as well as a violation of the student conduct code of rights and responsibilities. (Stony Brook University Police Department, 2005, p.1)

Boundaries for Acceptable Possession or Use

From Eastern Washington University:

> EWU residents may store two weapons at the Red Barn. Weapons brought to the Barn are to be unloaded, the weapon will be checked prior to acceptance. Any ammunition at the Red Barn will be in the original container,

clearly tagged with the owner's name and telephone number. You may transport your weapon from your vehicle to and from the Red Barn and your destination. Weapons must be in the trunk of your vehicle unloaded with the ammunition stored in a separate container. (Eastern Washington University, 2005, p. 1)

From the University of Arizona:

A request to use, possess, display or store a weapon on University property in connection with official University business must first be reviewed by the responsible Dean or Department Head. The Dean or Department Head may comment and shall forward the request to the Provost for review and comment. The request must then be forwarded to the Chief of Police of the University of Arizona Police Department in writing at least 10 days prior to the intended date of such use, possession, display or storage and must:

Identify the purpose of the request.
Identify how this request furthers the mission of the University.
Identify the weapon.
Identify the duration of the request.
Identify a responsible person.
Identify how the weapon will be secured.
Identify how the weapon will or may be used.
Penalties associated with policy infractions.
Procedures for allowable demonstration, possession, or storage of weapons.

The University of Arizona policy also accommodates weapons storage and use that may be a part of academic programs or shooting clubs and organizations. (University of Arizona Police Department, 2005, pp. 1–4)

Effective Policies Require Enforcement

Members of the community seem to feel safest in those environments where weapons are not observed on a regular basis. It is not clear whether the lack of weapons leads to a sense of safety or the general sense of safety negates the motivation for carrying weapons. In either case, the impact of weapons on the social and learning environment leads most campuses to take a strong policy stance regarding them.

Another dimension of weapons policy enforcement relates to the nature of the accountability for the various different populations on a campus. For instance, the student code of conduct is an obvious source of weapons policies. Faculty, staff, contractors, and visitors are also important populations to consider when discussing a weapons policy. For instance, if a contract employee working on a construction project violates a "no weapons on campus" policy, there are a number of important issues:

- Is the campus policy written to apply to all parties—visitors, students, staff, and others?
- Does the contracting language specifically include an expectation of adherence to these policies?
- Is the policy information reasonably available to contractors and their employees?
- What campus entity takes on the enforcement responsibility—and is it prepared to address these types of policy infractions?
- Has the policy been enforced consistently with other visitors?
- What is the basis for penalties or action taken with the individuals involved?
- Is there a deterrent effect or incentive for compliance?

Similar questions might be asked of employees or other types of visitors in regard to weapons situations. Working through the accountability and enforcement authority before an incident can be particularly important in making the policy effective.

Another potentially important dimension of enforcement is the level of communication between firearm licensing authorities and campus officials. For instance, in communities where a county sheriff issues concealed weapons permits, he or she often has the discretion to share this information with campus authorities. While the extent to which this is publicly available information varies across jurisdictions, it is generally possible to share this information among law enforcement agencies with a reasonable need to know. In practical terms, this means that campus officials may be able to follow up on rumors or emerging threats associated with weapons.

A specific component of the University of Puget Sound's Firearms/Weapons Policy, for example, defines the procedures for a search (University of Puget Sound, 2005). By anticipating the potential need to search offices, briefcases, bags, and vehicles, campus administrators have made policy implementation more likely to be effective.

Campus Outreach and Education

While a well-developed campus policy is a necessary foundation for an effective violence prevention strategy, most efforts to regulate behavior fail without some commitment to public education. A "no weapons" message is simple and increasingly consistent with policies in other schools and workplaces. Notices can be posted on building entrances, in orientation materials, and where visitors can easily see them. Vigorous public notice, along with occasional reminders in newsletters or news items, can be effective in ensuring that accidental policy violations are minimized. These efforts are important; however, to truly minimize weapons on campus, a more comprehensive effort can be developed on the basis of traditional community policing strategies.

Community Policing Models

Community policing is a well-developed philosophy of police operations (Community Oriented Policing Services, 2003). Community policing philosophies are founded on principles that include engaging community members in addressing community problems (Ledee, 2005). The principle of engagement transfers well to the emerging problem of weapons. As noted earlier, thoughtful creation of policy is a good foundation for a violence reduction program if it reflects the attitudes and feelings of the citizens. In this case, most citizens value an environment where weapons are not used to settle disputes. Campus officials can engage the campus population in processes of informal monitoring and support of the policy. Students and faculty often know about weapons that are brought to campus. If they have a sense of ownership over the campus and feel they can approach enforcement officials, then they are more likely to call violations to the attention of authorities before a weapon is displayed as part of a dispute. Without that sense of trust and cooperation, public reporting lags and policies become less effective. Developing this level of trust and cooperation demands a substantial commitment of resources (Community Oriented Policing Services, 2005).

The concept of engaging the community in the development and enforcement of policies reflecting their shared values is traditionally a hallmark of undergraduate residence halls. This continues to be the kind of environment where citizen-student awareness of and support for policies ensures that the community respects the policy.

Conclusion

Weapons challenge the traditional safety and security of college campuses. Families, students, staff, and visitors to campus have an expectation of safety and nonviolence. Many share the notion that campuses are a safe haven from the complicated and occasionally violent communities beyond their boundaries. Unfortunately, the experience of many campuses suggests that the contemporary campus is increasingly affected by many of the same challenges that occur in other communities. The presence of weapons and acts of violence are an unfortunate addition to the challenges of campus life.

While the typical campus is still safer than many of the communities surrounding it, the intrusion of weapons calls for leadership from campus administrators. Most campus policies have prohibited weapons possession, particularly among students. In recent years, campus policies have become more sophisticated, regulating weapons among faculty, staff, and visitors as well as among students. Policies increasingly recognize that instructional activities and public safety functions may require weapons and acknowledge these exceptions in their policies. In practice, the effectiveness of these policies can be substantially enhanced by involvement of the community and vigorous public education. Most campuses also share the challenge of increasing numbers of visitors coming to campus. These visitors may have little affiliation with the campus and, consequently, little incentive to comply with institutional regulations.

Campus administrators are responding to these challenges by creating more sophisticated policies, enhancing their attention to public safety services, and ensuring a sense of involvement in the campus commitment to a safe living-learning environment. Like many other challenges in campus life, the degree of student awareness and involvement are often powerful contributors to the success or failure of these efforts.

References

Bureau of Alcohol, Tobacco, Firearms and Explosives. (2005). *2005-26th Edition, ATFP. 5300.5 state laws and published ordinances—firearms*. Washington, DC: Author.

Bureau of Alcohol, Tobacco, Firearms and Explosives (2003). *Annual firearms manufacturing and export report*. Washington, DC: Author.

College of Charleston. (2005). *Weapons.* Retrieved October 10, 2005, from http://www.cofc.edu/publicsafety/helpfulinfo/weapons.php

Community Oriented Policing Services, U.S. Department of Justice. (2003). *Community oriented policing in action! A practitioner's eye view of organizational change.* Retrieved October 3, 2005, from http://www.cops.usdoj.gov/default.asp?Item = 893

Community Oriented Policing Services, U.S. Department of Justice (2005). *National summit on campus public safety, strategies for colleges and universities in a homeland security environment.* Washington, DC: Author.

Coyne-Beasley, T., Baccaglini, L., Johnson, R. M., Webster, B., & Wiebe, D. J. (2005). Do partners with children know about firearms in their home? Evidence of a gender gap and implications for practitioners. *Pediatrics, 115*(6), e662–e667.

Eastern Washington University (2005). *Weapons on campus.* Retrieved September 16, 2005, from http://www.ewu.edu/x7005.xml

Federal Bureau of Investigation (FBI), U.S. Department of Justice. (2003a). *2003 crime in the United States.* Table 2.8, Murder, Types of Weapons Used, Percent Distribution by Region, 2003.

Federal Bureau of Investigation (FBI), U.S. Department of Justice. (2003b). *2003 crime in the United States.* Table 2.9, Murder Victims by Weapon 1999–2003.

Federal Bureau of Investigation (FBI), U.S. Department of Justice. (2003c). *2003 crime in the United States.* Table 2.12, Murder Circumstances by Weapon, 2003.

Federal Bureau of Investigation (FBI), U.S. Department of Justice (2005). *Law enforcement officers killed & assaulted 2004.* Table 28, Law Enforcement Officers Feloniously Killed.

Hemenway, D., Azrael, D., & Miller, M. (2001). National attitudes concerning gun carrying in the United States. *Injury Prevention, 7*(4), 282–285.

Kachur, S. P., Stennies, G. M., Powell, K. E., Modzeleski, W., Stephens, R., Murphy, R., et al., (1996). School-associated violent deaths in the United States, 1992 to 1994. *Journal of the American Medical Association 275*(22), 1729–1733.

Kieck, G. D. (2005). Firearms, violence, and self-protection. *Science, 309*(5741), 1675–1676.

Ledee, M., (2005). Building relationships between university police, student affairs, and the campus community. *Student Affairs Law and Policy Weekly, 2*(6), 1–4.

Lockyer, B. (2005). *California firearms laws, California Department of Justice.* Retrieved September 16, 2005, from http://www.ag.ca.gov

Miller, M., Hemenway, D., & Wechsler, H. (1999). Guns at college. *Journal of American College Health, 48*(1), 7–12.

Miller, M., Hemenway, D., & Wechsler, H. (2002). Guns and gun threats at college. *Journal of American College Health, 51*(2), 57–65.

Pennsylvania State University (2000). *Penn State Pulse: Guns and weapons on campus*. University Park, PA: Pennsylvania State University Division of Student Affairs.

Presley, C. A., Meilman, P. W., & Cashin, J. R. (1997). Weapon carrying and substance abuse among college students. *Journal of the American College Health Association*, *46*(1), 3–8.

Stony Brook University Police Department. (2005). *Weapons on campus*. Retrieved September 16, 2005, from http://www.sunysb.edu/police/weapons.shtml

University of Arizona Police Department. (2005). *Weapons on campus*. Retrieved September 12, 2005, from http://www.uapd.arizona.edu/weapons%20on%20campous%20info%20for%20web.pdf

University of North Carolina-Charlotte. (2001). *Weapons on campus*. Retrieved September 12, 2005, from http://www.legal.uncc.edu/policies/ps-32.html

University of Puget Sound. (2002). *Firearms/weapons on campus*. Retrieved September 12, 2005, from http://www2.ups.edu/humanresources/zzzz/manual/cplcy FireArms.htm

University of Texas at Austin Police Department. (2003). *Weapons on campus*. Retrieved September 12, 2005, from http://www.utexas.edu/police/prevention/weapons.html

U.S. Department of Education. (2003). *Illegal weapons possessions*. Retrieved September 16, 2005, from http://www.ed.gov/admins/lead/safety/crimedisciplines/edllite-weapviolations.html

11

THE LEGAL IMPLICATIONS OF CAMPUS CRIME FOR STUDENT AFFAIRS PROFESSIONALS

John Wesley Lowery

As institutions of higher education and divisions of student affairs seek to address campus safety issues, it is vital that compliance with federal laws and attention to institutional liability be carefully considered. This chapter examines these legal implications of campus crime for student affairs professionals. When considering compliance with federal laws, at least three main areas must be carefully considered:

- Jeanne Clery Disclosure of Campus Security and Campus Crime Statistics Act (1990),
- Family Educational Rights and Privacy Act (1974), and
- Drug-Free Schools and Communities Act of 1989.

In addition to considering compliance, institutions should carefully consider institutional legal liability, particularly issues related to institutions' potential liability for the criminal acts of third parties. This chapter discusses the roles of specific student affairs functional areas in responding to campus crime.

Compliance with Federal Laws

Jeanne Clery Disclosure of Campus Security Policy and Campus Crime Statistics Act (1990)

In April 1986, Jeanne Clery was raped and murdered by another student in her residence hall room at Lehigh University. Her parents, Howard and

Connie Clery, came to blame Lehigh University for their daughter's death, alleging that the university had hidden facts about campus crime. They concluded, "Our daughter died because of what she didn't know" (Clery & Clery, 2001). The Clery family brought a lawsuit against Lehigh University, which was ultimately settled out of court. After settling the lawsuit, Connie and Howard Clery founded Security On Campus, Inc., to address the following goals:

- To educate prospective students, parents, and the campus community about the prevalence of crime on our nation's college and university campuses
- To compassionately assist victims and their families with guidance pertaining to laws, victims' organizations, legal counsel, and access to Security On Campus, Inc., files
- To foster security improvements through campus community initiatives
- To provide effective procedures and programs to reduce alcohol and drug abuse (*About Security On Campus*, 2002)

Security On Campus was initially successful in having legislation passed at the state level in Pennsylvania and then succeeded in having legislation passed at the federal level. In 1990, Congress passed the Student Right-to-Know and Campus Security Act. The portions of the act related to campus safety were formally renamed the Jeanne Clery Disclosure of Campus Security Policy and Campus Crime Statistics Act in 1998.

Compliance with the Jeanne Clery Disclosure of Campus Security Policy and Campus Crime Statistics Act (1990) is far more complicated than Security On Campus and other advocates have recognized. Part of the complexity of compliance stems from great variability in American higher education and the limited guidance provided by the U.S. Department of Education (U.S. General Accounting Office, 1997). Gregory and Janosik (2002) noted that the task of compliance was further complicated by the repeated amendments to the legislation after its initial passage. The problem of limited guidance on compliance with the legislation was addressed in large with the publication of *The Handbook of Campus Crime Reporting* by the U.S. Department of Education (ED) in 2005. This handbook is the single best guide for compliance with the Jeanne Clery Disclosure of Campus Security Policy and Campus Crime Statistics Act. A copy has been sent to all institutions of higher education required to comply with the act, and the full document is available through the ED's website (http://www.ed.gov/ admins/lead/safety/campus.html).

The U.S. Department of Education (ED, 2005) summarized compliance with the Jeanne Clery Disclosure of Campus Security Policy and Campus Crime Statistics Act in the following terms:

> Compliance with the *Clery Act* is not simply a matter of entering statistics into a Web site or publishing a brochure once a year. Compliance is a whole system of developing policy statements, gathering information from all the required sources and translating it into the appropriate categories, disseminating information, and, finally, keeping records. Many people at your institution—from the president on down—should be involved. (p. 1)

Given these complexities of compliance, it is impossible to cover every possible situation that might arise in meeting the requirements of law. However, this chapter seeks to outline the broad requirements of the law.

The requirement of the Clery Act with which student affairs professionals are most familiar is the Annual Security Report. All higher education institutions that participate in any federal financial aid program are required to publish an Annual Security Report by October 1 of each year. This Annual Security Report must be sent to each current student and employee, and a summary of the report must be shared with prospective students and employees. In 1999, the regulations were changed to allow institutions to meet most, but not all, of its distribution requirements by publishing their Annual Security Report on the Internet. Institutions seeking to meet their requirements through use of the Internet are still required to send notice of availability of the annual report and a summary of its contents to all current students and employees. The ED (2005) has offered the following sample notice of availability:

> A copy of [name of institution's] Annual Security Report. This report includes statistics for the previous three years concerning reported crimes that occurred on-campus; in certain off-campus buildings or property owned or controlled by [name of institution]; and on public property within, or immediately adjacent to and accessible from, the campus. The report also includes institutional policies concerning campus security, such as policies concerning sexual assault, and other matters. You can obtain a copy of this

report by contacting [name of office] or by accessing the following website [address of website]. (p. 113)

For many institutions of higher education, using the Internet to distribute the Annual Security Report is a far more cost-effective method of sharing this information. Some institutions have gone so far as to stop printing an annual report and only printing the materials from the website upon request.

The Annual Security Report must contain disclosures of various policies related to campus safety. To meet the requirements of the law fully, institutions must develop the policies themselves and provide required disclosures. The Appendix lists the policy disclosures that must be included in the Annual Security Report, and a number of these required policy disclosures are directly related to student affairs practice and specific functional areas traditionally associated with divisions of student affairs.

Student affairs professionals should carefully consider whether student affairs offices are, or should be, listed as individuals to whom crimes on campus should be reported. Residence life professionals should be involved in the development of policies regarding access to campus residence halls. Counseling center staff should be involved in the discussion of whether to adopt a policy under which counselors inform clients who report being victims of crime of their voluntary, confidential reporting options. The regulations do not require that institutions have a policy of this type; instead, they only require that the institution disclose whether such a policy exists. Many offices within student affairs may well be involved in programming related to crime prevention, including orientation, student activities, and residence life. The Greek life staff should be knowledgeable about and involved in the development of policies regarding monitoring criminal activity occurring in off-campus housing locations of recognized student groups, as the vast majorities of these facilities are fraternity and sorority houses.

Staff in alcohol and drug programs should be involved in meeting the requirements related to alcohol and drug education. Student judicial affairs professionals have very specific requirements when addressing sexual assault allegations. Under the Clery Act, institutions are required to provide for both the accused and the accuser to have the same rights to have others present during the hearing and to be involved in the final outcome of the disciplinary proceeding. Residence life staff also need to be involved in helping the institution assist victims of sexual assault to change their living arrangements upon request. Members of the division of student affairs at the highest

levels should be involved in discussion regarding the development of appropriate policies for handling situations that arise when students or employees
are registered sex offenders.

Higher education institutions are also required to collect crime data and
present them for the preceding three calendar years in the Annual Security
Report. Data must be collected for all reports to campus security authorities
and local polices of the following crimes: criminal homicide, including murder and non-negligent or negligent manslaughter; sex offenses including
forcible and nonforcible; robbery; aggravated assault; burglary; motor vehicle
theft; and arson. Institutions must also collect information about any of the
crimes listed above or any other crimes involving bodily injury that were hate
crimes. Furthermore, data must also be collected for arrests and referrals for
disciplinary action for illegal weapons possession and violation of drug and
liquor laws.

The definition of campus security authority for the purposes of collecting crime statistics is very broad and includes almost all student affairs professionals. In addition to campus police and individuals listed in the Annual
Security Report, the definition of campus security authority includes:

> An official of an institution who has significant responsibility for student
> and campus activities, including, but not limited to, student housing, stu-
> dent discipline and campus judicial proceedings. An official is defined as
> any person who has the authority and the duty to take action or respond
> to particular issues on behalf of the institution. (ED, 2005, pp. 49–50)

The only student affairs staff members likely to be excluded from this definition are licensed counselors acting within the scope of their licensure, medical professionals providing health care, and administrative support staff. The
institution should develop a system to collect these data from all staff within
the definition of campus security authorities and should provide training to
these staff members regarding their obligations.

Within the Annual Security Report, the crime data for the preceding
three calendar years must be presented. Institutions are required to provide
these data for the following geographic areas: on campus, residence halls,
noncampus building or property, and public property. The ED defines as on
campus,

> Buildings and property that are in the same general location and that fit
> into one of two types: a) owned or controlled by the school and used to

meet or support the school's educational purposes . . . b) owned but not controlled by the school, frequented by students, and used to support the institution's purposes. (pp. 12–13)

Under the regulations, crime statistics for residence halls on campus are double-counted in both the on-campus and the residence hall categories, which are subsets of on-campus. Noncampus building or property includes "Any building or property owned or controlled by a student organization that is officially recognized by the institution" (p. 13) as well as "any building or property owned or controlled by an institution that is used in direct support of, or in relation to, the institution's educational purposes, is frequently used by students, and is not within the same reasonably contiguous geographic area of the institution" (p. 14). However, in presenting information about hate crimes, the regulations allow an institution to provide a narrative summary of the reported hate crimes, including the location and category of prejudice (e.g., victim's race, gender, religion, sexual orientation, ethnicity/national origin, or disability).

Institutions have ongoing reporting obligations in addition to the Annual Security Report. Under the timely reporting requirement, institutions must report all Clery Act crimes that are "considered by the institution to represent a serious or continuing threat to students and employees" (p. 61). The regulations do not specify the form timely warnings must take, but do require that the "notice must be timely and reasonably likely to reach the entire campus community and aid in the prevention of similar crimes" (p. 62). Approaches used by institutions vary greatly and include fliers, ads in the student newspaper, notices on the institution's website, and e-mail messages to the campus community. All institutions with a campus police or security office are also required to maintain an open campus police log, which must contain information about all crimes, not just those required for statistical reporting or reported to the campus police or security office.

The elements of the police log include the nature of the crime; when the crime was reported; the date and time the crime occurred; the general location of the crime; and the disposition of the complaint, if known. Generally, this information should be available within two business days of receiving the report, but the regulations allow for the release to be delayed if release would:

- jeopardize an ongoing investigation;
- jeopardize the safety of an individual;
- cause a suspect to flee or evade detection; or
- result in the destruction of evidence. (ED, 2005, p. 70)

The reporting requirement for the campus police log is more limited than that for general crime statistics.

The ED (2005) has the authority to fine institutions for noncompliance with the Clery Act. Institutions may be fined up to $27,500 for each "substantial misrepresentation of the number, location or nature of the crimes required to be reported" (p. 7). While fines have been rare, the ED recently reached a settlement in the complaint filed against Salem International University in which the institution agreed to pay a fine of $200,000 over five years (Brush, 2005).

There has been only limited research on the impact of the Clery Act. Janosik (2001) and Janosik and Gehring (2001) found that publication of the Annual Security Report had virtually no impact on student behavior, but they did note that other activities, educational programming and timely reports, did lead some students to change their behavior to better protect themselves. Given the report's stated purposes, Fisher, Hartman, Cullen, and Turner (2002) concluded, "In the end, the intentions of the Clery Act were a noble step toward providing the campus community with information about the extent of crime and the institutional response. In practice, however, the actual results of the Clery Act have been more symbolic than substantive" (p. 89).

Family Educational Rights and Privacy Act (1974)

While clearly the Jeanne Clery Disclosure of Campus Security Policy and Campus Crime Statistics Act (1990) is the most significant piece of federal legislation related to campus safety, the impact of the Family Educational Rights and Privacy Act (FERPA) (1974) should also be considered. Since the passage of the Clery Act, there has been considerable debate regarding the protections afforded to student disciplinary records under FERPA (Lowery, 2004). Several state supreme courts (*Red & Black Publishing Co. v. Board of Regents*, 1993; *State ex rel The Miami Student v. Miami University*, 1997) determined that FERPA was not intended to protect student disciplinary records and ordered the release of records under state open-records laws. However, a number of other courts declined to reach this conclusion (*DTH v. University of North Carolina at Chapel Hill*, 1998; *Shreveport Professional Chapter of the Society of Professional Journalists and Michelle Millhollon v. Louisiana State University et al.*, 1994; *The Burlington Free Press v. University of Vermont*, 2001). Many advocates for greater media access to these records had originally predicted that other states would reach similar decisions to the Georgia high court's (Gregory, 1998).

Ultimately, the federal government brought suit against Miami University and Ohio State University to prevent those institutions from complying with the Ohio supreme court's ruling (*United States v. Miami Univ.*, 2002). The Court of Appeals for the Sixth Circuit upheld the district court's ruling and determined:

- FERPA prohibits the release of education records.
- Disciplinary records are education records.
- There is no First Amendment right of access to student disciplinary records.
- Student disciplinary records are not criminal in nature.
- Public access might be harmful to the disciplinary process.
- The public interest in crime prevention does not require open records.

This decision would seem to put rest debate about whether student disciplinary records are protected under FERPA.

There were also numerous amendments to FERPA in the 1990s allowing greater access to student education records related to campus safety. First in 1990, the Clery Act included an amendment to FERPA allowing release of the final results of disciplinary proceedings to the victim of an alleged crime of violence. In 1992, FERPA was amended to exclude from the definition of education records the records of a law enforcement unit. Two significant additional changes were included in the Higher Education Amendments of 1998. FERPA was amended to allow for the release of final results of disciplinary proceedings to the public when an accused student was found responsible for a crime of violence or a nonforcible sex offense. The other change to FERPA allowed the release of information about underage students' alcohol and drug offenses to their parents or legal guardians (Lowery,

1998, 1999, 2000, 2004). Following this change, almost half of the institutions surveyed in 2000 and 2002 had implemented some form parental notification policy (Lowery, Palmer, & Gehring, 2005; Palmer, Lohman, Gehring, Carlson, & Garrett, 2001; Palmer, Lowery, Wilson, & Gehring, 2003). There continue to be calls for additional changes to FERPA to allow even greater access to student disciplinary records.

Drug-Free Schools and Communities Act (1989)

The Drug-Free Schools and Communities Act of 1989 requires that higher education institutions distribute information annually to college students about alcohol and other drugs. The requirements of the Jeanne Clery Disclosure of Campus Security Policy and Campus Crime Statistics Act (1990) regarding alcohol and other drugs are, in fact, the same. However, institutions are also required to conduct a biennial review of alcohol and drug programs that has two primary objectives:

1. To determine the effectiveness of, and to implement any needed changes to, the alcohol and other drugs (AOD) program
2. To ensure that disciplinary sanctions for violating standards of conduct are enforced consistently

The biennial review represents an opportunity to formally assess the institution's efforts in this important area.

Institutional Liability for Crime on Campus

Since the Massachusetts Supreme Court's ruling in *Mullins v. Pine Manor College* (1983), institutions have been deeply concerned about institutions' potential legal liability for the criminal activity of third parties. In *Mullins*, the court found Pine Manor College legally liable for the rape of an undergraduate student by an unknown assailant. The *Mullins* case stood in stark contrast to the legal trend of that era to reject virtually any legal liability for institutions—a trend best characterized by *Bradshaw v. Rawlings* (1979). Bickel and Lake (1999) characterized this period as the "no-duty-to-student bystander" (p. 105) era.

The emerging student/university relationship has been described by

Bickel and Lake (1999) as the rise of the duty era. Bickel and Lake summarized their assessment of this transitional period:

> One fact appears clear: The duty era has effectively ended almost all aspects of college insularity except with respect to alcohol use on and off campus. The pendulum has swung away from extreme student freedom models. The duty era has been an implicit search for a balance between university authority and student freedom and for shared responsibility for student/safety risk. (p. 157)

In considering whether to assign liability to an institution, Bickel and Law identified seven relevant factors the courts consider:

1. foreseeability of harm;
2. nature of the risk;
3. closeness of the connection between the college's act or omission and student injury;
4. moral blame and responsibility;
5. the social policy of preventing future harm (whether finding duty will tend to present future harm);
6. the burden on the university and the larger community if duty is recognized; and
7. the availability of insurance. (p. 202)

The authors suggested a conceptualization of the role of the university in the arena of campus safety—the Facilitator University. Each institution that embraces this model is "especially sensitive to the risk it creates when it aggregates students in collective situations" (p. 203) and seeks to "use reasonable care to prevent foreseeable risks" (p. 203).

Nero v. Kansas State University (1993) is an instructive example of how the courts consider these factors. In *Nero*, the Kansas Supreme Court considered the duty owed by the university to residential students and the university's duty to address foreseeable risks, including those posed by other students (Kaplin & Lee, 1995, 1997). The *Nero* court noted,

> We emphasize that a university is not an insurer of the safety of its students. Nonetheless, a university has a duty of reasonable care to protect a

student against certain dangers, including criminal actions against a student by another student or a third party if the criminal act is reasonably foreseeable and within the university's control. (p. 780)

The lesson to be drawn from these cases is not that colleges and universities are liable for every unfortunate incident to befall students. Instead, institutions must acknowledge some shared responsibility and develop reasonable responses to these foreseeable risks. Bickel and Lake noted:

> A facilitator model embraces appropriate opportunities to supervise student activities and affairs and interact with students. By following a no-duty paradigm and intervening only after injury occurred, the modern university increasingly distanced itself from students in the day to day ways that prevent danger . . . The lesson of *Beach* [1986] should not be to become uninvolved but to foster strong involvement with students in ways that can prevent harm. (p. 199)

This shared responsibility on the part of the institution will certainly include properly maintaining its facilities and addressing dangerous alcohol abuse on campus. Bickel and Lake (1999) stressed that this model is not a return to the *in loco parentis* mentality of the past, but a middle ground between the extreme views of the institution as parent or as bystander.

Conclusion

Over the past two decades, the traditional view of college and university campuses as idyllic safe havens from the crime that besets the outside world has been shattered. Lawsuits and tragic cases, which gave rise to legislative proposals, have certainly contributed to this changing view. However, the very statistics collected under the Jeanne Clery Disclosure of Campus Security Policy and Campus Crime Statistics Act (1990) have demonstrated that college and university campuses are generally safer than their surrounding communities (Volkwein, Szelest, & Lizotte, 1995). The ED reached a similar conclusion in a 2001 report to Congress mandated by the Higher Education Amendments of 1998. After reviewing the 1999 data regarding location, the report noted, "The data collected suggest that students are safest while on campus" (p. 11). After reviewing the data, the ED (2001) concluded,

The campus crime statistics collected by the U.S. Department of Education suggest that our nation's college campuses are safe. In nearly every category of crime for which data were collected, college campuses show lower incidence of crime than comparable data for the national as a whole. (p. 13)

To address the serious issue of crime on campus effectively, institutions should seek to ensure compliance with both the letter and spirit of the federal laws related to campus safety—a task made easier with the release of *The Handbook of Campus Crime Reporting*. Furthermore, by implementing the strategies discussed in this book, institutions can move toward the vision of the facilitator university articulated by Bickel and Lake (1999).

References

About Security On Campus, Inc. (2002). Retrieved October 29, 2005 from http://www .securityoncampus.org/aboutsoc/index.html

Beach v. Univ. of Utah, 726 P.2d 413 (Utah 1986).

Bickel, R. D., & Lake, P. F. (1999). *The rights and responsibilities of the modern university: Who assumes the risks of college life?* Durham, NC: Carolina Academic Press.

Bradshaw v. Rawlings, 612 F.2d 135 (3d Cir., 1979).

Brush, S. (2005, May 13). University to pay $200,000 in fines for not reporting campus crimes. *Chronicle of Higher Education*, A20.

The Burlington Free Press v. University of Vermont, 779 A.2d 60 (Vt. 2001).

United States v. Miami Univ., 294 F.3d 797 (6th Cir. 2002).

Clery, C., & Clery, H. (2001). *What Jeanne didn't know*. Retrieved October 29, 2005, from http://www.securityoncampus.org/aboutsoc/didntknow.html

Drug-Free Schools and Communities Act, 20 U.S.C. § 1011i (1989).

DTH v. University of North Carolina at Chapel Hill, 496 S.E.2d 8 (N.C. App.1998).

Family Educational Rights and Privacy Act (FERPA), 20 U.S.C. § 1232g (1974).

Fisher, B. S., Hartman, J. L., Cullen, F. T., & Turner, M. G. (2002). Making campuses safer for students: The Clery Act as a symbolic legal reform. *Stetson Law Review*, *32*, 61–89.

Gregory, D. E. (1998). Student judicial records, privacy, and the press's right to know. In B. G. Paterson & W. L. Kibler (Eds.), *The administration of student discipline: Student, organizational, and community issues* (pp. 55–73). Asheville, NC: College Administration Publications.

Gregory, D. E., & Janosik, S. M. (2002). The Clery Act: How effective is it? Perceptions from the field—The current state of the research and recommendations for improvement of the act and campus safety. *Stetson Law Review, 32,* 7–59.

Higher Education Amendments of 1998, 112 Stat. 1581 (1998).

Janosik, S. M. (2001). The impact of the Crime Awareness Act of 1998 on student decision-making. *NASPA Journal, 38,* 348–360.

Janosik, S. M., & Gehring, D. D. (2001). The impact of the Jeanne Clery Disclosure of Campus Security Policy and Campus Crime Statistics Act on student behavior. *EPI Policy Paper* Number 10. Blacksburg, VA: Virginia Polytechnic Institute and State University.

Jeanne Clery Disclosure of Campus Security Policy and Campus Crime Statistics Act [originally passed as part of The Student Right-to-Know and Campus Security Act of 1990], 20 U.S.C. § 1092 (1990).

Kaplin, W. A., & Lee, B. A. (1995). *The law of higher education* (3rd ed.). San Francisco: Jossey-Bass.

Kaplin, W. A., & Lee, B. A. (1997). *A legal guide for student affairs professionals.* San Francisco: Jossey-Bass.

Lowery, J. W. (1998, Fall). Balancing students' right to privacy with the public's right to know. *Synthesis: Law and Policy in Higher Education, 10,* 713–715, 730.

Lowery, J. W. (1999, Fall). Understanding and applying the Campus Security Act. *Synthesis: Law and Policy in Higher Education, 11,* 785–787, 799–800.

Lowery, J. W. (2000, Fall). FERPA and the Campus Security Act: Law and policy overview. *Synthesis: Law and Policy in Higher Education, 12,* 849–851, 864.

Lowery, J. W. (2004). Battling over Buckley: The press and access to student disciplinary records. In D. Bakst & S. Burgess (Eds.), *Student privacy review: An annual review and compendium for higher education leaders* (pp. 40–45). Palm Beach Gardens, FL: Council on Law in Higher Education.

Lowery, J. W., Palmer, C., & Gehring, D. D. (2005). Policies and practices of parental notification for student alcohol violations. *NASPA Journal, 42,* 415–429.

Mullins v. Pine Manor College, 449 N.E. 2d 331 (Mass. 1983).

Nero v. Kansas State University, 861 P.2d 768 (Kan. 1993).

Palmer, C. J., Lohman, G., Gehring, D. D., Carlson, S., & Garrett, O. (2001). Parental notification: A new strategy to reduce alcohol abuse on campus. *NASPA Journal, 38,* 372–385.

Palmer, C. J., Lowery, J. W., Wilson, M. E., & Gehring, D. D. (2003). Parental notification policies, practices, and impacts in 2002 and 2003. *Journal of College and University Student Housing, 31*(2), 3–6.

Red & Black Publishing Co. v. Board of Regents, 427 S.E.2d 257 (Ga. 1993).

Shreveport Professional Chapter of the Society of Professional Journalists and Michelle Millhollon v. Louisiana State University et al. (La. Dist. Ct., Caddo Parish, March 4, 1994).

State ex rel. The Miami Student v. Miami Univ., 680 N.E.2d 956 (Ohio, 1997), cert. denied 118 S. Ct. 616 (1997).

U.S. Department of Education (ED). (2005). *The handbook of campus crime reporting*. Washington, DC: Author.

U.S. Department of Education (ED), Office of Postsecondary Education, Policy, Planning, and Innovation. (2001). *The incidence of crime on the campuses of U.S. postsecondary education institutions*. Washington, DC: Author.

U.S. General Accounting Office. (1997). *Campus crime: Difficulties meeting federal reporting requirements* (GAO Publication No. GAO/HEHS-97-52). Washington, DC: Author.

Volkwein, J. F., Szelest, B., & Lizotte, A. (1995). The relationship of campus crime to campus and student characteristics. *Research in Higher Education. 36*, 647–670.

Appendix

Disclosure of Policy Statements

I.   Procedures for reporting crimes and other emergencies.
  a. Timely warnings
  b. Policies for preparing the annual disclosure of crime statistics
  c. Titles of persons to whom crimes should be reported. This statement must also disclose whether the institution has any policies or procedures that allow victims or witnesses to report crimes on a voluntary, confidential basis for inclusion in the annual disclosure of crime statistics, and, if so, a description of those policies and procedures.

II. Policies concerning security of and access to campus facilities, including campus residences, and security considerations used in the maintenance of campus facilities.

III. Policies concerning campus law enforcement including:
  a. Enforcement authority
    i. Relationship with local and state police
    ii. Arrest authority
  b. Policies and procedures encouraging accurate and prompt reporting of all crimes to campus police and local police.
  c. Policy encouraging pastoral and professional counselors to inform clients

of voluntary, confidential crime reporting procedures. If no such policy exists, that must be disclosed.

IV. Programs to inform students and employees about campus safety procedures and to encourage students and employees to be responsible for themselves and others with regard to safety.
   a. Types of programs
   b. Frequency of programs

V. Programs to inform students and employees about crime prevention.

VI. Policy concerning the monitoring and recording through local police agencies of criminal activity in which students are engaged at off-campus locations of student organizations, officially recognized by the institution, including student organizations with off-campus housing facilities.

VII. Policy regarding the possession, use, and sale of alcoholic beverages and enforcement of State underage drinking laws.

VIII. Policy regarding the possession, use, and sale of illegal drugs and enforcement of Federal and State drug laws.

IX. A description of any drug or alcohol-abuse education programs. An institution may cross-reference the materials the institution uses to comply with Drug Free Schools and Community Act Amendments.

X. A statement of policy regarding the institution's campus sexual assault programs to prevent sex offenses, and procedures to follow when a sex offense occurs.
   a. A description of educational programs to promote the awareness of rape, acquaintance rape, and other forcible and nonforcible sex offenses.
   b. Procedures students should follow if a sex offense occurs, including:
      i. Who should be contacted,
      ii. The importance of preserving evidence for the proof of a criminal offense, and
      iii. To whom the alleged offense should be reported.
   c. Information on a student's option to notify appropriate law enforcement authorities, including on-campus and local police, and a statement that institutional personnel will assist the student in notifying these authorities, if the student requests the assistance of these personnel.
   d. Notification to students of existing on- and off-campus counseling, mental health, or other student services for victims of sex offenses.
   e. Notification to students that the institution will change a victim's academic and living situations after an alleged sex offense and of the availability of those changes, if requested and reasonably available.
   f. Procedures for campus disciplinary action in cases of an alleged sex offense, including a clear statement that:

      i.   The accuser and the accused are entitled to the same opportunities to have others present during a disciplinary proceeding.

     ii. Both the accuser and the accused must be informed of the outcome of any institutional disciplinary proceeding brought alleging a sex offense.

  g. Sanctions the institution may impose following a final determination of an institutional disciplinary proceeding regarding rape, acquaintance rape, or other forcible or nonforcible sex offenses.

XI. Statement advising the campus community as to where information provided by the state listing registered sex offenders who are students and/or employees may be obtained.

INSTITUTIONAL RESOURCES

12

EXEMPLAR PROGRAMS AND PROCEDURES

Best Practices in Public Safety

Jerry D. Stewart and John H. Schuh

olleges and universities in this country have 11,000 full-time peace officers with arrest powers and another 9,000 without arrest powers (Deisinger, Cychosz, & Jaeger, 1998). These officers and the police agencies they represent endeavor to provide places where students, faculty, staff, and others can go about their daily activities in an atmosphere of safety and security. Our view is that without such law enforcement officers, no matter how effective or creative the other members of the campus community are with regard to providing for a safe community, people and property are at risk. The lack of a modern law enforcement agency is a fatal flaw in a comprehensive campus safety strategy, and if institutional members do not "feel free from threat fear and anxiety, attempts at other more advanced learning goals will likely fail" (Strange, 2003, p. 310). In preparing this chapter, we assume that virtually all institutions of higher education have some form of a police agency, and that by having such an agency on campus, "The law recognizes that if an institution voluntarily renders a service for the protection of another and the other person relies on that service, reasonable care must be exercised in providing it" (Prosser 1971, cited in Gehring, 2000, p. 351).

We address this contemporary public safety issue from two perspectives. First, Jerry Stewart is the director of a comprehensive, sophisticated campus law enforcement agency. He has dedicated his career to providing a campus environment where students, faculty, staff, and others can go about their daily business in an atmosphere that is as safe and secure as human beings can provide. John Schuh is a faculty member who spent 27 years as a student affairs administrator. During that time, he worked closely with police agencies on three campuses.

The purpose of this chapter is to discuss selected best practices in public safety on college campuses. It examines contextual issues that frame the environment in which campus police agencies work and discusses how the effectiveness of public safety agencies can be measured. Ideas related to practice and resources are provided as well.

Contextual Factors

Three contextual factors influence the nature of public safety practices: the nature of the institution (e.g., public or private); its location—the extent to which students commute to the campus or are residents of the institution; and its surrounding area. Each of these factors is discussed in more detail in the following sections.

Public or Private?

The corporate nature of the institution, meaning that it is either a public or a private institution, influences the nature of public safety practices. For example, an institution that is operated by a state very well may be considered to be state property for legal purposes. That would imply that certain police agencies could conduct their work as they would on all state property, including parks, highways, and other forms of state property. The campus police agency could be an independent agency or it could be, in a legal sense, an arm of the state police or the county sheriff's department. Alternatively, it also could be a freestanding agency with police authority similar to that of a municipal police department or other political entity.

A private college or university may have a public safety arm that is organized differently from what is found at a state-operated institution. For example, the safety department may not include peace officers with authority similar to the local police department or sheriff's office. Laws vary from state to state, but when a public safety department with police authority is necessary because of the dynamics of the campus, the agency has to meet certain requirements to be empowered. The campus public safety department has to go through a rigorous process to be authorized to exercise police authority (see Indiana University Police Department, 2006; University of Colorado at Boulder, 2006; University of New Mexico Police Department, 2006; University of Texas at Austin Police Department, 2006), to include such actions as arrests, investigations of crimes, and so on. Certainly the days of "night watchmen" at many colleges and universities are past, but when a modern public safety department is desired, the institution has to do more than simply announcing that it has one. In addition, after being authorized to have a public safety department with full police powers, the institution may need to develop agreements with local police agencies (e.g., city police and the sheriff's department) so that activities of mutual interest can be as seamless as possible. That might include, but would not be limited to, pursuit of potential criminals, investigations on- and off-campus, and other areas of mutual interest.

Location

Where a college or university is located influences the nature of the security services provided, since violent crimes against persons are more common in metropolitan statistical areas, and property crimes and burglary are more common in cities outside metropolitan statistical areas (Federal Bureau of Investigation [FBI], 2004). For example, an institution in a rural location may have to deal with different kinds of issues from those facing one located in an urban or suburban area. Additionally, exigencies related to location can require adjustments in the kinds of security services that are provided.

Urban locations may present a variety of security challenges for a college or university because of the nature of violent crimes committed in these areas, as referenced above. For example, open events, that is, events that do not require a ticket or other form of admission, may attract a variety of people from the urban area, which may be exactly what event planners desire. Large numbers of attendees can mean everything from parking problems, to having emergency medical personnel available on short notice, to crowd control issues. Urban areas also may require certain security measures such as locking buildings early at night and on the weekends to protect institutional property and individuals who use laboratories or offices when buildings are relatively empty.

Urban locations also may require extra care in supervising parking lots, wooded areas, or other dimensions of the campus where crimes might be committed against persons. While this is the case regardless of where a campus is located, extra work needs to be done with newcomers to the campus community to explain how they can take advantage of security services that are available to them. These might include escort services from buildings to their vehicles, how to use emergency call boxes where a direct call can be placed to the campus police department, or how to take advantage of other services such as vehicular assistance when their cars do not start or they encounter other problems.

Rural locations may not attract as many people from the surrounding community as urban locations do, but that does not mean security services are any less important. Students may choose to walk to the local community at night and need assistance to return to campus. Sometimes campuses in rural areas seem so safe that members of the campus community are not as vigilant as they ought to be in terms of locking offices, dormitory rooms, and other areas where valuables are kept. Therefore, the challenges at rural institutions may not appear to be as great in a day-to-day sense, but they require no less vigilance.

Some aspects of an institution's location have special campus security requirements. For example, one of the authors worked on a campus where a major railroad line ran on the southern perimeter of the campus close to a residence complex. Consequently, during warm weather months people riding in boxcars would disembark at the residence halls and break in to spend the night or worse. This situation warranted extra security services and constant reminders to students who lived on that part of the campus to pay attention to people who were not residents and to call the campus police department if they noticed people who did not appear to belong there.

A corollary to campus location is the special events that are unique to a campus. For example, at some colleges and universities, Halloween is a major event that attracts many visitors to the campus. At other institutions, a spring festival attracts a large number of visitors. In other cases, winning a major athletic event can trigger a celebration that, if not planned for carefully, can result in injuries to people and damage to property.

Residential or Commuter?

Residential institutions present a series of challenges for security services. Our definition of "residential" is when a large percentage of the student body lives in campus housing or in residences within a short walk from campus. With so many people living in close proximity to one another, there is the potential for crimes against persons. Students often leave the exterior doors to their residence halls open when they are supposed to be locked, or they prop them open so others can get into the buildings. They also tend to leave the doors to their rooms open. The consequence of this behavior may result in certain problems. Theft from campus residence hall rooms occurs and, in the worst cases, crimes against persons are possible. So at least two general approaches (i.e., education and direct services) to providing security services need to be provided in a residential environment.

Education. First, students need to be given strategies they can use to protect their property and themselves. The educational process is an excellent opportunity for a partnership to form between the campus police department and residence life staff. Everything, from table tents in dining halls, to hanging notices on student room doors, to holding floor meetings related to security services, is an element to remind students that they need to be careful about how they protect themselves and their property. In addition, electronic messages can be sent to students during times of high activity, such as just before breaks in the academic calendar, to remind them to take appropriate measures.

Direct services. Second, the campus police department can provide direct services to students, such as foot patrols in parking lots adjacent to residence halls, assuring that exterior doors are locked, and periodically checking lounges to make sure that people who are not residents or guests are not using the facility. The presence of campus security officers can reassure students, and parents that security services are important to the institution.

Commuter institutions present a different set of challenges. Parking is at quite a premium at commuter institutions, and motorist assistance becomes an important function of the campus police. If classes are held at night, escorting students to their cars as a safety measure becomes an ongoing function of the police. In addition, since commuter institutions tend to be located in larger urban areas, some of the challenges described earlier in this chapter need to be addressed.

Education. Among the challenges faced at commuter institutions is staying in touch with members of the campus community, especially students. Since many of them attend part time, getting information to them about campus security services and helping them understand how they can protect themselves is not easy. One strategy is to include campus security services as part of various orientation programs for both students and new employees. Time is precious in orientation programs, but the information that can be shared by campus police representatives is essential for students and others new to the campus. Even a brief presentation, followed by providing each student and each new staff member with printed material, can be a good start. Similar to residential dining halls, table tents and other promotional material can be provided to commuter students in snack bars, lounges, and other places where they congregate.

Direct services. As suggested above, many direct services are related to transportation. Assistance to motorists whose cars do not start or who have had minor accidents or other problems is essential. Safety escort services at night from classrooms, laboratories, and the library are typical forms of assistance provided at a commuter campus. Less emphasis is placed on student activities, since they are typically less pervasive, especially on weekends, but many commuter institutions have some residential students, so their needs, too, have to be addressed, but the scale of the work is not as complex as what one might find on a residential campus.

Measuring Effectiveness of Campus Public Safety Agencies

The relative effectiveness of campus public safety agencies can perhaps best be determined by measuring performance against the following criteria: (a) responsiveness to community needs; (b) quality of the workforce; (c) adherence to professional standards; (d) collaborative efforts to address safety issues; and (e) identification of future trends. The following provides an overview of various programs that policing organizations might implement, in whole or in part, to better meet community service needs.

Responsiveness to Community Needs

Crime Prevention and Community Involvement

Campus law enforcement agencies must be committed to developing and perpetuating proactive crime prevention programs. The scope of departmental activities should be limited to those that best serve the needs of the university community. All officers, especially those engaged in field assignments, should be acquainted with the general philosophy and specific techniques associated with the crime prevention function. The methods used by municipal agencies may not be effective in a campus setting, where transient residents are the norm. Public safety agencies may wish to consider employing electronic campus watch groups for disseminating crime prevention and alert information rather than using the traditional neighborhood watch approach.

Prevention programs should be targeted by crime type and geographic area based on ongoing analyses of local crime data. Departmental personnel should then decide which crime types pose the greatest concern; where identified problems are most severe; how organized crime prevention activities could be implemented most effectively; and what types of programs would be most effective in combating crime. The effectiveness of all crime prevention programs should be evaluated on fixed and logical schedules. After each review, personnel may decide whether each program should continue to function as is, be modified to address identified needs, or be discontinued.

Public safety agencies must devote the resources necessary to establish and maintain direct contact with the members of their respective communities. Officers and civilian staff should establish formal relationships with key organizations and assist with organizing safety groups where they are needed. By establishing an effective liaison with residents, law enforcement agencies may be apprised of concerns and respond before they escalate into larger problems. An ongoing awareness of community needs is a prerequisite to eliciting public support and providing appropriate services.

Contingency Planning

College campuses are not immune from the effects of natural or human-made disasters. Given their complex structure, population, and density, these communities may arguably be more prone to experience such events than other entities. Unusual occurrences are generally considered to be emergencies resulting from the following: hurricanes, floods, tornadoes, major fires, hazardous material exposure, and active shooter or hostage/barricaded persons situations. Civil disturbances, a very real threat for campus communities, may arise from athletic celebrations, political rallies, concerts, or organized protests.

Contingency plans for unusual occurrences should be formulated to ensure that the university community is protected in the event of a disaster. This preparation requires a realistic and concerted effort by everyone involved, regardless of affiliation. A law enforcement organization may have responsibility for initial response and control of a situation, or it may be asked to facilitate activities for another department. When a public safety entity does not have responsibility for primary control, it should be prepared to assist, expedite, and protect agencies directly engaged in situation-management efforts.

Prompt and orderly mobilization of resources is required to manage any emergency effectively. A multitiered system is often used to alert and activate personnel when an unusual occurrence is either anticipated or in progress. The mobilization plan should contain provisions for alert stage criteria; communications; assembly areas; equipment distribution; special task force activation; key personnel designations; transportation; management control measures; coordination with emergency management personnel; and rehearsals.

The expanding scope and sophistication of emergency operations require that personnel act immediately to stabilize and control disaster scenes. First responders must act decisively to minimize loss of life, reduce property damage, and permit involved authorities to fulfill their respective responsibilities. The Incident Command System (ICS) has been proven to enhance emergency communication and response. This organized approach permits a clear point of control and can be expanded or contracted to escalating or diminishing situations. The command system selected should be adaptable in several areas, including terminology, modular organization, integrated communications, and unity of command.

Compatibility among agencies is imperative for ICS to work effectively. It is important, therefore, for officers and civilian staff to work collaboratively with other agencies using the ICS, familiarizing all personnel with associated structures before crises arise. Component activation and deactivation should depend on existing and/or changing circumstances.

Medical Assistance

Because law enforcement officers are often first to arrive at crime and accident scenes, they must have the necessary skills and equipment to provide emergency medical services. A professional agency should employ officers who are certified in basic first aid techniques, including establishing an airway, performing rescue breathing, administering cardiopulmonary resuscitation, clearing an obstructed airway, treating for shock, and controlling bleeding. Proactive capabilities are enhanced by having a contingent of certi-fied first responders or emergency medical technicians on staff.

Many public safety agencies are equipping patrol vehicles with auto-mated external defibrillators (AEDs). The more sophisticated devices guide personnel through the defibrillation process using electronic timers and re-corded voice commands. Grant and student government funding may be used to purchase these vitally important devices.

Safety Escort Program

Many campus public safety agencies operate safety escort programs during hours of darkness. Typically, a person calls a designated, well-advertised tele-phone number to request a walking or vehicular escort between on-campus locations. Some jurisdictions require that users be registered with the depart-ment before requesting service; identity is confirmed at the point of contact or when the call is made. Nonsworn personnel are often used to staff this program; it is imperative that appropriate background and driver license checks be performed before they are hired.

Motorist Assist Program

When no other resources are available, the public often relies on law enforce-ment agencies for routine emergency assistance and advice. For this reason, officers regularly respond to incidents where an arrest or other enforcement action is required. Public safety organizations provide many ancillary traffic services, including general and emergency services; protection to stranded persons; facilitating mechanical and towing services; unlocking vehicles; cor-recting hazardous highway conditions; and providing traffic safety educa-tional materials and presentations.

Many agencies, through their respective parking or police operations, offer free motorist assist programs that provide one or more of the following: jumper cables and related assistance; jacks, lug wrenches, tire sealant, and other tools needed to repair or change a tire; and transportation to and from a service station to obtain fuel or other mechanical assistance. Legal counsel and risk management officials should be consulted regarding the type and scope of services offered before a motorist assist program is implemented. To reduce liability concerns, appropriate waiver forms should be developed and training programs conducted.

Quality of the Workforce

Educational Preferences

Responding to increased concerns regarding crime and the professionalism of law enforcement, President Lyndon Johnson established the Commission on Law Enforcement and Administration of Justice in 1965. The commission advocated system-wide reform and endorsed a variety of strategies, including establishing entry-level standards, increasing training requirements, ensuring better supervision, improving overall managerial skills, and allocating funds to formally educate personnel. The commission also encouraged recruitment of college-educated officers and dedicated nearly $200 million in financial assistance to criminal justice students. The percentage of sworn officers possessing college degrees has increased steadily since that time.

Certain law enforcement agencies may be precluded by regulation or policy from requiring officers to possess an undergraduate degree before appointment. Nonetheless, it may be advantageous for public safety administrators to consider implementing a degree preference in the recruitment and selection process. A college degree is certainly not the sole predictor of a successful career in law enforcement; however, it does ensure an officer is attuned to the nature and dynamics of a higher education institution.

Physical and Psychological Examinations

Following a conditional offer of employment, a physical examination of each entry-level candidate for sworn positions should be conducted to determine fitness for duty. State statutes often require that applicants be examined by a licensed physician or surgeon to certify general health as well as compliance with established standards pertaining to hearing and eyesight.

All applicants should complete a psychological assessment during the final selection process for law enforcement positions. Following administration of any written instrument, an interview with a licensed psychologist or other qualified mental health professional should be conducted to clarify or reinforce earlier findings.

Any medical or psychological examination required of a person already employed in a permanent full-time job should be provided at no cost to the individual. Records relating to physical and psychological examination results should be filed securely. Access to, and retention of, such records should be in accordance with applicable federal laws, state statutes, and university regulations.

General Health and Physical Fitness

The functions of law enforcement require a level of fitness not demanded by many other occupations. Sworn employees should be required to maintain a satisfactory level of general health and physical fitness. Many public safety agencies require a physical fitness assessment of each sworn employee at least annually.

Physical fitness assessments often are based on state-mandated entrance requirements and consist of various strength, endurance, and agility tests. The required standards may be listed scales that are adjusted to consider age and gender. Employees unable to participate due to medical reasons should be referred to appropriate administrative personnel who then make appropriate testing accommodations.

Agencies with sufficient shift strength or overlap may wish to consider allowing employees reasonable exercise time while on paid status, preferably near the end of their respective tours of duty. Additional incentives may include purchase of recreation center passes or issuing rewards for those who successfully complete all assessment components at or above designated percentiles.

Adherence to Professional Standards

Accreditation

To enhance professional competency, four major law enforcement associations cooperatively provided input to form the Commission on Accreditation for Law Enforcement Agencies (CALEA). This national accreditation program is viewed by many as an excellent vehicle to professionalize police agencies and thereby improve the overall delivery of law enforcement services. During its formative years, the commission researched, tested, and approved a comprehensive set of standards for law enforcement administration and operations. The number and content of these standards has been revised since their inception; however, they still serve as the basis for law enforcement agencies to voluntarily demonstrate compliance with established professional criteria.

Additional accreditation programs have been developed by the International Association of Campus Law Enforcement Administrators (IACLEA) and a number of individual states. Most are similar to the CALEA program and involve external review to determine compliance with established standards. Because these processes tend to improve the overall quality of policing, they often elicit extensive support from federal, state, and local policymakers.

Existing literature clearly indicates law enforcement accreditation to be a growing and important national influence. The structure of accreditation processes requires both internal and external evaluation to determine whether an agency meets the standards developed by law enforcement experts. Numerous accounts of those familiar with accreditation support the process, believing that it serves as a liability shield, promotes pride among employees, and stimulates community confidence.

Training

It is essential for public safety agencies to provide employees with the finest entry-level, in-service, and advanced instruction available. Well-trained staff are more likely to act professionally when confronted with a variety of routine and unusual situations. Failure to provide adequate initial or remedial training may result in the agency being held legally accountable for any subsequent improper actions of its personnel.

The departmental training function should include the following activities: monitoring attendance; reimbursing employees; coordinating lesson plan development; scheduling personnel; planning, developing, implementing, and evaluating programs; coordinating remedial, shift briefing and specialized, advanced, and in-service training; selecting instructors; coordinating recruit and field training; and overseeing career development.

Organizational Membership

Maintaining active membership in recognized professional organizations brings numerous benefits. These groups provide administrators, supervisors, and line staff with a means of receiving and disseminating current information about various law enforcement topics. Newsletters, websites, conferences, and listserves allow members to interact efficiently, thereby increasing knowledge and professionalism. Particularly worthwhile organizations include the International Association of Chiefs of Police (IACP), International Association of Campus Law Enforcement Administrators (IACLEA), American Society of Industrial Security (ASIS), and American Society of Law Enforcement Trainers (ASLET).

Collaborative Efforts to Address Safety Issues

Critical Incident Response Team

Campus public safety agencies often benefit from participating in multidisciplinary teams that addresses myriad important issues. These groups integrate available services, including law enforcement, counseling, media relations, human resources, legal counsel, environmental health and safety, risk management, residence life, and student affairs, into functional units. This approach has proven to provide more timely, comprehensive, and accessible support when responding to a variety of critical incidents.

Critical incidents may include threats or acts of violence; suicides; major demonstrations or riots; floods, major fires, tornadoes, aircraft crashes, train derailments, major chemical spills, hostage/barricaded persons situations, building collapses, explosions, bomb threats, or other disasters; deadly diseases; and food contamination incidents. A coordinated response can more effectively anticipate and, when possible, prevent incidents involving violence or injury. Regular meetings and exercises help ensure the implementation of effective proactive and postincident recovery services.

Establishing and maintaining a critical incident response team provides the following outcomes: a coordinated and rapid incident response, a venue for promptly identifying and supporting key decision makers, a system for evaluating incident response, a planning vehicle for protecting lives and property, a reduction in vicarious liability, and an improved method of managing public information. The designated core group may benefit from expanding its membership to include additional departments as particular needs are identified.

Sexual Assault Response Team

Campus law enforcement agencies should be firmly committed to providing an environment free from the threat of unwanted sexual conduct. Sexual assault is a crime as well as a violation of institutional disciplinary regulations, faculty standards, and employee policies.

To address this complex issue effectively, consideration should be given to forming a multidisciplinary Sexual Assault Response Team (SART), designed to identify barriers that prevent survivors from seeking services, and to overcome obstacles through a sensitive, victim-centered approach. Team members should represent law enforcement, health care, advocacy, counseling, and prosecution. Agencies from both the campus and local community are often members of these response organizations.

When a survivor of sexual assault contacts a SART agency, a three-person team, consisting of a sexual assault nurse examiner, an advocate, and a law enforcement officer, is dispatched. Team members explain their respective roles and outline the services they provide. The survivor then decides which resources to use or may decline to meet with any professionals if so desired.

Drug Task Force

Campus public safety agencies should consider a multijurisdictional investigative approach when attempting to reduce the use, sale, distribution, and manufacture of controlled substances. Implementing a task force, controlled by appropriate cooperative agreements, has proven to be an effective and efficient method of addressing drug-related issues. The advantages associated with task force projects include sustaining enforcement and prosecutorial efforts; reducing addictive behavior; coordinating investigations and intelligence information with federal, state, and local authorities; identifying and limiting gang-related activity; and reducing community concern.

Grant funding may be obtained to subsidize organization of a multiagency drug task force. Once such a task force is established, money obtained through court-related forfeiture proceedings may be used to sustain operational needs. Obtaining the support of local businesses or other campus entities to provide office equipment, unmarked vehicles, and office space may assist in the cost effectiveness of such a venture.

Interaction with Other Agencies

Campus law enforcement organizations must establish and maintain positive working relationships with federal, state, county, and local agencies. Colleges and universities often host large conferences, along with entertainment, athletic, and political events. A community so diverse and technologically sophisticated attracts interest from a variety of federal, state, and local law enforcement agencies. To retain some degree of information and case control, campus law enforcement officials would be well served by working closely with these organizations on a continual basis. Administrators may wish to consider providing federal and state agencies with office space and participating in multijurisdictional efforts such as a Joint Terrorism Task Force (JTTF) or an Internet Crimes Against Children (ICAC) investigative group.

Identification of Future Trends

Multiyear Plans

Agency administrators must identify future law enforcement trends in an accurate and timely manner. Multiyear plans are valuable tools in these processes when they include, at a minimum, long-term goals and objectives, anticipated workload needs, projected population trends, anticipated personnel levels, equipment needs, and scheduled capital improvement projects. Completed planning documents should be reviewed at least annually and revised as needed.

Forensic Computer Examination

Computers are increasingly involved in law enforcement casework by being targets of crime, incidental to illegal acts, or instruments of crimes. It is therefore beneficial for any public safety agency to have a computer forensic laboratory at its immediate disposal. Equipment necessary to recover deleted data and analyze files can often be obtained through grant funding or collaborative efforts with academic departments. Having an officer trained and certified in examination techniques has many advantages and reduces reliance on federal, state, or private laboratories.

Access Control

Higher education institutions throughout the country are moving quickly to upgrade building and facility access from metal keys to electronic access control technology. Computerized systems greatly enhance control capabilities and reduce the need to replace lost or stolen keys. They track employee use, provide an audit account, and can be programmed to specific individuals, locations, and times. Should a computerized key be lost or stolen, subsequent use can be programmed to activate an alarm. Sophisticated access control systems are especially useful in areas requiring high levels of security, such as sensitive laboratories, computer facilities, and medical facilities.

Environmental Design Input

Proactively, it is advantageous for campus public safety officials to be involved during the design phase of new construction and remodeling projects. Having an employee trained in Crime Prevention through Environmental Design (CPTED) principles involved during planning and construction can help address a number of security-related concerns before project completion. Law enforcement officials are then able to review blueprints and attend construction meetings to provide appropriate input. One key concept of this approach is to enhance natural surveillance capability to reduce the likelihood of future criminal activity.

Electronic Surveillance

Many campuses use electronic surveillance equipment in areas where safety and security are of particular concern. When considering this technology, officials must determine whether cameras are placed overtly, covertly, or in combination. Officials should understand the fatigue factor and personnel commitment required when monitoring cameras on a real-time basis. Agencies and private companies are increasingly using digital technology when installing surveillance systems. Regardless of the recording methods used, institutional policies should clearly address installation authority, access rights, and retention requirements.

Threat Assessment

Law enforcement continues to become more sophisticated in its response to interpersonal violence. It is recommended that agencies adopt strategies pertaining to threat assessment and management. Such proactive approaches are designed to evaluate the severity of threatening situations and to develop and implement appropriate interventions to deescalate particular situations. Experience has shown the multidisciplinary case management approach to be most effective. The overriding philosophy of this approach is to look beyond the existence of criminal elements and focus on recognizing and responding to problematic behavior before an incident occurs.

Mental Illness

Many jurisdictions report an increase in calls for service relating to persons exhibiting signs of mental illness or significant emotional distress. Because law enforcement is often the only entity providing a 24-hour response to persons in crisis, it is imperative that officers receive specialized training in recognizing and responding to these situations. A collaborative approach involving personnel from law enforcement, corrections, and mental health services better enables early identification of and response to mentally ill or distressed individuals.

Computerization

Campus public safety agencies, like other law enforcement organizations, are becoming more computerized with regard to dispatch and records management systems. Administrators may wish to consider consolidating or technologically linking their information databases with municipal counterparts when contemplating system upgrades. This approach not only increases the quantity and quality of available information, but also provides for redundancy in the event of system failure. Agencies should also consider using computerized mapping programs when analyzing incidents and selectively directing enforcement efforts.

Conclusion

This chapter has identified several contextual issues that influence the approach taken to providing contemporary campus police services and has discussed criteria that can be used to evaluate the effectiveness of campus police services. A cross-cutting theme of this chapter is the importance of collaboration between various elements of the institution and the campus police agency (for further discussion of collaboration on campus, see Deisinger et al., 1998). As the higher education environment becomes increasingly complex, a notion implicit in this chapter, members of the campus community must work together to devise and deliver services related to safety and security. In addition, our view is that it is crucial that the agency charged with delivering safety and security services measure the quality of its work against contemporary standards.

References

Deisinger, E., Cychosz, C., & Jaeger, L. A. (1998). Strategies for dealing with violence. In A. M Hoffman, J. H. Schuh, & R. H. Fenske (Eds.), *Violence on campus* (pp. 327–345). Gaithersburg, MD: Aspen.

Federal Bureau of Investigation. (2004). *Crime in the United States 2004.* Washington, DC: Department of Justice. Retrieved March 27, 2006, from http://www.fbi.gov/ucr/cius_04/

Gehring, D. D. (2000). Understanding the legal implications of student affairs practice. In M. J. Barr, M. K. Desler, and Associates, (Eds.), *The handbook of student affairs administration* (2nd ed.) (pp. 347–376). San Francisco: Jossey-Bass.

Indiana University Police Department Police Academy. (2006). Main. Retrieved March 27, 2006, from http://www.indiana.edu/~iupd/academy.htm

Strange, C. C. (2003). Dynamics of campus environments. In S. R. Komives, D. B. Woodard, Jr., & Associates, (Eds.), *Student services: A handbook for the profession* (4th ed.) (pp. 297–316). San Francisco: Jossey-Bass.

University of Colorado at Boulder. (2006). *Police authority and training.* Retrieved March 27, 2006, from http://www.colorado.edu/police/about/authority.html

University of New Mexico Police Department. (2006). UNM police home page. Retrieved March 27, 2006, from http://police.unm.edu/home.htm

University of Texas at Austin Police Department (2006). About UTPD. Retrieved March 27, 2006, from http://www.utexas.edu/police/about/

13

YOU ARE NOT ALONE

Resources for the College Administrator

Robert D. Reason and Brenda R. Lutovsky

C ollege administrators, particularly those who ascended to administration via traditional academic routes, may not be formally trained
in creating and maintaining safe campus environments. New administrators may not have any experience dealing with the types of crises that
occur each day on college campuses. While other chapters provide invaluable
information to make up for this lack of training, this chapter is meant to
provide a jump-start for new administrators by identifying resources commonly available during times of crisis. Much like a leaky roof that only gets
our attention when it rains, identifying resources for dealing with campus
crises is not likely a high priority for campus administrators—unless, of
course, a crisis has occurred. By identifying some common resources, we
hope to encourage campus administrators to be proactive, by seeking out and
building relationships with professionals on campus or joining professional
organizations external to campus, before a crisis occurs.

We use the term, *crisis*, in this chapter as all encompassing, relating to
any event that disrupts normal institutional operations and hinders educational pursuits. A crisis, therefore, can take many forms: hurricane, residence
hall fire, racist/homophobic incident, or violent crime. Regardless of the type
or degree of the crisis, however, many resources are available to help administrators manage or, preferably, prevent it. Many of these resources are currently available on campus, such as student affairs, public safety, counseling
centers, and public relations or closely related offices such as the campus
attorney. Others are national organizations and electronic resources available

via the Internet. In this chapter, we identify resources administrators may find useful for both *managing* and *preventing* crises.

Resources for Managing Crises

College administrators will find it too difficult to search for previously un-known resources in the middle of managing a crisis. They should spend time *before* a crisis identifying and building relationships with people who can assist them, perhaps as part of a crisis response plan (as we discuss briefly later). Proactively identifying relationships with other professionals on cam-pus who have the training and personal characteristics to handle crises will reap rewards for the busy administrator when the inevitable crisis occurs. In this section, we offer some suggestions about whom a busy college adminis-trator might want to know and how to work with each group of professionals during a crisis.

Working with Student Affairs Professionals

Practically every college campus has professional staff persons trained in crisis management (or skills translatable and useable during a crisis). Although the campus police office is the most obvious on-campus resource, we begin this section by highlighting the division of student affairs and the many func-tional areas within this division. Although the perception of student affairs professionals as "those people who play games with the students" is chang-ing, we begin with the assumption that most academic administrators have little familiarity with the type of training these professionals undergo. Be-cause of the level of contact they normally maintain with students, student affairs professionals can be valuable in communicating with current students, providing accurate information to quell rumors, and pulling together groups of students when necessary.

The authors of a widely used textbook (Barr, Desler, & Associates, 2000) identify 12 "essential skills and competencies" for student affairs pro-fessionals. Of these 12, 4 are directly related to our topic: understanding the legal implications of student affairs work (Gehring, 2000), developing rela-tionships with external constituencies (Sandeen, 2000), managing conflict (Moore, 2000), and dealing with campus crisis (Duncan & Miser, 2000). Further, the Council for the Advancement of Standards in Higher Education

(CAS) includes as one of its required areas of "professional studies" in student affairs preparation programs, "instruction in individual and group techniques and practices for addressing personal crises" (CAS, 2003, n.p.). Campus administrators therefore may assume with some confidence that student affairs professionals—educated at the master's degree level in a CAS-compliant program—possess both practical and academic training in crisis management.

The role of student affairs professionals during crisis is dictated to a large degree by the administrative organization of any given campus (Duncan & Miser, 2000). The division of student affairs, however, is a large and heterogeneous group of offices and professionals (Reason, 2001). On our campus, Penn State University, for example, the division of student affairs includes such a diverse group of professionals: medical doctors, computer programmers, mental health counselors, residence hall directors, and research and assessment specialists. Other campuses include campus police, academic advising, and athletics under the rubric of student affairs. Obviously, not all of these individuals are trained or experienced in crisis management; however, by identifying those who are, campus administrators will greatly enhance the human resources available during times of crisis. Writing about dealing with crises as student affairs professionals, Duncan and Miser (2000) state, "student affairs professionals are trained to work with people, and from these foundations, they become key leaders in responding to campus crises" (p. 465).

Given the diversity of organizational structures within student affairs divisions on different campuses, we cannot identify by title and responsibility all professionals with whom a campus administrator will need to work during a time of crisis. We do offer, however, brief descriptions of some of the student affairs professionals who may be the most helpful. We necessarily use common titles and descriptions to make them applicable to the widest array of campuses. Specific titles may be different on your campus, but responsibilities will be similar.

Director of residence life. The director of residence life is likely someone with whom most campus administrators are familiar. The director is responsible for all residence life staff and for students who live on campus; as such he or she can help in coordinating emergency response efforts with staff and students. Residence life professionals train staff, particularly student resident assistants (RAs), to respond to crises and plan educational programs for students aimed at preventing crises. As the person with the most direct access to all on-campus students, the director of residence life is vital to managing a crisis that could easily escalate without trained personal and coordinated communication efforts.

In addition to the director of residence life, we suggest campus administrators form relationships with individual residence hall directors. A key component of managing a crisis situation is conveying accurate information in a timely manner to those who need it. Current students, particularly those who live on campus, comprise one group that needs such information. Residence hall directors live and interact with the students, making them effective partners in communicating information to students. This is true not only because of proximity to and accessibility for students but because residence hall directors are trained to communicate with students effectively. Because of their existing relationships with the students in their halls, students will likely respond well to any directions or unpleasant information that may accompany a crisis if it comes from a residence hall director. These individuals can also quell rumors and provide preventive education for students.

Residence hall directors likely deal on some level with crisis situations almost daily, making them active crisis interveners who can train others. They also may be the most committed to preventing crisis or managing a crisis well, so they will be eager to become involved in prevention strategies or groups. However, residence hall directors are usually fairly new professionals whose lack of extensive experience and limited scope of job may cause their focus to be narrow. Including them in campus-wide efforts, with the help of their supervisors, can broaden their focus and create a group of crisis intervention specialists on campus.

Director of residential facilities. The person who is responsible for residence life may also be responsible for campus housing facilities, but this is not the case on all campuses. The director of residential facilities is responsible for maintenance, equipment contracts, and related concerns of residence halls. Usually this person coordinates fire safety inspections in addition to equipment and furnishings checks and upgrades. As such, the director of residence facilities knows a great deal about the "inner workings" of a building, which may be invaluable in times of crisis. If an emergency occurs within a residence hall related to the facility itself, such as a fire, elevator malfunction with students inside it, or a student falling through a window, the director of residential facilities should be one of the first people contacted.

Director of the student union. Like the director of residence life, the director of the student union can be a great resource for coordinating communication efforts to the campus community and in organizing an information center, emergency response headquarters, or alternative student sleeping spaces inside the student union building. A student union is typically a hub of both on- and off-campus student interaction. Students are accustomed to seeking information in a student union and may feel more comfortable going there than a campus police office or administration or academic building. In a time of a crisis when students are displaced or need assurance of safety, the student union offers comfortable furniture, familiar surroundings, dining facilities, multiple spaces for various groups or services, and distraction from the crisis at hand. In addition, the director of the student union may have several means of conveying information, such as bulletin boards, electronic signs, or televisions that display information, and a building-wide public address (PA) system.

Director of student activities. Depending on the size and scope of an institution, the person who oversees student activities may be the director of the student union. If this is not the case, the director of student activities is also a valuable resource in managing a crisis. Like other student affairs staff members, the director of student activities likely has quick access to large groups of students and student leaders, which can aid in organizing communication efforts. In addition, the director of student activities likely has equipment and supplies for events, movies to be shown, and the knowledge of how to plan these activities very quickly. Perhaps a casino night or a midnight showing of *Grease* is not the first thing to enter your mind during a crisis, but keeping students' minds off a major crisis or providing something to do in a blizzard or power outage can be important.

Fraternity/sorority life advisor. Like the director of student activities, the fraternity/sorority life advisor is a helpful resource, because this person works with a large population of students. The fraternity/sorority life advisor has the ability to reach the organizations' leaders very quickly, which is important for communicating accurate and timely information to students. Like residence hall directors, these people are likely adept at dealing with crises quickly and calmly. Second, because fraternities and sororities often are viewed as the source of many crisis situations, the fraternity/sorority professional staff member is a valuable resource in mitigating those situations. This staff member can help form relationships between organization leaders and institutional leaders, educate the students on policies and risk prevention efforts, and build relationships with national fraternity/sorority staff members.

Director of counseling services. Depending on the type of crisis, students—individually or in groups—may need to talk to campus counselors. While there is usually at least one counselor on call at all times, an emergency plan should include creation of a makeshift counseling center in the student union, a residence hall, or a fraternity or sorority house. Coordinating this plan with the director of the counseling center before a crisis can aid greatly in the calm management of an emergency situation.

Directors of special population services/advocacy units. Often, a crisis occurs that affects one group of students more directly or more significantly than another group. Some examples of these crises are stranger rapes or sexual assaults, hate crimes (on- or off-campus), or an incident in a country from which you have a large international student population. Most campuses have student affairs offices that work with specific campus populations, such as a women's center; a lesbian, gay, bisexual, and transgender (LGBT) center; a multicultural student center that works with specific racial or ethnic groups; and an office of international student affairs. The professionals who run these offices already have relationships and rapport with various student populations. In the event of a crisis, these students are more likely to go to these offices and individuals than to a central information center in a student union. The student affairs professionals from these offices may have an easier time communicating with the specific groups than would other professionals. Working with these professionals regularly and getting to know the students they serve will aid in crisis management.

Professional who works with students with disabilities. Students with disabilities may require specific services during times of crisis that other students do not require. Professionals who work with this group of students should be consulted in crisis prevention planning to ensure that proper attention is given to plans created for students with disabilities. Situations such as building fires and power outages may require distinct services to ensure the safety of students with disabilities. We suggest that such plans should be in place well before a crisis occurs.

The aforementioned is a list of the primary student affairs professionals we feel are good resources for administrators, but it is not exhaustive. There may be other people in specialized student affairs positions who could be quite valuable for campus administrators to know. The trained student affairs professionals on any campus have the experience and knowledge to assist with managing campus-based crises. In particular, campus administrators should look to student affairs professionals to work closely with students during times of crisis. Using these professionals' existing relationships with students will yield dividends for the campus administrator.

Working with Campus Police

Campus police officers are an obvious and valuable resource for college administrators dealing with crises. Deisinger, Cychosz, and Jaeger (1998) estimated that approximately 75% of campuses employ professional police officers with full arrest powers. These campus police officers are fully trained—meeting the same requirements for credentialing as any municipal police officer. Further, campus police officers often receive specific training for issues more prevalent on college campuses through the International Association of Campus Law Enforcements Administrators (IACLEA).

What can we expect when working with these trained police officers? First, campus administrators can assume that campus police demonstrate the same degree of professionalism and responsibility as any police force. Campus police officers work in close partnership with college administrators before and during a campus crisis (Deisinger et al., 1998). If the crisis involves a crime (or the potential for a crime), campus police will likely assume responsibility for the crime scene, coordinate evidence and gather information, and protect all involved. At other times, campus police officers may take their lead from educational administrators—although this relationship must be discussed well before a crisis arises. When in doubt, campus administrators will do well to defer to the police officers.

Working with Local/Municipal Police Departments

On those 25 percent of campuses with no professional police force, administrators are likely to work more closely with the local police during times of crisis. In this case, a strong working relationship may be even more important, and potentially more difficult to build, than when working with campus police. Local police departments and officers likely will focus less on the educational efforts of law enforcement and have less training in campus-specific incidents. If appropriate, campus adminstrators may do well to introduce local police officers to IACLEA or provide other training opportunities for local police officers on common issues on campus.

International Association of Campus Law Enforcement Administrators (IACLEA)

IACLEA is the primary professional organization focused on campus-related and campus-specific law enforcement. According to its website (www.iaclea.org), IACLEA "advances public safety for educational institutions by providing educational resources, advocacy, and professional development services." IACLEA offers multiple forms of individual and institutional memberships with varying dues. Member services include a variety of training programs for campus officers, an accreditation program with campus-specific standards, and listservs and consulting services. IACLEA holds an annual conference during which educational programming and exhibitor displays keep attendees up to date on the latest trends and developments in campus safety.

Working with Public Relations and the Media

Reflecting on a tragic fire at Seton Hall University, Allen (2001) concluded that communication was the most critical component of managing this tragedy. Although the student affairs professionals he led were not directly involved with the media, Allen recognized the importance of providing accurate and timely information for constituents external to the university. Public relations (PR) professionals, as long as they are well informed by campus administrators, can provide service during a crisis by communicating a coherent message to external constituencies, including parents, alumni, the local community, and trustees.

In collaboration with campus administrators, public relations professionals are responsible for coordinating and disseminating information about a crisis. While the PR professionals become the voice of the college, campus administrators are responsible for providing details to the professionals in the public relations office. Because of the importance of communication and information dissemination, formal briefings to the public relations staff should occur regularly throughout the crisis and its aftermath.

Strategies for Effective Communication

Fannelli (1997) and Siegel (1994) both suggest assuming a "cause and effect approach" to this communication during crises by clearly and concisely providing descriptions of the events and the institution's reactions. Clarity and precision of details are enhanced by selecting one person to serve as the designated information officer (Siegel, 1994). This person becomes the public face of the institution during the crisis. Siegel also suggests that information be provided that seeks to increase the sense of control and safety of campus community members by quelling rumors and providing contact information for available resources. Coordinating the message through a trained communication professional may go a long way toward alleviating the stress that arises during times of crisis.

Working with Campus Attorneys

College administrators today are likely to have well-worn relationships with the college attorney. The ever-changing and more litigious relationship of student and institution requires college administrators to keep a close eye on the law (Barr et al., 2000; Duncan & Miser, 2000; Gehring, 2000). Issues such as student group recognition, freedom of speech, Title IX, and affirmative action have focused attention on the intersection of higher education and the law. While these issues may garner more attention, college administrators should also be familiar with tort law as it relates to injury (broadly defined) resulting from a crisis or security breach.

Working with a campus attorney to limit liability and mitigate security issues is an essential part of the job for a campus administrator (Duncan & Miser, 2000). During times of crisis or its aftermath, administrators may necessarily take their lead from the attorney, who understands how to limit legal liability. Before a crisis, however, administrators should consider the relationships with campus attorneys as reciprocal, often involving a "give and take" in finding an appropriate balance between educating students and limiting liability. At times, the campus administrator may need to advocate for the educational environment, teaching the campus attorney about educational processes. The National Association of College and University Attorneys might be one resource in managing this relationship.

National Association of College and University Attorneys (NACUA)

The mission of NACUA is to "advance the effective practice of higher education attorneys for the benefit of the colleges and universities they serve" (www.nacua.org). To its members, NACUA offers a variety of services, including an annual conference; continuing professional development and training opportunities; online resources, which include up-to-date dissemination of information related to campus legal issues through an e-mail distribution network; and print publications, including the *Journal of College and University Law*. NACUA offers both institutional and individual memberships.

National Conference on Law and Higher Education

A discussion of legal issues in higher education would not be complete without mentioning the National Conference on Law and Higher Education, held annually at Stetson Law School in Florida. For almost three decades, the National Conference has brought together legal scholars and practitioners for an interdisciplinary dialogue on law and policy issues currently affecting the administration of student life and academic programs. The conference is designed for mid- or upper-level administrators and legal staff who need professional development related to the intersection of law and policy. This conference is normally held immediately following the national conference of the Association for Student Judicial Affairs (ASJA), which we discuss later in this chapter. Information about the National Conference is available at the Stetson Law School website (http://www.law.stetson.edu/CLE/).

Being Prepared: The Importance of a Crisis Management Plan

While we have focused thus far on managing a crisis, a discussion of precrisis preparation is needed here as well. A crisis management plan that provides action steps for foreseeable crises is an essential component of all colleges and universities' long-term strategic plans (Gutierrez Kenney, 1997). Because Delight Champagne's chapter, which follows, includes a more comprehensive discussion of planning for campus safety, we touch on the topic here only briefly.

Crisis management plans should include written procedures for suicides and suicide attempts, crimes with victims, fires, natural disasters, and student rioting (Siegel, 1994). Siegel also suggests plans to evacuate each building on campus safely and efficiently. However, because anticipating all contingencies is not realistic, a complete crisis management plan should also provide a framework for decision making during the crisis itself, focusing on clarifying who has responsibility and authority to act (Duncan & Miser, 2000).

Several authors suggest building a crisis management team to react rapidly during times of crisis (Bornstein & Wilson, 2004a, 2004b; Gutierrez Kenney, 1997; Siegel, 1994). Bornstein and Wilson suggest a team of approximately seven to nine people to allow for "manageable discussion and idea generation and a strong knowledge base" (Bornstein & Wilson, 2004a, n.p.). Individuals and offices discussed in the previous sections of this chapter should be represented on such a team as well. The chief student affairs officer and other high-ranking campus administrators should be included in the crisis management team to provide leadership and guidance (Reason & Saunders, 2003; Sandeen, 2000). Individuals on the crisis management team serve as first responders to any crisis and initiate the process of coordinated communication of information.

Resources for Preventing Crises

We turn now to an examination of resources available to *prevent* a crisis from occurring. Although the majority of these resources are external to the college or university (e.g., national organizations, web-based resources), we begin where we began in the previous section: student affairs professionals. These professionals, particularly those responsible for advocacy and educational programming, can provide guidance in creating a safe environment on campus. Before we leave student affairs, we also highlight several related professional organizations through which a campus administrator might find training and support for crisis prevention efforts.

Student Affairs Professionals and Organizations

Many of the same personnel just discussed as resources to *manage* a crisis are also invaluable in *preventing* crises from occurring. Certainly, educational efforts by student affairs professionals, campus police officers, or college attorneys play a major role in creating an environment in which crises are averted or at least mitigated. In particular, we suggest that campus administrators build relationships with those student affairs professionals who work in "advocacy" roles on their campuses (e.g., directors of the women's center, LGBT center, multicultural affairs). These professionals represent groups of students who may be at greater risk of being disenfranchised or victimized on campus (Rankin & Reason, 2005; Reason & Rankin, 2006). These professionals often also are charged with educating majority students about diversity and multiculturalism issues. A recent survey revealed that most students believe greater educational efforts are needed to improve the campus climate for underrepresented and underserved populations (Rankin & Reason, 2005). Knowing and supporting those professionals who are responsible for educating students about such issues will go a long way toward building safe college campuses. Visible administrative support for all students and the student affairs professionals charged with advocating for them sends a strong message to students, faculty, and external constituents (Nicoletti, Spencer-Thomas, & Bollinger, 2001).

Professional Organizations for Student Affairs Professionals

Several organizations exist at the state, regional, and national levels to support and educate student affairs professionals. In this section, we highlight only four: two because of their national scope, and two because of their specific focus on safety issues germane to our discussion. We encourage campus administrators to find out about other organizations from the student affairs professionals on their campuses. Professional organizations, like those we discuss below, play an important role in the professional and administrative development of student affairs professionals and, as such, can be resources for creating safe and educational campus environments.

National Association of Student Personnel Administrators (NASPA). With its mission to provide professional development opportunities for its members, NASPA (www.naspa.org), one of two national student affairs associations, boasts a membership of more than 9,000 professionals (including over 3,000 senior student affairs officers). NASPA hosts a public policy forum that keeps members current on national and regional student affairs–relevant policy matters. Members may also join "knowledge communities" that connect individuals with similar interests and concerns. Of particular note are the knowledge communities related to alcohol and other drug use and those related to specific institutional types (e.g., community and two-year institutions, small colleges and universities). Finally, NASPA publishes an online academic journal, several books, and monographs, all focused on administrative issues, many of which are relevant to campus crises.

American College Personnel Association (ACPA). Like NASPA, ACPA (www.myacpa.org) is a national association of student affairs professionals dedicated to educating its members about contemporary student affairs issues. Like NASPA's knowledge communities, ACPA members can join one or more "commissions" that represent functional areas or campus settings in which a member has an interest. Commissions of particular interest for our topic include: Administrative Leadership, Alcohol and Other Drug Issues, Campus Judicial Affairs and Legal Issues, and Counseling and Psychological Services. Most commissions offer informative websites, electronic updates, and newsletters. In addition, it provides opportunities for educational programs and networking at the ACPA Annual Convention and offers programs and services to members.

Association for Student Judicial Affairs (ASJA). ASJA (www.asja.tamu .edu), which began in 1986 to bring together student affairs professionals with interest in or responsibility for student conduct, has a membership of about 1,200 in the United States and Canada, representing more than 750 higher education institutions. According to its constitution, ASJA strives to facilitate integration of student development concepts with principles of judicial practice in a postsecondary educational setting and to promote, encourage, and support student development professionals who are responsible for student judicial affairs. The organization focuses on building communication networks for its members to exchange ideas and concerns related to campus judicial codes and practices.

ASJA presents an annual conference immediately before the National Conference on Law and Higher Education each February in Clearwater, Florida. Both events provide intensive, focused attention on matters of law, safety, and security on college campuses. Further, ASJA provides an annual training session on campus judicial and mediation skills for beginning and advanced student judicial officers.

Stopthehate.org (a program of the Association of College Unions International (ACUI). Stopthehate.org is a hate crime education and prevention program that, according to its website (www.stopthehate.org), supports colleges and universities in preventing and combating hate on campus and in fostering development of community and serving as the premiere source of antihate educational resources for higher education. The program is action-oriented with multiple downloadable resources for planning and implementing hate crime prevention efforts on a college campus. A centerpiece of the stop-the-hate effort is a "train the trainer" program that brings experts to campus to train 25–50 personnel who are then able to train others.

In addition to the numerous educational and training resources on stop thehate.org, the website features a comprehensive listing of links to other diversity-related websites (www.stophate.org/stophate/relatedlinks.htm). These links fall in six categories: university initiatives, national organizations, community programs, statistics, law and legal issues, and government. The site also features publications related to hate crime prevention. Although some of the links on this page are dated or no longer active, the site remains a broad and inclusive listing of resources.

Other Resources for Preventing Crisis

It was interesting to note that, as we compiled the resources for this section, we realized that campus administrators might see as adversarial or antagonistic many of the individuals and groups that could be resources for preventing a crisis on campus. As with the student affairs resources just discussed, the groups identified below are often seen as advocates for one group of students (e.g., fraternity/sorority members, crime victims). It would be easy for college administrators to view these groups as "opponents" when they assume their advocacy roles. For each group, however, part of its advocacy role is the support of student learning and safety. Viewed this way, these groups can be allies to college administrators.

Fraternity and Sorority National Offices

National fraternity and sorority leadership and related organizations may seem to be unlikely resources for helping prevent campus crises, but creating relationships with national leadership and understanding how fraternities and sororities operate can be highly beneficial to campus administrators. Fraternity/sorority life professionals likely have relationships with these organizational leaders already. We suggest that you meet with these persons to learn about the organizations. Although campus fraternity/sorority advisors are responsible for the day-to-day relationships with fraternities and sororities, if a crisis occurs, upper-level administrators likely will conduct the majority of discussions with both local and national fraternity/sorority members.

Before a crisis, creating relationships with local chapter advisors and regional and national advisors/staff is recommended. Creating a joint and mutually beneficial relationship is in the interest of all involved. Often, national office staff do not fully know what is happening in the chapters with which they work, and they usually appreciate the relationship with campus administrators. The campus fraternity/sorority life professional likely meets with advisors regularly. Attending these meetings is an excellent means for upper-level administrators across academic and student affairs units to begin to build necessary relationships with fraternity/sorority advisors. Furthermore, including local chapter advisors on emergency response teams or in campus-community coalitions ensures that all players are on the same page if a crisis occurs. If the local chapter advisors are unresponsive, contact the national offices.

If regional or national staff persons visit your campus, upper-level administrators should take the time to meet with them and find out how their organizations operate. All national fraternities and sororities have their own risk management policies and crisis management plans. These policies and plans usually dovetail well with existing campus policies, but sometimes portions of them may be at odds. Knowing this information and deciding with the group which policy to defer to will mitigate potential problems with local leadership. National fraternity and sorority leaders want to prevent crises as much as college administrators do. If they know that the organization they represent is not acting in accordance with its own policies on your campus, and they have had discussions with you about the matter, they will be more likely to address the situation before it escalates into a crisis. Undergraduate fraternity and sorority members may be more responsive to their own leadership than to the college or university administrators. Involving fraternity/sorority leaders in policy discussions and crisis prevention planning is beneficial for the institution and the individual organizations.

We also suggest that upper-level administrators meet undergraduate leaders of the fraternities and sororities. Unfortunately, many undergraduates and some local advisors lump all administrators into the amorphous entity of "The University" or "The College" and view this group in an antagonistic manner. Interacting with the undergraduates can help build trust and rapport, which are vital in a crisis situation. Often, undergraduates do not fully understand their own policies or those of the college or university. By meeting with students and showing that you know their policies, you can help them understand how they fit into the institution. In addition, if the undergraduates know you have forged a positive working relationship with their advisors and national staff, they may be more wary about acting irresponsibly.

Many resources exist to help you learn about fraternity and sorority policies and procedures. Most national organizations place many of their documents on their websites. Affiliated organizations also provide valuable information on the Internet. Below is a list of fraternity/sorority resources on the Internet.

Association of Fraternity Advisors (AFA). AFA is the professional organization for student affairs professionals who specialize in fraternity and sorority life as well as many national and volunteer fraternity/sorority staff. Its website, www.fraternityadvisors.org, has links to almost all of the national fraternities and sororities and their umbrella organizations and other affiliated organizations. In addition, AFA offers virtual seminars on topical issues, many of which are related to risk management. If you cannot participate in a seminar, audio tapes of them are available, as are many other resources. If your campus fraternity/sorority life professional is a member of AFA, most of these resources are available at a reduced rate.

Fraternal Information & Programming Group (FIPG) (http://www.fipg .org/). FIPG, a resource organization for fraternities and sororities and those who work with them, addresses alcohol and drug use issues; hazing; sexual abuse and harassment; fire, health, and safety; and education. FIPG's risk management policy is used by 47 groups and is the standard for most other groups' policies. Understanding fraternity and sorority risk management policies will aid you and your staff in helping the groups manage themselves. Additionally, knowing their policies will help in the development of your campus policies and judicial proceedings, if necessary. Often, the individual organizations' policies are much stricter than the college's or university's policies. The FIPG website offers links to numerous other websites and organizations that work with the issues listed above as well as an online newsletter.

Fraternity/sorority insurance companies and risk management resources.

Most national fraternities and sororities are insured by one of two companies, Kirklin & Co. or M-J Insurance, Inc. These companies seek to prevent crises within the organizations they insure and offer valuable resources online to aid in risk and crisis management.

HRH/Kirklin & Co., LLC (www.kirklin.com), provides insurance to many fraternities and produces or provides access to numerous resources about risk management and safety. On the company's website are links to the Fraternal Property Management Association, resources, and FRMT, Ltd. The Fraternal Property Management Association (FPMA) provides assistance to campus professionals and local chapter advisors to help in managing fraternity and sorority properties. The FPMA publishes a semiannual newsletter. FRMT, Ltd., the arm of the company that provides insurance to fraternities, also publishes a useful semiannual newsletter that is available on the Internet.

M-J Insurance, Inc. (www.mjinsurance.com or to link directly to the Sorority Division homepage www.mjinsurance.com/mji/mj.nsf/), provides insurance coverage for many sororities. Its website provides information on insurance policies as well as educational resources and links to other risk management-related websites.

Victims' Rights Organizations

Security On Campus, Inc. Perhaps the most visible and active victims' rights organization is *Security On Campus, Inc.* (www.securityoncampus.org). Founded in 1989 by Howard and Connie Clery in response to the 1986 murder of their daughter, Jeanne, at Lehigh University, Security On Campus has grown into a powerful lobbying and educational organization. The group most notably advocated for and championed passage of the Jeanne Clery Disclosure of Campus Security Policy and Campus Crime Statistics Act in 1998, which requires full disclosure of campus crime statistics.

Beyond lobbying and advocacy, Security On Campus maintains an updated listing of "campus crime news" and a comprehensive educational resource library on its website, which also features links to other resources (www.securityoncampus.org/schools/links.html), including several of the sites discussed below. Administrators can enroll in an e-mail distribution list, which sends timely periodic updates on legislation and court proceedings. Security On Campus provides a one-stop-shop for college administrators who wish to remain current on issues of campus crime prevention.

StopHazing.org. Unfortunately, hazing is a problem on many campuses today. From the band to Reserve Officers' Training Corps (ROTC), fraternity/sorority chapters to athletic teams, and honor societies to secret societies, some students choose to create conditions that lead to physical, emotional, and psychological trauma for other students. Even though many people defend hazing as a fun activity that promotes group bonding, all hazing harms those who must endure it, and many hazing activities can lead to violations of the law, assaults on students (outside the group), or physical injury or death. Such crises can be prevented, and the web-based StopHazing .org (www.stophazing.org) seeks to educate about the risks associated with hazing, offer prevention strategies, and eliminate hazing of all types. The site offers educational and prevention resources, information on research conducted on hazing, recent articles, links to books and videos about hazing, and information on hazing as it relates to the law. In addition, it maintains a listserv to subscribe for regular updates on news regarding hazing and to communicate with others about strategies to prevent hazing.

College Parents of America (CPA). A more recent advocacy group to the college scene is *College Parents of America* (www.collegeparents.org). In 2005, the CPA listed approximately 75 member institutions and about 50,000 member families. Although the organization focuses primarily on college financing issues, its website provides a useful link for resources related to health and safety issues on college campuses (www.collegeparents.org/cpa/resource-current-health.html).

Higher Education Center for Alcohol and Other Drug Abuse and Violence Prevention (HEC) (http://www.edc.org/hec/). This organization helps college and university leadership prevent and address problems associated with student alcohol and drug use and violence. The HEC provides valuable resources on how to work with community leaders and begin campus-community prevention initiatives, environmental management strategies, and educational programs. Each fall HEC holds an annual National Meeting on Alcohol and Other Drug Abuse and Violence Prevention in Higher Education. In addition, the organization offers training for campus and community leaders, publications, and electronic updates and resources. We suggest subscribing to HEC's publication services and using HEC as a resource for your campus-community coalition. If you do not have a functioning campus-community coalition on your campus, HEC members will come to your campus and provide training on how to start and build your coalition. The

HEC also offers information on statewide initiatives on the problems of student alcohol and drug use and violence. Connecting with the network of campuses and individuals in your state may give you local insights into how to address campus-specific problems and put you in contact with state officials or law enforcement officers with whom you need to build relationships.

Conclusion

In this chapter, we discussed resources available to campus administrators for preventing and managing crisis. We approached this topic with the belief that most college campuses have on-site human resources who have valuable training and experience in working with crises. The preceding discussion highlighted those groups of professionals common to most college campuses, highlighting how and why a college administrator would work with each group. Similarly, we identified resources external to the campus with which administrators should be familiar. These resources, primarily professional organizations, can provide training in working with campus crises and guidance to lessen the chances of a crisis occurring.

We hope you take away the knowledge that the resources and those with crisis management expertise are at hand, either on campus or "a click away." To use an old adage, "An ounce of prevention is worth a pound of cure." Indeed, spending an hour or two becoming familiar with the people and resources outlined in this chapter will assist you in managing crises, and we believe that many crises will be averted as well.

References

Allen, C. D. (2001, May 31). *Lessons learned in a time of crisis.* Retrieved May 29, 2005, from http://www.naspa.org/membership/mem/nr

Barr, M. J., Desler, M. K., & Associates (Eds.). (2000). *The handbook of student affairs administration* (2nd ed.). San Francisco: Jossey-Bass.

Bornstein, J., & Wilson, A. (2004a, December 7). *Creating a crisis management plan: Using the all-hazards approach (part I).* Retrieved May 29, 2005, from http://www.naspa.org/membership/mem/nr

Bornstein, J., & Wilson, A. (2004b, December 14). *Creating a crisis management plan: Using the all-hazards approach (part II).* Retrieved May 29, 2005, from http://www.naspa.org/membership/mem/nr

Council for the Advancement of Standards in Higher Education (CAS). (2003). *2003 masters-level graduate program for student affairs professionals standards and guidelines.* Retrieved December 27, 2005, from http://www.cas.edu/

Deisinger, E., Cychosz, C., & Jaeger, L. A. (1998). Strategies for dealing with violence. In A. M. Hoffman, J. H. Schuh, & R. H. Fenske (Eds.), *Violence on campus: Defining the problems, strategies for action* (pp. 327–346). Gaithersburg, MD: Aspen.

Duncan, M. A., & Miser, K. M. (2000). Dealing with campus crisis. In M. J. Barr, M. K. Desler, & Associates (Eds.), *The handbook of student affairs administration* (2nd ed.) (pp. 453–474). San Francisco: Jossey-Bass.

Fannelli, S. A. (1997). When crisis occurs: A president's perspective. In I. M. Weisman & G. B. Vaughn (Eds.), *Presidents and trustees in partnership: New roles and leadership challenges* (pp. 63–72). San Francisco: Jossey-Bass.

Gehring, D. D. (2000). Understanding the legal implications of student affairs practice. In M. J. Barr, M. K. Desler, & Associates (Eds.), *The handbook of student affairs administration* (2nd ed.) (pp. 347–376). San Francisco: Jossey-Bass.

Gutierrez Kenney, P. (1997). When a crisis occurs: A trustee's perspective. In I. M. Weisman & G. B. Vaugn (Eds.), *Presidents and trustees in partnership: New roles and leadership challenges* (pp. 73–80). San Francisco: Jossey-Bass.

Moore, L. V. (2000). Managing conflict constructively. In M. J. Barr, M. K. Dresler, & Associates (Eds.), *The handbook of student affairs administration* (2nd ed.) (pp. 393–409). San Francisco: Jossey-Bass.

Nicoletti, J., Spencer-Thomas, S., & Bollinger, C. (2001). *Violence goes to college: The authoritative guide to prevention and intervention.* Springfield, IL: Thomas.

Rankin, S. R., & Reason, R. D. (2005). Differing perceptions: How students of color and White students perceive campus climate for underrepresented groups. *Journal of College Student Development, 46*(1), 43–61.

Reason, R. D. (2001). Supervisory responsibilities of senior student affairs officers. *ISPA Journal, 13*(1), 51–67.

Reason, R. D., & Rankin, S. R. (2006). College students' experiences and perceptions of harassment on campus: An exploration of gender differences. *College Student Affairs Journal, 26*(1), 7–29.

Reason, R. D., & Saunders, K. P. (2003). The conflict between personal and professional roles of senior student affairs officers during a time of national crisis. *College Student Affairs Journal, 22*(2), 137–149.

Sandeen, C. A. (2000). Developing effective campus and community relationships. In M. J. Barr, M. K. Desler, & Associates (Eds.), *The handbook of student affairs administration* (2nd ed.) (pp. 377–392). San Francisco: Jossey-Bass.

Siegel, D. (1994). *Campuses respond to violent tragedy.* Phoenix, AZ: American Council on Education and The Oryx Press.

14

ELEMENTS OF A
COMPREHENSIVE SAFETY PLAN

Delight E. Champagne

Planning for the safety of a campus community in a complex and sometimes violent world creates many challenges for colleges and universities across our nation (Pezza, 1995). In response to Columbine, the attacks of September 11, current crime rates, and recent natural disasters, various emergency planning, law enforcement, and advocacy groups have offered safety plan advice to a wide range of institutions, including colleges and universities. The U.S. Department of Homeland Security (U.S. Department of Education, 2003), the Federal Emergency Management Association (2002), and the National Advisory Council on Violence Against Women (NACVAW) (2002) are examples of national organizations that have responded to the need for developing plans to protect our institutions from violence and other threats to personal safety. However, these safety plans may be limited by the scope of their interventions or by their lack of direct application to the college environment. Furthermore, measures that have been created specifically for collegiate settings are sometimes developed without the leadership of student affairs divisions (Wilkinson & Rund, 2002).

Some colleges and universities have risen to this challenge by creating comprehensive plans that address a multitude of threatening situations and offer extensive intervention and prevention strategies. In an effort to provide information to institutions about potential programs and strategies that might be included in campus safety plans, I conducted a content analysis of more than 100 campus safety plans and website resources related to violence and safety issues (American College Personnel Association, 2004). Using a major computer search engine to locate campus safety and campus security websites, 100 websites were examined initially. I then examined an additional 25 campus security websites for institutions located near recent disaster areas under the assumption that those institutions would be highly motivated to enhance their security measures with regard to disaster response.

Content analysis measures included recording all elements of each safety plan, listing common elements, and grouping elements into categories by types of situations and types of response measures. As a result, several elements of comprehensive safety plans were ascertained. These elements include response, prevention, communication, and educational measures that span a wide range of potentially violent or threatening situations. In this content analysis, no single institution's plan was considered a model or a prototype representing the "ideal" comprehensive plan. Rather, all observed components were considered equally valid elements in developing a comprehensive plan. Therefore, I mention all components as possible elements of a comprehensive plan, but each institution should evaluate components based on its own needs and the resources available for implementing the safety plan.

The types of threatening situations that may be encountered at a particular location also determine safety plan components. Violent or threatening situations that require consideration in campus safety plans may be of a personal or interpersonal nature and include, for example, rape, assault, harassment, use of weapons, and cyberstalking. Violence that affects colleges may also have community origins, such as off-campus crime, intrusions, and hostage situations, or global origins, such as terrorism and responses to war. Additionally, campus safety plans must include responses to natural disasters or such nonviolent disruptive activities as power outages.

Common Elements Found in Comprehensive Safety Plans

In an overview of campus safety plans, common elements have emerged that take into consideration sources of threats, targets of threats, and type of intervention needed. The most comprehensive plans appear to be collaborative enterprises that cut across departments, personnel levels, and interest groups. In so doing, these plans appear to recognize the uniqueness of their institutions and the communities within which the institutions are located. Additionally, they include responses to crises caused by natural disasters.

Comprehensive plans, then, appear to be ones that take the broadest view of the possibilities for danger and for intervention. Taken as a whole, this information suggests that the following components of a campus safety plan are essential for ensuring the safety of the college community:

1. coherent organizational structures developed through collaborative efforts of many departments and constituent groups;
2. recognition of multiple sources of threats;
3. the ability to address the needs of potential victims or targets of the threats on a particular campus;
4. planning for prevention and response measures, interpersonal threats, and natural crises;
5. effective communication systems;
6. comprehensive education and training measures; and
7. ongoing appraisal and reworking in light of new developments.

These eight essential elements are found in the most extensive safety plans and, to some degree, in less comprehensive plans. Institutions vary in the extent to which they give consideration to each of these components.

Coherent Structures

The first element of comprehensive safety plans that emerged from examination of campus security websites is the development of coherent organizational structures. Safety plans appear to evolve from campus security departments and from committees or task forces whose primary focus is on ensuring the safety of the campus community at all levels. Amherst College (2005), for example, has a security advisory committee comprised of the dean of students, the assistant dean of students, a faculty member, the chief of campus police, the director of facilities planning and management, and three students. At other institutions, administration of the plan may fall under the auspices of the campus security department or a combination of administrative personnel. A vice president of administration or head of campus police may serve as the overall administrator of the plan, and a student affairs administrator may be part of the organizational team.

Campus safety "programs" emerge as an outgrowth of safety plans to provide proactive efforts for preventing and responding to crisis situations.

They are established to make sure that "plans" do not simply become hand-books that are dusted off in haste at the time of an emergency. Student affairs departments often serve as vehicles for implementing these programs in residence hall, orientation, and judicial programs. Additionally, the student affairs division commonly provides links between parents and the institution with regard to safety measures. Campuses with the most comprehensive plans also appear to have an emergency response team that is responsible for implementing crisis plans. Communication protocols and reporting lines among members of this team are clearly defined.

Overall, these structures provide the foundation for developing and implementing a comprehensive safety plan. These structures may differ substantially, depending on the type, size, and location of the institution.

Recognition of the Various Sources of Threats to Campus Safety

The content of each campus safety plan also appears to differ, depending on the characteristics of the institution. Nonetheless, some consistent elements emerge in an overview of various plans. Comprehensive safety plans commonly take into account three aspects of safety: (a) the source or domain of the threat; (b) the target or victim involved in the threat; and (c) the type of intervention needed. In examining the domains of threats to safety, three sources have been ascertained: personal or interpersonal, community, and global. Personal domain issues encompass acts of violence or threats to individuals and groups that evolve from interactions with others within the campus environment. The focus of many campus safety plans has been on this particular domain. The American College Health Association has delineated violent acts that threaten the personal safety of students and other members of the campus community (Carr, 2005), including sexual violence such as stalking, sexual assault, and dating violence; racial-, ethnic-, and gender-based violence and homophobic intimidation; hazing and celebratory violence; suicide and attempted suicide; murder; non-negligent manslaughter; aggravated assault; arson; and attacks on faculty and staff. Cyberthreats have recently been added to this list on many campus safety websites.

Personal safety issues are not limited to acts of violence between and among members of the campus community. They may be threatened by acts of nature and other dangers as well. Fires, floods, hurricanes, tornadoes, and severe power outages require strategies for prevention and emergency response to protect members of the campus community. Sweet Briar College in Virginia (2005) offers a comprehensive online resource manual with information about a variety of unusual occurrences, such as inclement weather, aircraft disasters, blood-borne pathogens, bomb threats, infectious disease outbreaks, curtailment of utilities, civil disturbances, international emergencies, and other crisis situations. The online manual contains standardized procedures for dealing effectively with each of these occurrences with a description of college actions, personnel involvement, and follow-up activities for the event. For example, in the event of a severe power outage, the typical problem is described, the point person is named, team members who would be involved are listed, and college actions are presented in detail.

A second domain or source of threats that has gained attention in campus safety plans in recent years is the local and regional community within which the institution is located. Neighborhood environments, local legal issues, town/gown relationships, relationships with state and local police, economic conditions in the regional and local areas, and the unique characteristics of a local community all may have a bearing on the types of threats and concerns in the area. As a specific example, James Madison University (2005), beset by area threats that included sniper assaults, anthrax threats, and the 9/11 attacks in nearby Washington, D.C., has developed substantive crisis response procedures in its safety plan. The National Association of Student Personnel Administrators Task Force on Crisis Management and Violence Prevention (Zdziarski, 2003) has recommended that all institutions conduct a crisis audit to determine their vulnerability as targets of terrorist threats or activities.

Local and regional environments harbor other dangers that threaten personal safety on a smaller, but nonetheless disconcerting scale. For example, institutions in very rural areas may have concerns related to having an expansive campus with many unlit areas, while urban institutions may be plagued by problems related to the availability of drugs and other substances. In suburban areas, where students frequently live in close proximity to homeowners, town/gown relationships may be strained to the point of hostility. Community residents, troubled by noise, inappropriate behaviors brought on by alcohol consumption, and incivility on the part of students, may resort to calling local police to settle their disputes. Local laws and relationships with police are also strong forces in determining how alcohol policies are enforced on college campuses.

In addition to acts of interpersonal violence, threats from natural disasters may evolve from the local or regional vulnerabilities. Hurricane Katrina was a harsh reminder of the need for all institutions to assess regional propensity for environmentally dangerous situations. In recognition of its vulnerability to hurricanes, Florida Atlantic University (2005) has a separate section on hurricanes in its campus safety website, while the University of Iowa (2004) devotes a portion of its campus safety website to tornado information.

Finally, a third source of possible threats is the global community. Within this domain are the many threats stemming from our international relationships and from events that have worldwide significance. Terrorism, bioterrorism, nuclear threats, and war are examples of the threats to safety that affect each of us. Because of its proximity to landmarks of international significance, George Washington University (2005) has developed an extensive online procedural manual for identifying and responding to a variety of potentially catastrophic events. This manual contains specific information about incident planning, response, and recovery, including evacuations, sheltering-in-place, alert levels, incident severity, and specific threats. The manual is updated regularly. Having an assistant vice president for public safety and emergency management who coordinates crisis management at the university emphasizes the importance of safety measures at the institution.

For all colleges and universities, regardless of location, threats arising from tensions in the global community profoundly affect study abroad programs and the safety of international students. Our awareness of how intrinsically interwoven we are with the international community has been heightened by the occurrence of natural disasters in recent years. Increasingly, campus safety committees have integrated global issues into their safety plans.

Attention to Potential Victims or Targets of Threats

The target of the threat is an additional consideration in comprehensive safety plans. Those involved in campus security planning take into account the probable victim in a number of scenarios on their campuses. Questions may arise for security planners about the types of persons most at risk for harm on their campuses. As suggested by the literature in the field (NACVAW, 2002), are women on some campuses frequent targets of violence? Are subgroups of students particularly vulnerable to harassment or assault on campus, as indicated by some studies (Carr, 2005)? Are students in fraternities, sororities, or sports likely to experience hazing violence or alcohol-related injuries, as one might assume based on current statistics (Carr, 2005)?

The unique nature of individual institutions would appear to dictate the propensity of certain types of victimization. One way to assess this propensity is to examine prior incidents of violence using campus crime statistics. All colleges are required to include this information in public documents (Nichols, 1997), and it is most often included on campus security websites. This information is most helpful to campus safety planners in developing prevention and protection measures in the safety plan.

Effective Prevention and Response Measures for Interpersonal and Natural Crises

Taking into account both the sources of threats and the targets of those threats, those involved in developing campus safety plans must create measures to actually deal with the threat or crisis. Two major types of measures have been ascertained in the literature and from institutional reports: prevention and response; a comprehensive safety plan includes both. Response measures include establishing a crisis response team, emergency preparedness, crisis management, policing measures, judicial measures, policy development, procedural measures, and counseling and emotional support measures. Included in the response measures should be plans and procedures for persons with disabilities. Although few institutions currently provide safety information for persons with disabilities on their websites, it is presumed that such information is provided elsewhere in some other format. George Washington University (2005) is one institution that has provided clear and comprehensive evacuation procedure information for students with disabilities on its website.

Avoiding harm through prevention measures is undoubtedly the most desirable approach to dealing with violence and other dangers. Measures observed in a review of campus safety plans include educational programs, policies that support safety, campus facility and design planning, outreach programs, adequate staffing, and extensive services. Skidmore College (2004), for example, offers bicycle patrols, blue light telephones, escort services, alarm systems, silent witness opportunities, and whistle defense programs. Rape defense programs are also offered on many campuses. Langford (2004) has suggested that comprehensive safety plans should also include approaches that address attitudes underlying violence and support healthy group norms.

Effective Communication Systems

If we have learned anything from Hurricane Katrina and September 11, it has been that communication is essential for ensuring the safety of any community in a time of crisis. The lack of effective communication before and the breakdown of communication during an event can result in harm to numerous individuals. A "plan" without communication will never be implemented properly. In examining the websites of numerous colleges and universities, I observed the following components of campus safety plans related to communication:

1. The institution is receptive to information regarding possible threats and provides a safe vehicle for members of the campus community to convey information about potentially threatening situations.
2. The institution has a clear communication and response protocol that has been conveyed to all members of the campus community.
3. There is a clear communication protocol for members of the response team.
4. The campus has alternative sources of communication available during emergencies, such as lighted emergency telephones, alarms, radios, and broadcast systems.
5. Members of the campus community are aware of the communication alternatives that can be used in times of crisis.
6. Literature is available that highlights safety policies and procedures, and posters and signs that direct students to appropriate safety resources in times of threat are visible throughout the campus.
7. Communication systems for students and members of the campus community with disabilities are available and functional.

8. The campus safety plan has high visibility on the college website and provides easy access for students, staff, prospective students and their families, and visitors.

9. The website is easy to navigate and provides clear and easy-to-follow instructions and information.

10. Website information is up to date with current alerts and contact people.

11. Website information includes links to local, state, and federal resources outside college or university.

In its Emergency Response Guide, which contains specific protocols and procedures for responding to an array of threatening situations, Arizona State University (2005) has demonstrated efforts to establish clear communication lines, particularly through its well-thought-out website.

Education and Training Measures

While communication is a core component of a campus safety plan, particularly in response to threats, education and training are key components for prevention and protection. Without awareness of safety procedures, protocols, and policies, individual members of the campus community are at risk for suffering unnecessary personal harm in crises and threatening situations. Therefore, education and training are the primary vehicles for informing students and other members of the campus community about all personal safety issues. Educational programs may take the form of retreats, workshops, institutes, panel presentations, speakers, and role-play activities.

Possible topics for educational programs are endless, but those most commonly seen in the safety programs at institutions examined in this review are:

1. knowing one's rights in various circumstances;
2. understanding the nature of specific crimes;
3. knowing ways to avoid and protect oneself from harm;
4. knowing what to do to in the event of specific emergencies;
5. having information about resources available on and off campus; and
6. being informed of methods for reporting suspicious activities.

Educational programs related to campus safety include those sponsored by human resources, campus security, residence life, academic affairs, counseling centers, continuing education, disability offices, student activities, judicial affairs, international affairs, postal services, health centers, multicultural affairs, Information and Technology (ITT), and academic affairs. However, coordination is needed to ensure that programs do not overlap or give conflicting information. The campus safety task force or steering committee can play a key role in coordinating educational programs.

One important observation about the educational components of comprehensive safety plans is that all members of the campus community, including nonresident students, have opportunities to attend and are involved in these educational programs. Such opportunities should be well publicized through multiple resources, including websites, bulletin boards, e-mail announcements, and personal mail. Student affairs division heads, continuing education offices, commuter program directors, and liaisons for students with disabilities play pivotal roles in this publicity.

Educational programs are targeted for student groups on most campuses. Training, however, is offered to different constituent groups, such as professionals and paraprofessionals, and thus requires different approaches. Often training involves staff and personnel who will be directly involved in response and prevention measures. Their learning needs are related more specifically to providing leadership in protecting others from harm during a crisis or in preventing an event from occurring. Depending on the personnel involved, training may be offered on the following topics:

1. interviewing and counseling techniques for speaking with victims of violence;
2. recognizing substance abuse signals;
3. understanding policy and judicial interventions related to safety violations;
4. awareness of protocols for specific security breaches;
5. how to conduct a safety audit;
6. legal issues related to campus security; and
7. rapid response rehearsals and role-plays.

Follow-up training sessions may also be offered to reinforce learning or to provide the opportunity for discussion about specific safety issue concerns.

Ongoing Appraisal and Reworking of the Plan in Light of New Developments

Appraising the campus climate, the infrastructure of the institution, interrelationships between the institution and the local and regional communities, communication systems, and the potential for different types of threats at any given point in time should be ongoing. Ever vigilant to new or potentially violent situations, campus security advisory boards and committees require frequent reviews of policies and procedures. Institutions with comprehensive campus safety plans appear to have this appraisal built into the structure of their plans.

One important task of campus safety committees is gathering and screening current risk management information gathered from various emergency planning organizations and advocacy groups. Many campus security departments include this information on their websites and update it when needed. Additionally, surveys of students help to determine their perceptions of safety on campus. Campus and community crime reports provide a barometer for the current state of security on any particular campus. Judicial reports and reports from residence life offices can also be used as resources in developing preventive and response measures. The student affairs division can play a vital role in informing the campus safety advisory boards about many safety issues at the institution.

Conclusion

In examining the overall content of comprehensive safety plans, some general observations can be made. First, comprehensive plans contain prevention and response procedures for dealing with threats and occurrences across a range of activities, including personal, community, and global threats to safety. These plans complement other emergency plans in place for events such as natural disasters. Second, these plans have been developed with input from many departments and divisions at the institution. Although campus police or campus security may ultimately implement the plan, responsibility for campus safety does not fall wholly in the hands of that department; the student affairs division plays an integral role in developing and implementing the plan. Third, there are structures in place for education, training, and staff development related to campus safety and the plan itself, and training programs are updated as new information and situations occur. Finally, appraisal and review of the plan are ongoing in light of new developments. Outcomes assessment can be an effective tool in the appraisal process.

As colleges and universities review their established safety plans and attempt to develop more comprehensive designs that accommodate the complexity of today's tenuous environments, information gleaned from other institutions can be quite helpful. No single institution's plan can serve as a model for any other institution, but these guidelines may be deemed highly desirable to meet the unique needs of a particular campus. Clearly, outcomes assessment is needed in the development of such plans. With a definitive statement of desired outcomes for the institution, campus security planning committees can proceed to develop the best and most comprehensive safety plans for their institutions.

References

American College Personnel Association. (2004). *Professional issues core council violence and personal safety resources page*. Retrieved April 12, 2004, from http://www.acpa.nche.edu/corcouns/PI/violrscs.htm

Amherst College. (2005). *Amherst college campus police home page*. Retrieved September 30, 2005, from http://www.amherst.edu/~campuspolice/sac.html

Arizona State University. (2005). *ASU emergency response guide*. Retrieved September 28, 2005, from http://www.asu.edufm/Risk/emresponseguide.htm

Carr, J. I. (2005, February). *American College Health Association campus violence white paper*. Baltimore, MD: American College Health Association.

Federal Emergency Management Association. (2002). *The disaster resistant university project*. Retrieved April, 17, 2004, from http://training.fema.gov/emiweb/edu/highlinks2.asp

Florida Atlantic University. (2005). *Emergency information*. Retrieved September 29, 2005, from http://www.fau.edu/notices/

George Washington University. (2005). *University police department*. Retrieved September 30, 2005, from http://gwired.edu/upd/

James Madison University. (2005). *Comprehensive safety plan*. Retrieved March 29, 2004, from http://www.jmu.edu/safetyplan/terrorism/index.shtml

Langford, L. (2004). *Preventing violence and promoting safety in higher education settings: Overview of a comprehensive approach*. Washington, DC: U.S. Department of Education.

National Advisory Council on Violence Against Women (NACVAW). (2002). *Toolkit to end violence against women*. Retrieved April 2, 2004, from http://www.tool kit.ncjrs.org/vawo_7.html

Nichols, D. (1997). *Creating a safe campus: A guide for college and university administrators*. Springfield IL: Charles C. Thomas.

Pezza, P. (1995). College campus violence: The nature of the problem and its frequency. *Educational Psychology Review, 7*(1), 93–103.

Skidmore College. (2004). *Skidmore College Department of Campus Safety*. Retrieved September 29, 2004, from http://www.skidmore.edu/administration/business/se curity/security.html

Sweet Briar College. (2005). *Sweet Briar College comprehensive safety and crisis management plan*. Retrieved September 28, 2005, from http://www.police.sbc.edu/ comprehensivesafetyplan.htm

University of Iowa. (2004). *Department of Public Safety critical incident management plan*. Retrieved, August 26, 2005, from http://www.uiowa.edu%7epubsfty/

U.S. Department of Education. (2003). *Campus public safety: Weapons of mass destruction, terrorism, and protective measures*. Retrieved April 1, 2004, from http:// www.ed.gov/admins/lead/safety/emergencyplan/campussafe.html

Wilkinson, C. K., & Rund, J. A. (2002). *Addressing contemporary campus safety issues*. San Francisco: Jossey-Bass.

Zdziarski, E. L. (2003, March 17). *Responding to the threat of campus terrorism. Net results: NASPA's e-zine for student affairs professionals*. Retrieved March 26, 2003, from http://www.naspa.org/netresults/article.cfm?ID = 995&category = feature

ABOUT THE EDITORS AND CONTRIBUTORS

Editors

Jerlando F. L. Jackson, Ph.D.

Dr. Jackson, whose interests lie in the study of administrative diversity, executive behavior, and academic entrepreneurship in higher and postsecondary education, is an assistant professor of higher and postsecondary education in educational leadership and policy analysis, faculty associate for the Wisconsin Center for the Advancement of Postsecondary Education, and faculty affiliate in the Weinert Center for Entrepreneurship (School of Business) at the University of Wisconsin-Madison. Dr. Jackson's central interest has been to contribute to administrative science, with a focus on administrators' impact on higher and postsecondary education. In addition, he serves as executive director of the Center for African American Research and Policy, which is developing and publishing a new generation of research on policy issues confronting African Americans in both the academy and society at large for Brothers of the Academy Institute.

Since receiving his Ph.D. in educational leadership and policy studies from Iowa State University, Dr. Jackson has become renowned for shaping the literature on diversifying the higher education workforce. Deeply appreciated by researchers, policymakers, and practitioners nationally, Dr. Jackson's work benefits people of color and higher education institutions across the United States. His sophisticated scholarship offers rich insights on critical topics in higher education, including diversity, multicultural influences, university and college governance, and student affairs leadership.

Dr. Jackson is credited with more than 60 publications and 100 presentations, and he edited *Strengthening the African American Educational Pipeline: Informing Research, Policy, and Practice* for SUNY-Albany Press (2007).

Melvin Cleveland Terrell, Ph.D.

Dr. Terrell, vice president for student affairs and professor of counselor education at Northeastern Illinois University in Chicago, earned his B.S.Ed.

(1971) in history and secondary education from Chicago State University and his M.Ed. (1974) in college student personnel from Loyola University (Chicago). Dr. Terrell's doctorate in higher education administration and Black studies is from Southern Illinois University-Carbondale (1978), and he has continued postdoctoral studies at Harvard University and the University of Virginia. In addition, he served as an American Council on Education (ACE) fellow at Florida State University in 1993–1994.

Currently, Dr. Terrell is president of the National Association of Student Affairs Professionals (NASAP) and the past director of the American College Personnel Association's (ACPA) Core Council for Professional Issues. He has served as editor of the *NASAP Journal* since 1997 and serves on the editorial board of the *Illinois Committee on Black Concerns in Higher Education (ICBCHE) Journal*.

In 2002, Dr. Terrell co-authored the groundbreaking *How Minority Students Experience College: Implication for Planning and Policy* (Stylus). Recipient of the 2004 NASPA Outstanding Contribution to Literature or Research Award, Dr. Terrell is one of the leading names in student affairs scholarship and practice today and has authored more than 30 publications, including monographs, book chapters, and articles in refereed journals.

Contributors

Anna Ah Sam, Ph.D., provides research, planning, and administrative support for student service programs that implement the University of Hawai'i's strategic goals of access and diversity through the Office of Student Equity, Excellence, and Diversity. She has presented and published widely in diversity, disability, grant writing, and evaluation and has more than 15 years of experience as a researcher. Previously Dr. Ah Sam coordinated health and educational research and training projects in Hawai'i and the U.S. Pacific jurisdictions, including American Samoa, the Commonwealth of the Northern Mariana Islands, Guam, the Federated States of Micronesia, Palau, and the Marshall Islands.

Aaron M. Brower, Ph.D., is professor of social work at the University of Wisconsin (UW)-Madison. His scholarship and teaching focuses on the transition from high school to college and on a variety of issues related to college student life. In August 2006, he completed a 10-year project funded by the Robert Wood Johnson Foundation addressing high-risk college student drinking. At UW-Madison, he created the Bradley Learning Community in 1995, helped create all subsequent living-learning communities at UW-Madison, and has consulted with many universities on the evaluation and development of living-learning programs. He received the university's Chancellor's Award for Distinguished Teaching in 2001.

Sudakshina L. Ceglarek, who received her B.A. and M.S.W. from the University of Michigan, Ann Arbor, coordinates a 10-year initiative, the PACE (Policy, Alternatives, Community & Education) project, funded by the Robert Wood Johnson Foundation, which addresses high-risk drinking issues at the University of Wisconsin-Madison. Ms. Ceglarek is also working on her doctorate with the federally funded Chicago Longitudinal Study at the UW Waisman Center, which examines the effects of primary prevention efforts on enhancing health behavior and health status of individuals into adulthood.

Delight E. Champagne, Ph.D., is professor of psychology and director of the Student Personnel Administration in Higher Education Program at Springfield College in Massachusetts, where she has taught courses in student personnel administration and college student development for over 20 years. She has been actively involved in national associations in leadership positions and has been a frequent presenter at national conferences. Currently, she is on the editorial board of the *NASPA Journal* and is faculty representative to the NASPA Region I conference planning committee. In the American College Personnel Association, she is the coordinator of the Annuit Coeptis Award program and serves on the Professional Issues Core Council. While serving as director of the Professional Issues Core Council, she developed a website dealing with campus safety issues and conducted presentations on campus safety. Her publications include articles and book chapters on topics related to career development and developmental issues of young adults and college athletes.

Darnell G. Cole, Ph.D., is an associate professor of education with an emphasis in higher education and education psychology at the University of Southern California. His areas of research include race/ethnicity, diversity, college student experiences, and learning. Earlier he served as an associate professor in the Department of Educational Administration at the University of Hawai'i at Mānoa (Honolulu). He has also been a member of Marquette University's faculty. Dr. Cole, who is on the review board of Journal Educational Foundations, has published more than 25 articles and book chapters and is featured in major higher education journals. His most recent article, "Do Interracial Interactions Matter?" will appear in the *Journal of Higher Education*.

Charles Cychosz, Ph.D., is the support services manager for the Ames Police Department. In addition, he served four years as crime prevention, research & training manager in the Iowa State University Department of Public Safety. As a former faculty member and assistant to the vice president for student affairs, he led strategic planning and assessment in student retention and student life. Dr. Cychosz has also managed and evaluated several local and regional substance abuse prevention activities. He has published research findings on health education issues and is actively involved in the evaluation of projects examining leadership development, social norms, and violence prevention.

Noah D. Drezner is an advanced Ph.D. candidate in higher education in the Policy, Management, and Evaluation Division at the University of Pennsylvania Graduate School of Education in Philadelphia. His research interests include philanthropy in minority and special serving institutions. Recently, Mr. Drezner published "Thurgood Marshall: A Study of Philanthropy Through Racial Uplift" in *Uplifting a People: African American Philanthropy and Education* edited by Marybeth Gasman and Katherine V. Sedgwick (Peter Lang, 2005).

Charlene M. Dukes, Ed.D., who earned her doctorate in administrative and policy studies from the University of Pittsburgh, has 25 years of progressive leadership experience and administrative responsibility in student affairs. Her scope of knowledge includes student development services, strategic and operational planning, and program administration and implementation. In addition, she serves as a founder and lead faculty for the Community College Student Development Leadership Institute under the auspices of the National Council on Student Development. She is currently vice president for student services at Prince George's Community College in Largo, Maryland.

Marybeth Gasman, Ph.D., is an assistant professor of higher education in the Graduate School of Education at the University of Pennsylvania. Her research focuses on historical and contemporary issues at historically Black colleges. Her most recent book is *Envisioning Black Colleges: A History of the United Negro College Fund* (Johns Hopkins University Press, 2007). She wrote the chapter, "Fund-Raising," in *Black College Alumni: Successful Strategies for Supporting Alma Mater* (CASE Books, 2003).

Tracy A. Harris, a doctoral candidate in the Walden University School of Education with 21 years of professional experience in higher education administration, is currently dean of enrollment services for Prince George's Community College in Largo, Maryland. He is a member of several professional organizations and frequently presents at regional and national conferences/forums on such topics as strategic enrollment management, student recruitment and retention, and assessment testing and implications. He has published journal articles on such topics as enrollment management and marketing, student retention, and small college strategic enrollment planning.

Richie L. Heard, who served as a graduate assistant for Dr. Jerlando F. L. Jackson in 2005–2006, graduated from the University of Illinois at Urbana-Champaign with a B.A. in speech communication, and he received an M.S. in educational leadership and policy analysis from the University of Wisconsin-Madison in May 2006. His research interests focus on the retention of at-risk and underrepresented postsecondary student populations.

Walter M. Kimbrough, Ph.D., 12th president of Philander Smith College in Little Rock, Arkansas, has served in administrative capacities at Albany State University, Old Dominion University, Georgia State University, and Emory University. Based on a strong fraternity experience, Dr. Kimbrough has forged a national reputation as an expert on historically Black fraternities and sororities. He is the author of the book, *Black Greek 101: The Culture, Customs and Challenges of Black Fraternities and Sororities* (2003; Fairleigh Dickinson University Press), currently in its sixth printing.

John Wesley Lowery, Ph.D., an associate professor in the School of Educational Studies at Oklahoma State University, earned his doctorate in higher education administration at Bowling Green State University and has held administrative positions at Adrian College and Washington University. Dr. Lowery is actively involved in numerous professional associations, including the American College Personnel Association (ACPA), American Society for the Study of Higher Education (ASHE), and National Association of Student Personnel Administrators (NASPA). He is a frequent speaker and author on student affairs and higher education, particularly legislative issues and judicial affairs, on which he is widely regarded as an expert.

Brenda R. Lutovsky, a doctoral student in higher education at Pennsylvania State University, earned her master's degree in English from Ball State University in Muncie, Indiana. Before returning to graduate school, she served five years as director of Greek affairs at Shippensburg University of Pennsylvania.

Christian Matheis, M.A., is assistant director of the LGBTA Student Resource center at Pennsylvania State University. He has co-authored chapters for several anthologies on topics ranging from institutional climate and administrative leadership to pedagogy and curriculum transformation. As a trainer, Mr. Matheis provides professional development and training sessions in human relations facilitation, experiential dialogue, and community-based conflict resolution. His research interests include ethics, epistemology, philosophies of community, feminist critical social theory, models of applied leadership and organizational development, pedagogy, and curriculum development.

Elizabeth M. O'Callaghan is a Ph.D. student in the Educational Leadership and Policy Analysis Program at the University of Wisconsin-Madison. Mrs. O'Callaghan's scholarly interests include women's leadership and persistence in historically male-dominated domains and disciplines. Her recent publications include a review of recruitment and retention barriers for women and people of color in the science and engineering disciplines. Mrs. O'Callaghan currently serves as a research assistant in her department and is a fellow with the Wisconsin-Spencer Doctoral Research program.

Meechai Orsuwan, a Ph.D. candidate in the Department of Education Administration at the University of Hawai'i at Mānoa, earned a bachelor of international economics from Bangkok University (Thailand); a master of business administration in finance and marketing from Hawai'i Pacific University; and a master of art in economics and a master of education in educational administrations, both from the University of Hawai'i at Mānoa. His research interests include student outcomes, economics of education, diversity in higher education, college enrollment pathways, and community college student retention. Mr. Orsuwan has lectured in economics and he has served as a senior consultant for Actuaries of America.

James A. Perrotti, chief of University Police at Yale University since 1998, has been a member of the Yale police force for more than 30 years. A graduate of the University of New Haven, where he earned a bachelor's degree in criminal justice administration, Chief Perrotti received his police training from the New Haven Police Academy and was the first member of the Yale Police Department to graduate from the FBI's National Academy. He has been instrumental in developing Yale's community policing approach and has worked with New Haven's Police Department in coordinating community policing and other activities.

Susan R. Rankin, Ph.D., is a senior diversity planning analyst in the Office of the Vice Provost for Educational Equity and an assistant professor in higher education at Pennsylvania State University, from which she earned a Ph.D. in higher education administration in 1994. She has presented and written several papers and books on the impact of sexism, racism, and heterosexism in the academy and in intercollegiate athletics. Her current research focuses on providing program planners and policymakers with recommended strategies to improve the campus climate for underserved communities. Dr. Rankin has collaborated with more than 50 institutions/organizations in developing social justice issue strategic plans.

Robert D. Reason, Ph.D., an assistant professor of education (College Student Affairs/Higher Education) at Pennsylvania State University, is also a research associate at Penn State's Center for the Study of Higher Education. Dr. Reason's area of research is student development in college environments, specifically related to the development of social justice attitudes. He has also researched the role of the senior student affairs officer in higher education.

Elizabeth A. Roosa Miller, Ph.D., recently completed her doctoral work in higher education at Pennsylvania State University, where she now serves as interim director for the Center for Student Activities and Programming and teaches first-year seminars as an adjunct faculty member in the Smeal College of Business. Dr. Roosa Millar's research focuses on the influence of racial justice ally development during college, including formal and informal educational interventions. Before attending Penn State, she worked in student affairs at Montana Tech of the University of Montana as campus recreation director, then as student unions and activities director.

John H. Schuh, Ph.D., distinguished professor of educational leadership and policy studies at Iowa State University in Ames, is the author, co-author, or editor of over 200 publications, including 24 books and monographs, 60 book chapters, and more than 100 articles. His most recent books include *Promoting Reasonable Expectations* (with Thomas E. Miller and Barbara E. Bender; Jossey-Bass, 2005) and *Student Success in College* (with George D. Kuh, Jillian Kinzie, and Elizabeth J. Whitt; Jossey-Bass, 2005). Currently he is editor in chief of the *New Directions for Student Services* sourcebook series and associate editor of the *Journal of College Student Development*. Dr. Schuh received a Fulbright award to study higher education in Germany in 1994.

Jerry D. Stewart, M.S., director of public safety at Iowa State University, has extensive experience in municipal and university policing, especially in law enforcement accreditation, administration, policy writing, criminal investigations, and special event planning. He serves on numerous committees and provides assessment-related services to agencies throughout the country.